Event Processing: Designing IT Systems for Agile Companies

Event Processing: Designing IT Systems for Agile Companies

K. Mani Chandy
W. Roy Schulte

New York   Chicago   San Francisco
Lisbon   London   Madrid   Mexico City
Milan   New Delhi   San Juan
Seoul   Singapore   Sydney   Toronto

Cataloging-in-Publication Data is on file with the Library of Congress

McGraw-Hill books are available at special quantity discounts to use as premiums and sales promotions, or for use in corporate training programs. To contact a special sales representative, please visit the Contact Us page at www.mhprofessional.com.

Event Processing: Designing IT Systems for Agile Companies

1 2 3 4 5 6 7 8 9 0   DOC DOC   0 1 9

ISBN   978-0-07-163350-5
MHID   0-07-163350-2

Sponsoring Editor
    Roger Stewart
Editorial Supervisor
    Janet Walden
Project Manager
    Patricia Wallenburg
Acquisitions Coordinator
    Joya Anthony
Developmental Editor
    Heather Levy
Copy Editor
    Bill McManus
Proofreader
    Paul Tyler

Indexer
    Claire Splan
Production Supervisor
    Jean Bodeaux
Composition
    TypeWriting
Illustration
    Matrix Illustration Services
Art Director, Cover
    Jeff Weeks
Cover Designer
    Jeff Weeks

To our wives, Jean and Mary, who supported us and postponed family plans while we worked on the book.

Contents

About the Authors

K. Mani Chandy is the Simon Ramo Professor at the California Institute of Technology in Pasadena, California. He received his bachelor's degree from the Indian Institute of Technology, Madras, and his PhD from the Massachusetts Institute of Technology in Electrical Engineering and Operations Research in 1969. He was a professor at the University of Texas at Austin from 1970 to 1987, and has been at Caltech since then. Chandy has received numerous awards, including the CMG Michelson Award, the IEEE Kobayashi Award, the Babbage Award, and several teaching awards. He is a member of the U.S. National Academy of Engineering. His research is on distributed systems, event processing, and performance analysis with an emphasis on smart systems and sense-and-respond systems.

W. Roy Schulte is Vice President and Distinguished Analyst at Gartner, Inc. in Stamford, Connecticut. Schulte was the lead author of the 1996 Gartner report that introduced the term service-oriented architecture (SOA) to the industry. He also originated the research in the field of message brokers, coined the term business activity monitoring (BAM), and wrote the first analyst reports on the zero-latency enterprise and the enterprise service bus (ESB). Schulte has more than 25 years of experience as an application developer, software system programmer, database administrator, product manager, and analyst. He is a member of the Event Processing Technical Society steering committee, is a frequent speaker at industry events, and contributes to web forums. He has a BS from MIT and an MS from MIT's Sloan School of Management.

Introduction

Event processing makes dramatic improvements in business processes and IT systems possible. It has a direct, tangible impact on the lives of businesspeople. Event processing changes the way they do their jobs by giving them better visibility into what is happening in their company and its external environment. It also improves a company's reaction time to unforeseeable situations, reduces the end-to-end elapsed time of business processes, and improves the quality and availability of information.

When you can see what is going on in your sales operations, customer contact center, supply chain, or service network in near real time through a dashboard on your web browser, you are using event processing. When an insurance company condenses a 25-day process for paying a claim down to 9 days, it is using event processing. When an application system can be adapted in days rather than weeks to support a new set of requirements, it is likely using event processing as well.

Event processing is an increasingly important part of enterprise service-oriented architecture (SOA) and business process management (BPM) strategies. Event processing is synergistic with SOA and BPM, making them more effective and better able to respond quickly to escalating business requirements.

Defining Event Processing

An *event* is just what you think it is—anything that happens. We react to events every day, and we're always learning better ways to handle them. Events are all around us and have always been all around us, like the air we breathe and the winds that we exploit to fill our sails and create windmill power. For many centuries, people used sails and windmills without understanding the Bernoulli principle or much else about the scientific properties of airflow. However, thanks to advances in the fields of aerodynamics, engine design, and material science, we now use the power of air currents to fly airplanes, helicopters, and spaceships. Even our windmills are more powerful and efficient because they use specially shaped impeller blades instead of using simple sails or blades mounted on wheels as in early designs.

In a similar way, companies that deal with millions of events in their daily operations can learn better ways to use events to their benefit. Analysts have an intuitive understanding of how to design business processes that are triggered by events. However, they could accomplish much more if they understood better how events actually work and used modern design patterns and software tools to harness the power of events.

We need to distinguish between the general concept of *responding* to real-world events, which is practiced more or less continuously by every company and person, and the design discipline known as *event processing,* which encompasses the principles, reference architectures, design patterns, and best practices that are the subject of this book. Many business analysts, managers, and application architects have only an informal and limited knowledge of this subject. Event processing is not included in many business and computer science courses and textbooks, and when it is, it is treated as a side issue rather than a focus. Most people are more familiar with the characteristics of systems that are not event based, such as time-driven and request-driven systems, because those design styles are more commonly used in business applications (although the terms *time-driven* and *request-driven* aren't explicitly recognized in many cases).

In some crucial ways, event processing changes the rules of the game. Event-driven design differs from conventional design in a way that can be compared to the difference between left-brain and right-brain thinking.

Why Event Processing Has Become Critical

If event processing is such a great idea, why hasn't everyone been doing it all along? Event processing is underutilized partly because relatively little data on current business events has been available in digital form until recently. In the past, many events either were undetected or were detected but not reported in a digital form that could be sent over a network or manipulated by a computer. Now, more events are detected and represented electronically, although, unfortunately, many are still not readily accessible to the people, devices, or IT systems that could benefit from them.

The amount of available event data is rapidly expanding because of the decreasing costs and increasing speed of computers and networks, and the unifying power of the World Wide Web and its communication standards. We are blessed with an explosion of event "streams" flowing over corporate networks—data from websites, enterprise application systems, e-mail systems, cell phones, RFID readers, GPS systems, and a variety of other sensors and devices. This wealth of event data will grow as the cost of the relevant technologies continues to drop and companies create new sources of event data in their operations and the outside environment. Our challenge is to make better use of this data.

The other reason that formal event processing has been used sparingly until now is that competition and customer demands were less urgent in the past. Companies had more time to respond to events than they have today. A person driving 30 miles per hour doesn't need as much advance warning of upcoming curves or obstructions on the road as a person driving 60 miles per hour. Companies today are operating at a faster pace, so early notification of emerging business threats and opportunities is increasingly important. Companies that know how to leverage event processing have an advantage over those that don't.

About This Book

The goal of this book is to make the knowledge of the event-processing design discipline more widely available. If you understand how event processing really works, you can design business processes and IT systems that will offer your company better timeliness, agility, and information availability.

The book is aimed at a broad audience, including business analysts, IT architects, CIOs, application managers, project leaders, process modelers, and technology-aware businesspeople outside of the IT department. It bridges the gap between the business literature, which describes the aspirations of agile companies, and the technical literature, which explains how to write event-driven programs. The book does not expound on the value of situation awareness, rapid response, accelerated business processes, or expanding the event horizon to see further into the future, because it assumes that you either already know about these concepts or can find an explanation elsewhere (Appendix A provides a reference to some of the better resources on those topics). This book focuses on *how* to achieve these, not why you'd want to.

The first three chapters of the book introduce the basic concepts and terminology so that you understand the gist of event processing. Chapters 4 and 5 explain the kinds of business problems that event processing addresses and give more examples of real-world applications. Chapters 6 and 7 explore logical design and architectural issues. (This book neither assumes that you have knowledge of a programming language nor delves into how to write code, but it does explain how things work. Wherever we need to dive into technical details, we'll give you the bottom line in plain language.) Chapters 8 through 11 address best practices, organizational issues, industry standards, and a bit about the software technology. We don't evaluate commercial software products because they change too frequently, but we identify the kinds of software that are relevant. Finally, Chapter 12 concludes the book with a look at current and future impact of this discipline. Appendix B includes a glossary of terms to help you navigate through this subject.

Event processing is one of the most interesting aspects of modern technology. It will bring fundamental—and favorable—shifts in the nature of business and the practice of IT.

Acknowledgments

This book was made possible by the cheerful support of Gartner Research management. Peter Sondergaard, Val Sriber, Jeff Schulman, and Anthony Bradley understood the value of event processing from the start. They believed in its importance to the industry enough to invest resources. Without their backing and personal encouragement, this project would not have happened.

The research that led to the writing of the book was also funded, in part, by the Lee Center at the California Institute of Technology (Caltech). Members of the Center listened to seminars, read papers, and gave constructive criticism over a decade. The research was also funded in part by the Air Force Office of Scientific Research Multidisciplinary University Research Initiative. Many students in the Infospheres group at Caltech worked on event-processing systems from the late 1980s; their influence is gratefully acknowledged.

The information for this book was drawn from many sources. As with any book, it is impossible to trace the origins of much of it, but some contributions stand out. We would like thank David Luckham for his book, insights conveyed through countless discussions, and friendship. Several other people contributed directly to this book by providing comments and valuable input as we worked, including John Bates, Opher Etzion, Dieter Gawlick, Alan Lundberg, Giles Nelson, Peter Niblett, Mark Palmer, Dale Skeen, Paul Vincent, and Jeff Wootton. We leaned heavily on the work done by many colleagues at Gartner, Inc., particularly Anthony Bradley, Bill Gassman, Yefim Natis, Massimo Pezzini, Dan Sholler, Jim Sinur, and Jess Thompson. Members of the Event Processing Technical Society helped directly and indirectly in many ways. We give special thanks to the participants in the EPTS Glossary Working Group: Jeff Adkins, Pedro Bizarro, H.-Arno Jacobsen, David Luckham, Albert Mavashev, Brenda M. Michelson, Peter Niblett, and David Tucker. Much of the vital information on the commercial use of event processing is drawn from discussions, conference calls, e-mails, and other interactions with Gartner clients (Roy notes he learned more from them than they did from him on many occasions).

We are also grateful to those who reviewed drafts of the material: Jeff Adkins, Carola Campbell, Jean Chandy, Thomas Chandy, Lesley Koustaff, Michael Schulte, William Sullivan, and Suzanne Swan. They took time from their busy schedules to provide feedback on the clarity and readability of the book from the practitioner's point of view.

Finally, we thank Heather Pemberton Levy, developmental editor at Gartner Inc., Roger Stewart, sponsoring editor at McGraw-Hill, and Patricia Wallenburg, project editor, for the work they did to make this project a success. It was truly a pleasure working with them.

1

Event Processing Overview

This chapter introduces you to events, event-processing systems, and event-driven architecture. You'll learn about the relevance of event processing to contemporary management strategies and begin to see how event processing can improve a company's timeliness, agility, and information availability.

Introduction to Events and Event Processing

An *event* is anything that happens. A *business event* is an event that is meaningful for conducting commercial, industrial, governmental, or trade activities. Examples include receiving a customer order, making a bank payment, experiencing a power outage, changing a customer address, suffering a network security breach, detecting signs of attempted fraud, hiring an employee, and spotting a change in a competitor's price. Events small and large take place all day, every day in every corner of a company and its environment.

A fundamental characteristic of events is that they cannot be entirely foreseen—a company doesn't know in advance when an event will occur or the details of the event's nature. Customers place orders, competitors change prices, and dishonest people attempt fraud according to their own wants and needs, not on a schedule or plan known to the company or its employees.

A company, person, or animal is said to be *event-driven* when it acts in direct response to an event. The event acts as a stimulus, triggering some reaction. Some events represent threats that must be addressed. For example, a zebra that encounters a lion on the savannah will be event-driven to run away as fast as possible. Or a bank that picks up signs of credit card fraud will be event-driven to stop accepting charges on that card immediately.

Other events are positive opportunities that can be exploited. For example, a sales manager who receives a report that snow blower sales in the New York region are exceeding expectations will be event-driven to order an extra shipment of snow blowers to take advantage of the market conditions. A trader who detects a price differential for a certain commodity in two different markets will be event-driven to buy in one market and immediately sell in the other to profit from arbitrage.

Every company or person exhibits event-driven behavior some of the time, but many activities are time-driven or request-driven. A typical corporate business process has event-driven, time-driven, and request-driven aspects. Event-driven behavior is the best approach when dealing with unpredictable factors and situations. The person or system who responds to an event may be guided by a general policy or standard operating procedure but might not know when to implement the policy or procedure or exactly how to apply it to a particular situation until the actual event is detected. Time-driven behavior occurs when the nature and timing of an activity can be planned in advance. Request-driven behavior is appropriate when the nature of the activity is understood and jointly agreed on by multiple parties but the timing is not predictable.

Because the world is full of events, airplanes need pilots, not just flight plans. A flight plan can describe a trip in advance, taking into account landmarks, distances, weight, historical data on fuel consumption, weather forecasts, and reported wind velocity. But a pilot is required to carry out the plan and make ongoing adjustments, as the plane will inevitably encounter other planes and changes in the weather, and perhaps have mechanical problems or experience other unforeseeable conditions while en route to its destination. Most of a pilot's job is event-driven. Drones and automatic pilots have become practical in recent years precisely because of the emergence of the technology described in this book. Our primary focus is on commercial business systems rather than on smart devices but the principles are the same.

All companies and people pay attention to events because the real world is complex and dynamic, and no one has complete foreknowledge of what will happen. Activities that are strongly affected by external factors—things that are outside the control of the company—are particularly suited to event-driven behavior. For example, field sales and service operations, customer contact centers, web-based sales and marketing, other customer-facing activities, supply chain management, transportation operations, and anything to do with competitive markets are fertile ground for event-driven behavior and event-processing systems. Internal processes that are more under the control of the company have more time-driven and request-driven aspects, but even they are sometimes event-driven because unexpected circumstances arise everywhere.

Being event-driven in a real-world sense is clearly nothing new. If your company is advised to become an event-driven enterprise, that doesn't mean that your company should start handling events—your company already does that. What it means is that your company should improve *how* its business processes and IT systems handle events. Too often, companies respond to events by using outdated processes that were designed for a slower-paced, less-automated world. They don't take full advantage of the wealth of event data that is available in enterprise application systems, on the Web, or from other potential sources of event data. People making minute-by-minute, operational decisions often don't get information on current events soon enough. In other cases, people are overwhelmed by the volume of event data that is sent their way so they miss the truly important observations. Most companies could streamline, simplify, accelerate, and improve operations in hundreds of ways by applying the discipline of event processing.

Business Context

Companies use the discipline of event processing to improve business performance, not to make their IT departments run better (although event processing can sometimes do that, too). Today's companies face escalating demands, as shown in the Business Pressures column in Figure 1-1.

Competition is growing as new companies emerge. Globalization is also increasing the number of competitors that any business is likely to encounter in a traditional geographic market. Many markets are consolidating as weaker players lose ground to stronger companies. Companies strive to outdo each other by providing faster and better customer service, new products, and, in many cases, lower prices. Customer expectations keep rising, putting pressure on every company to improve its operations. When someone applies for a loan or an insurance policy, she expects a quicker decision and more visibility into the process than was available in earlier days. When a customer submits an insurance claim, requests a repair service, or ships a package or letter, he wants quick action and may want to know the status of his work item at all times. When he places an order online, he expects that the goods will arrive sooner than in the past and wants a tracking number so he can anticipate the delivery time.

New requirements also arise from external regulators and internal decision-makers. Governments and other official bodies impose an ever-growing amount of regulation that requires more reporting and better transparency of operations. Executives, managers, and operational decision-makers on every level want fresher and better information from dashboard displays, e-mail, and other forms of alerts so they can have a clearer picture of what is happening. Operational control activities, such as

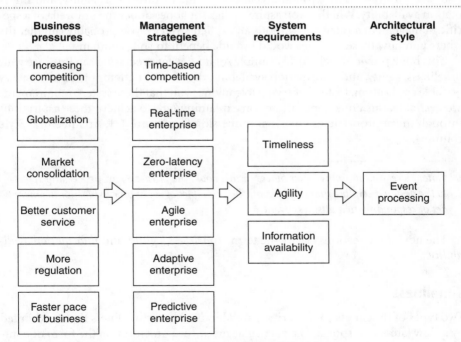

Figure 1-1: Business pressures affect application architecture decisions.

supply chain management, are far more effective today because of the increasing availability of current information about events. Technology makes it possible for companies to respond to all of these requirements, but it also encourages these requirements to grow even more over time.

These business pressures have inspired the development of numerous modern management strategies (see Figure 1-1, Management Strategies column). Time-based competition, real-time enterprise, and zero-latency enterprise strategies highlight the benefits of timeliness. Agile enterprise and adaptive enterprise strategies focus on the importance of flexibility and change. Predictive enterprise strategies emphasize a combination of information availability and timeliness. Each strategy has its own set of truths and benefits, but they all ultimately depend on improving a company's timeliness, agility, and information availability (see Figure 1-1, System Requirements column) to varying degrees. For example, fast action isn't much good if you are doing the wrong things quickly, so you need good information as well as timeliness. Doing the right thing quickly is good, but you also need agility so you can adjust your behavior when the business requirements change, because the "right thing" will change over time.

This is not a book on business architecture, so we won't dwell on business pressures and management strategies. We mention them here to explain why people pursue event processing. For the purpose of this discussion, we assume that you and others in your company already know which of these business requirements and management strategies apply to your situation, or you can discover them by other means. We also take for granted that you appreciate the value of timeliness, agility, and information availability. Whether you aspire to these qualities under the umbrella of a specific management strategy or without an explicit strategy, you probably can identify where and how these qualities would provide benefit to your company.

This book provides real-world examples of how event processing can improve your timeliness, agility, and information availability, but it won't attempt to identify every possible application. Instead of trying to convince you that these system requirements are desirable, this book concentrates on explaining *how* to achieve these aspirations through the appropriate use of event processing (see Figure 1-1, Architectural Style column).

Note: Here, and in many other places in this book, the phrase event processing *refers to the design discipline that implements the principles of event processing, not the mere act of responding to a business event.*

The next three sections clarify the terms *timeliness, agility,* and *information availability.*

Timeliness

Two types of timeliness (or "celerity") are identified here: timeliness that is exhibited by a "low latency" response to a particular input, and timeliness in the form of completing an end-to-end business process in a shorter elapsed time.

Reducing Latency for an Individual Activity

Latency is the time it takes for a system to respond to an input. Latency in the user interface is one of the most critical factors in the design of an interactive system. Software engineers pay an enormous amount of attention to latency because of the impact that it has on human productivity. When online application systems first became popular in the 1970s, studies showed that applications that returned results to the display terminal within 400 milliseconds (0.4 second) after the user pressed ENTER on the keyboard provided excellent user efficiency for transactional applications. More-common systems with 1- to 2-second latencies were a bit less valuable because people noticed the pause and their rhythm was disrupted in subtle ways. Systems with higher latencies were not only annoying, they damaged the productivity and effectiveness of the business.

Latency is still an important issue for surfing the Web and for social applications. Modern web designers know that if their site can't display a new web page within several seconds of a person clicking a hyperlink, many users will lose patience and abandon the thread they are pursuing (although their willingness to tolerate delay varies considerably, depending on the nature of the task—sometimes 2 seconds is too long!).

Latency is also an issue in other aspects of IT systems and in business activities that don't use computers at all. Reducing latency can help a person or company in myriad ways, most of which are fairly obvious. For most business activities, faster is better up to a point, but beyond that point timeliness has little or no additional value. Event processing, and particularly event-driven architecture (EDA), helps reduce latency, as we'll explain shortly.

Reducing Business Process Elapsed Time

An insurance company that used to pay 90 percent of automobile damage claims within 25 working days now pays 90 percent of those claims within 9 days. A computer vendor that previously filled orders for PCs within two weeks now ships PCs to customers within 24 hours. Banks that traditionally settled foreign currency trades overnight now settle some currency trades within seconds using real-time gross settlement (RTGS) systems.

These are examples of *multistep* business processes—sequences of activities carried out by one or more people, application systems, or business units. The benefit of reducing the end-to-end elapsed time for the process varies. In some cases, the benefit is increased customer satisfaction, leading to more revenue. In other cases, the company saves money by being able to hold less inventory, thereby reducing the carrying costs of inventory. In the case of RTGS, banks are reducing their risk.

If you consider process elapsed time closely, it turns out to be another way of looking at latency. The difference between a multistep process and an individual activity is in the eye of the beholder. Even the simplest activity can be considered a process because it can be decomposed into subactivities. For example, when you click a hyperlink to navigate the Web, you are initiating a short process that will end when the new page is displayed on your browser. To decrease the latency of an individual activity, you need to reduce the elapsed time of the process that constitutes that activity.

Latency is more useful than process elapsed time as a way to think about timeliness where you don't want to deal with the subactivities. On the other hand, process elapsed time is more appropriate when you have reasons to be aware of the component activities. People often think of latency for responses that occur within seconds or minutes and use elapsed time for things that consume hours or days, but the distinction is arbitrary and technically fictitious. Ultimately, the business only cares about minimizing the time between the beginning and the end of the activity or process, and EDA helps this in a wide range of business situations.

Agility

Enterprise agility is one of the most trite goals in business today, but it's trite for good reason. The world is changing faster than ever. An agile enterprise can readily adjust its behavior in response to environmental or internal changes—such as shifts in customer demand, competitors' activities, regulatory requirements, economic trends, supplier activities, and company circumstances. Agility is different from timeliness because it refers to a company's ability to change its activities rather than its ability to just perform them in less time.

Here we identify two forms of agility: instance agility and process agility.

Instance Agility

Instance agility is the ability of an entity to handle each instance (iteration) of a business process differently. For example, each car that comes off an assembly line can have its own unique combination of colors, tires, and audio equipment. In the extreme, no two cars may be alike. Another example is an insurance company cutting and pasting a different set of amendments ("endorsements") to create a custom insurance policy that is tailored to a customer's particular needs. Processes that allow decisions to be made by a person dynamically at run time exhibit instance agility. Activities can be skipped, inserted, executed out of order, or modified on the fly. Instance agility enables "mass customization," and when applied to marketing, people speak of it as "precision marketing" or selling to a "market of one."

Process Agility

Process agility is the ability of an entity to change a whole process to support new kinds of products or services. For example, if customer demand for sport utility vehicles (SUVs) drops, an automobile manufacturer may decide to convert an SUV assembly line to produce smaller, fuel-efficient cars. Another example is an insurance company that enters a new market to insure boats by adapting the process, forms, people, and application systems that it uses to insure cars.

The effect of process agility is more durable than the effect of instance agility. Process changes affect every instance that is undertaken in the revised process. Every vehicle that comes off the modified assembly line will be a car rather than an SUV. By contrast, instance agility doesn't change the process definition; it merely provides ad hoc variability for each instance within the bounds of a defined process.

In subsequent chapters, we explain how events play a role in enabling both kinds of agility.

Information Availability

This book addresses only a small part of the information management discipline, specifically focusing on three aspects that are most directly affected by event processing: data consistency, information dissemination, and situation awareness.

Data Consistency

The goal of *data consistency* initiatives is to get multiple business units and their respective application systems and databases to agree on the facts. For a variety of reasons, all companies inevitably have redundant versions of some data regarding customers, products, orders, employees, and other entities. We can bemoan the disadvantages of maintaining redundant data and strive to reduce it through strategies such as master data management (MDM), but maintaining redundant data sometimes is necessary and often is inescapable in practical terms. This gives rise to the perennial problem of keeping data consistent ("in sync") across the disparate data stores. When a person, department, or application system receives or generates new data or a revised version of the data, the person or entity updates the local database. The person or system should also forward a copy of the new data to other departments and systems that are keeping track of that data.

Business-to-business (B2B) relationships also depend on data consistency. For example, a company may need to send its product catalog and price information to its distributors or customers. This may entail bulk transfers or partial updates.

Information Dissemination

The need to pass on information is one of the most common situations in business and in life. A person or system detects that something happened and sends a report to one or more people or systems. Notifying a single recipient is a simple case of information dissemination. Some messages report routine events that are expected in the normal course of business, such as the arrival of a shipment. Other notifications report exceptions or abnormal situations, such as when a warning system notifies all the students on a campus through e-mail, Short Message Service (SMS) text messages, or a "reverse 911" network that the school will close early because of a snowstorm. A notification that is intended to cause a response is often called an *alert*.

Situation Awareness

Situation (or *situational*) *awareness* means knowing what is going on so that you can decide what to do. The term originated in military applications to describe the goals of advanced command and control systems, but it is relevant in many business scenarios as well. Companies seek to cut the fog of commerce just as generals seek to cut the fog of war. Almost every company has operational activities that run continuously and must respond quickly to changing conditions. Situation awareness implies that you have an up-to-the-minute understanding of the environment and your own internal circumstances. The purpose of situation awareness is to help you make faster and better decisions—it can be viewed as the ultimate goal of intelligent decision management initiatives. Situation awareness goes beyond mere dissemination because it implies that someone or something is able to synthesize multiple sources of input data to develop a holistic picture of what is happening.

Relating Business Drivers to System Design

Timeliness, agility, and information availability can't be achieved simply by speeding up traditional business processes or exhorting people to work harder and smarter with conventional applications. These goals generally require fundamental changes in the architecture of business processes and the application systems that support them. Often this involves more use of the event processing discipline.

Almost every step in every business process today is enabled in some direct or indirect manner by an IT system. You can't have timeliness, agility, and information availability in your business unless you also have timeliness, agility, and information availability in your IT systems. Of course, IT is only part of the solution. Improving the business also requires changes to the non-IT aspects of operations, including people's job descriptions, document and form design, the flow of work, corporate polices and procedures, the organizational chart, and corporate governance. These are all part of business *systems* in the larger sense of the word.

Summary

Events—things that happen—are a central fact of life for companies and people. Companies can improve the timeliness, agility, and information availability of their operations if they handle events in a systematic way that leverages advances in the contemporary understanding of how events work.

2

Event-Processing Patterns in Business

This chapter describes different types of interactions among people and among software components. The chapter analyzes use of these different interaction types at different times in the evolution of information technology, and shows why event-driven interactions are becoming more common today. The differences between different types of interactions are highlighted by studying contracts or expectations between people executing each type of interaction; contracts between people are extended to software contracts between components. The chapter explains why hybrid systems—systems that use different types of interactions for different functionalities—are becoming increasingly common. Understanding the basic types of interactions described in this chapter will help lay the foundation for more detailed analyses in later chapters.

Categories of Business Drivers for Event Processing

Chapter 1 discussed the business drivers for event processing and summarized them in Figure 1-1. Understanding those business drivers is also helpful to understanding trends in the use of information processing patterns in business and IT, as discussed in this chapter, so Figure 1-1 is presented again here as Figure 2-1 for your reference.

The business drivers shown in the first three columns of Figure 2-1 can be aggregated into three basic categories:

▶ **Celerity**—The pace of business keeps increasing. Celerity—swiftness of action—is an increasingly important competitive advantage.

▶ **Connectedness**—The world is increasingly interconnected. Events in Guangzhou impact prices in Peoria. Bands in Dublin impact music listening in Los Angeles.

▶ **Complexity**—The intricacy of business regulations in multiple jurisdictions, convoluted healthcare insurance, and labyrinthine financial instruments (such as credit default swaps and collateralized debt obligations) provide ample evidence of the increasing complexity of business and, indeed, daily life.

Celerity is fundamental to several of the components listed in Figure 2-1, including timeliness, the faster pace of business, time-based competition, and the predictive enterprise. Since more timely service to customers is also better service, celerity is also important in better customer service. The relationship between celerity and these components of Figure 2-1 is shown in Figure 2-2.

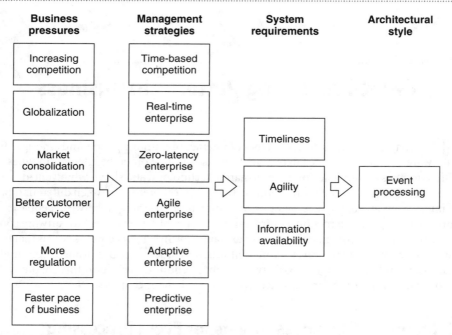

Figure 2-1: Escalating business pressures motivate the use of event processing.

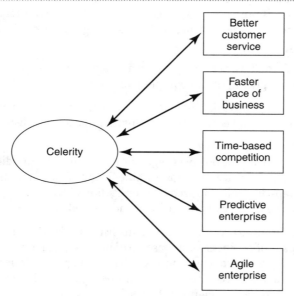

Figure 2-2: Celerity and business trends driving event processing.

Connectedness between enterprises and the outside world is a feature that appears in many of the components of Figure 2-1. Globalization requires interactions between components distributed across countries. Market consolidation requires connections between enterprises that are merged or acquired. Different countries and even different states within the same country have regulations dealing with the same issues, and so more complex regulation is also a demand for greater connectivity. Governments are issuing more regulations on the financial sector and other areas of business. Better customer service through the Web requires more attention to connectivity. People and components in different places and time zones help agile enterprises adapt to changing conditions. The relationship between connectedness and these components of Figure 2-1 is shown in Figure 2-3.

The business world is getting increasingly complex. Regulations are getting ever more detailed and regulators require businesses to detect and report noncompliance ever more quickly. Rules and processes become more complicated as markets and businesses are consolidated. Enterprises compete for each individual customer; for example, advertisements associated with keywords on web searches are targeted to satisfy the interests of smaller and smaller groups of customers as they treat each customer as a "market of one." The adaptive enterprise responds quickly to changes in the economic climate and government actions. People in enterprises are kept aware of situations and key performance indicators across multiple divisions. A few of the roles that complexity plays in business trends driving event processing are shown in Figure 2-4.

Celerity, connectedness, and complexity are characteristics of business trends that result in increasing use of event-driven patterns of interactions. These categories are

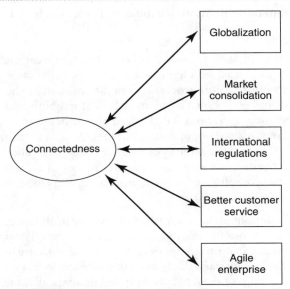

Figure 2-3: Connectedness and business trends driving event processing.

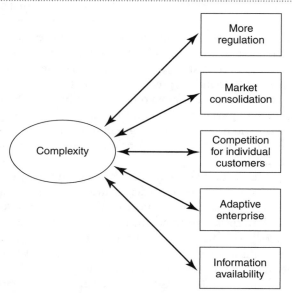

Figure 2-4: Complexity and business trends driving event processing.

examples of "consumer pull"—demand by consumers for more support for event-driven interactions.

Trends in technology also increase use of event-driven interactions. These trends are examples of "producer push" that increase usage of event-driven interactions by providing less expensive and more powerful technology. These trends include (see Figure 2-5):

▶ **Price**—Costs of most items, such as a year of college education, a car, and a kilo-watt-hour, have gone up at least tenfold in the last 50 years. In the same period, the dollar cost of an information processing operation, such as the cost of searching a database, has gone down by many orders of magnitude. The cost of information processing operations has changed even more dramatically in the last 50 years when measured not in dollars but in units such as the number of database searches that cost the same as one day of college education. There are many reasons for the decreasing cost of IT, such as Moore's Law, more powerful software, open source software for event processing, and global competition in the IT space; see Figure 2-5.

▶ **Pervasiveness**—IT components are increasingly pervasive in all aspects of our lives, including our safety, health, food, water, and energy needs. The densities of transistors on chips and data on storage devices, such as disks, have increased exponentially over the last 50 years. Partly as a consequence, form factors and power consumption ratings of devices have dropped dramatically, and this in turn is leading to increasing use of IT devices in cars, hospitals, and the smart

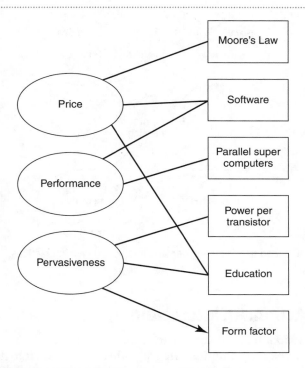

Figure 2-5: Technology push for event-driven interactions.

electric power grid. Billions of people are familiar with IT tools, such as the Internet and mobile phones, and this level of education about IT tools makes IT even more pervasive.

▶ **Performance**—The ease of access to immense computing power offered by cloud computing, such as Amazon's EC2, wasn't imagined even as recently as 10 years ago. The performance of information systems has grown dramatically over the last half century, and even small companies can get access to substantial computing power.

The combination of technology push—price, pervasiveness, and performance—and consumer pull—celerity, connectedness, and complexity—is making changing components of IT systems and enterprises interact in a more event-driven manner. We refer to this collection of trends as *PC-cubed*, after **p**roducer push and **c**onsumer pull, and after the components of producer push and consumer pull—price, pervasiveness, and performance, and celerity, connectedness and complexity (Figure 2-6). Let's begin our study of how event-processing interactions are impacted by the PC-cubed trends by looking at basic human activity.

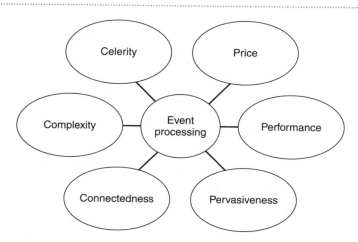

Figure 2-6: The PC-cubed trends driving demand for event-driven interactions.

The Basic Action: An Interaction

A simplistic description of human activity is that humans observe the world around them; learn from the past; communicate with others; decide what to do; and act (see Figure 2-7). When a group of prehistoric men hunted, they used their five senses to observe their environment; they learned that certain spoors indicated deer while others indicated tigers; they communicated with others in their hunting party; they decided what each of them would do; and they acted. The activities we carry out today and those that our ancestors carried out millennia ago have points in common. There are, however, profound changes in speed, scale, and complexity.

Our ancestors looked for threats and opportunities as far as the eye could see; today we use sensor networks to scan the planet. Our forefathers deciphered patterns of paw prints in the ground; today we use sophisticated business intelligence programs to identify subtle patterns. Our ancestors communicated with members of their hunting party by using sounds and signs; today we use the Internet to communicate to all points on the globe. Our forebears processed information in their brains; today we amplify our intelligence by using powerful algorithms, processors, and storage. Though the differences in scale are indeed profound, you can understand the continuing evolution of IT by focusing on how IT supports activities that humans have carried out from the beginning of history.

Let's begin by studying a basic unit of human activity: the interaction. How do people interact with each other and what do they gain from interactions? Many types of interaction occur among people and components in IT systems. Chapter 1 introduced the basic types of interaction—time-driven, request-driven, and event-driven interactions. People exchange information and decide what to do in these interactions. Each type of interaction offers some advantages over the oth-

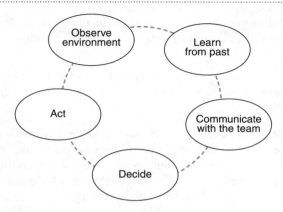

Figure 2-7: Stages in human activity.

ers in terms of celerity, agility, and information availability, so most IT systems employ combinations of the basic types. This chapter discusses different types of interaction in detail.

A study of types of interaction helps in identifying the fundamental concepts essential for designing in the event-driven architecture (EDA) style. A review of the historical contexts in which these interactions flourished helps us understand how different software styles developed in the past and where they are going in the future. Arguments about software architectures can get heated—discussions about whether a product is in the EDA style or whether service-oriented architecture (SOA) can be event-driven can get contentious. We can get to the heart of these issues by asking questions about the most elementary operations: How do people interact with each other? How do we expect software components to interact? Elucidating the differences between basic types of interaction gets to core issues without using terms that may be considered either pejorative or complimentary.

People with expertise in different areas of IT have different views of event processing. An expert concerned with only one stage of activity—such as an expert in sensor networks for observation, business intelligence for learning, message oriented middleware (MOM) for communicating, real-time pattern detection for deciding, or actuator design for executing actions—brings a valuable, but different, perspective to event processing. This discussion integrates different perspectives to help you understand how event processing helps across all stages of activity.

People and organizations have processed events since the beginning of history. IT has always supported event processing, though IT approaches have been problem-specific and ad hoc. A discipline of event processing that spans all branches of IT is only just emerging. This discipline will have a profound impact on the evolution of IT over the next few decades. A foundation for such a cross-discipline must start with the basics, and there is nothing more basic than an interaction. Let's identify features common to event processing in human organizations and IT by studying interactions among people in enterprises and among IT components. Indeed, most features of IT event-processing systems are mirrored in human organizations. The term *agent* is used to indicate both a person and a component of an IT system. A study of interactions among agents is thus a study of how people and IT components interact.

> Note: A discipline of event processing that spans all branches of IT is emerging. A foundation for such a discipline must start with the basics, and there is nothing more basic than an interaction.

People in an enterprise have expectations—formal or informal—of each other. An enterprise functions because people live up to shared expectations. We have expectations of one another at all stages of activity as we observe, learn, communicate, decide, and act. For example, we expect to be kept informed about important events. A parent on a business trip expects to be informed if an emergency occurs at home; the president of a country expects to be informed if the country is attacked; a CEO expects to be notified if a factory burns down. An example of shared expectations between a mother and her support system, while the mother is traveling, is shown in Figure 2-8. People interact partly to meet shared expectations, and components of IT systems interact to meet designers' expectations about component behavior. In software engineering, an expectation of a component is manifested as a formal *contract* specifying how that component must behave. Expectations and contracts provide a systematic framework for analyzing interactions.

> Note: An enterprise functions because people live up to shared expectations. Shared expectations of people in organizations and formal contracts for components in IT systems provide a systematic framework for analyzing interactions.

The next section analyzes basic types of interaction using the framework of shared expectations and contracts in the context of the PC-cubed trends.

Time-, Request-, and Event-Driven Interactions

Chapter 1 introduced the three basic types of interaction, *time-driven, request-driven,* and *event-driven*. This chapter explores the nature of these interaction patterns in more detail. The types of interaction are differentiated by what initiates the interaction and the set of participants in the interaction. The goal here is to identify the unique features of event-driven interactions as they occur in the context of human activity (refer to Figure 2-7) and as they occur between IT components.

▶ **Time-driven**—In a time-driven interaction, an agent, or a group of agents, initiates an interaction at a specified time. An example of such an interaction is a regular meeting of an executive committee that meets every Monday at 8 A.M. The interaction is initiated when a specific time (Monday at 8 A.M.) is reached. The participants in the interaction (the executive committee) are specified by the invite list.

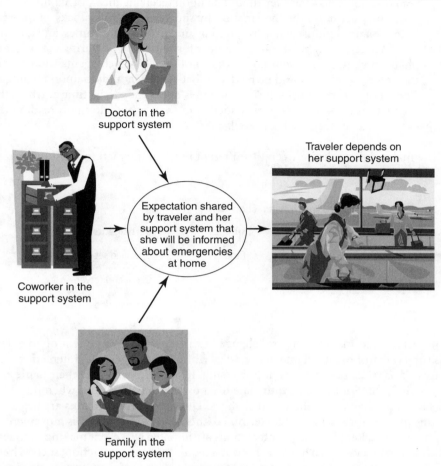

Doctor in the
support system

Coworker in the
support system

Expectation shared
by traveler and her
support system that
she will be informed
about emergencies
at home

Traveler depends on
her support system

Family in the
support system

Figure 2-8: Shared expectations in event-driven interactions.

▶ **Request-driven**—In a request-driven interaction, a client requests a service from a server and waits to receive a reply from that server. The interaction is initiated by the client and completes when the server replies. The participants in the interaction are the client and the server.

▶ **Event-driven**—In an event-driven interaction, an agent initiates an interaction by creating an object describing an event. Here's an example of an event: Lehman Brothers declared bankruptcy on September 15, 2008. Lehman started an event-driven interaction by creating an event object—the bankruptcy filing. The event object describes a state change: Lehman was not bankrupt on September 14 and became bankrupt on September 15. The bankruptcy filing does not specify which agents—organizations, individuals, and software—should read the filing and what they should do upon receiving the information. Hedge funds may act upon the information by short-selling bank stocks; employees in the financial industry may respond by updating their resumes; and government agencies may act upon the same information by preparing contingency plans. In general, an event object does not specify which agents should read the object, when it should be read, or what agents should do upon reading it. The set of participants in the interaction is open-ended, the time at which the interaction terminates is open-ended, and what agents do upon reading the event object is open-ended as well.

The major differences between the different types of interaction are summarized in Table 2-1.

Table 2-1: Basic Types of Interaction

Type of Interaction	Initiator	Participants
Time-driven	Time	Specified set of agents
Request-driven	Client	Client and server
Event-driven	Event	Open-ended

In technical terms, an event is a change in the state of a component of an enterprise or its environment. All interactions deal with state changes so all interactions can be treated as special cases of event processing. If you ask somebody their name and they reply "John Smith," then your state of knowledge changes; and when the clock ticks forward, the state of the world changes. Time-driven interactions are triggered by time moving forward to a predetermined interaction point, and this movement of time is an event. Request-driven interactions are initiated by a client making a request, which is also an event. When you carry out a request-driven interaction, such as buying an airline ticket, you do so because something happened—an event occurred—to make you start the interaction. Though time-driven and request-driven interactions can be thought of as special cases of event-driven interactions, the ways in which events are processed by each of these interactions are different.

The basic types of interaction can be illustrated by considering three simple commands from an investor to a commodities broker:

▶ **Time-driven example**—Buy 10 ounces of gold every morning at 8 A.M. provided the price is less than $800 until my funds are exhausted (see Figure 2-9).

▶ **Request-driven example**—Buy 10 ounces of gold right now provided the price is less than $800 per ounce (see Figure 2-10).

▶ **Event-driven example**—Until I tell you to stop buying, or my funds are exhausted, keep buying and selling gold according to a specified strategy. An example of a strategy is this: Exchange cash for gold when the 13-week mov-

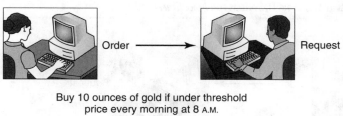

Buy 10 ounces of gold if under threshold
price every morning at 8 A.M.

Figure 2-9: Time-driven interactions.

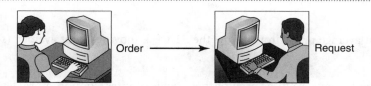

Buy 10 ounces of gold if under threshold price

Order has been fulfilled

Figure 2-10: Request-driven interactions.

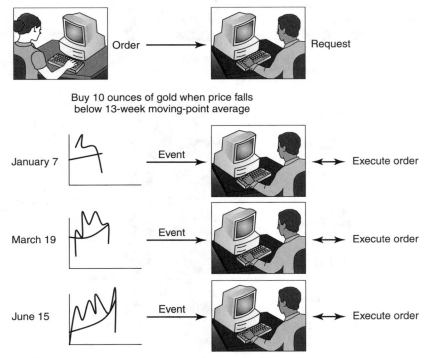

Buy 10 ounces of gold when price falls
below 13-week moving-point average

Figure 2-11: Event-driven interactions.

ing-point average price drops below the 52-week moving-point average (see Figure 2-11).

The following sections examine each of these types of interaction in more detail using the examples just described and shown in the figures. After that, each of these types of interaction is evaluated in turn. The examples are used to show the differences between the participants in different types of interaction, the start and end times of the interactions, and the business situations in which each type of interaction is used.

Time-Driven Interactions

In the time-driven interaction of the example (see Figure 2-9), the broker continues to perform tasks for the client, but does so at specified times. The broker's actions are triggered by time. Some time-driven interactions are executed once and some are executed repeatedly. Time-driven interactions are appropriate when tasks can be scheduled and rapid responses to unanticipated events are not critical. The benefits of time-driven interactions are evident from their ubiquity: for example, a CEO meets with the executive team every Monday at 8 A.M., or a batch computer job runs every night at 11 P.M. Organizations use time-driven interactions in combination with other interaction patterns. For instance, if a factory burns down on Tuesday, the factory manager doesn't wait till the following Monday to inform the CEO. Information about the event—factory burns down—is communicated to the CEO as soon as possible using event-driven interactions.

Request-Driven Interactions

In a request-driven interaction, such as depicted in the example in Figure 2-10, a server executes a service for a client and then does nothing on behalf of the client until the client makes another explicit request. Request-driven software interactions are better suited than time-driven interactions for meeting urgent needs. For example, a CEO may call a CFO to ask about the status of a line of credit rather than wait to find out the status at the next scheduled weekly meeting. The thread of interaction begins with the CEO making a request to the CFO and ends with the CFO responding to the request. In that context, the CEO is the client and the CFO is the server. A common example of a request-driven activity is a consumer looking up a bank balance at a website.

Advantages of request-driven interactions are that the interactions have clear initiation points (client makes a request), clear termination points (client receives a reply), and well-defined participants (the client and the server). These advantages are manifested in both human and software interactions. In some cases, the request and reply can be treated logically as a transaction—a single indivisible atomic operation: a transaction is either completed successfully or aborted. For example, when a bank is transferring funds to another bank, you want either the transaction to succeed and funds debited from the first bank and added to the second, or the transaction to be aborted and the amounts in both banks to remain unchanged. You would be perturbed if a transaction you initiated to move funds from one bank to another either lost your money or never terminated. Though transactions can be implemented as sequences of event-driven interactions, they are more commonly treated as request-reply interactions.

The request-driven interaction pattern has been used in IT since the dawn of computing with good reason. Programming languages, since the 1960s, have used procedure calls in which a program calls a procedure and waits for a response. Remote procedure calls, remote method invocations, client-server interactions, and most web service interactions are request-driven. The long history and current ubiquity of request-driven interactions provide evidence of their value.

Event-Driven Interactions

In the event-driven interaction example shown in Figure 2-11, the commodity broker continues to do tasks for the investor; however, the actions of the broker are triggered by events and not by the clock or by requests. The event of the 13-week moving-point average dropping below the 52-week moving-point average is a complex event; this event is detected by carrying out computations on a set of simple event objects such as an object that contains a price and a timestamp.

The event-driven interaction example, though very simple, has features that merit discussion. The investor and broker have long-term expectations of their interaction: the broker continues to carry out responses on behalf of the investor until told to stop. By contrast, a request-driven interaction terminates with the reply from the server. Indeed, the requester may not want the server to keep data about the request after the interaction is over. In an EDA application, the user expects the application to maintain information about the user so that the application can continue to execute tasks on the user's behalf. For example, you expect your doctor to remember your medical information so that the doctor can send you an alert when an event—such as the recall of a drug that you are taking—occurs. The differences in expectations impact designs of systems based on time-, request-, and event-driven interactions.

Note: Users expect event-driven applications to maintain information about them so that the applications continue to work on their behalf. A user of a request-driven application may prefer that the application delete information about the user after the application has replied to the user's request.

The following sections evaluate how the PC-cubed trends impact the usage of different types of interaction. Later in this chapter, we compare expectations of components—or, in software engineering terms, formal contracts for components—that participate in each type of interaction.

Evaluation of Time-Driven Interactions

IT relied mostly on time-driven interactions in the 1960s. Computing jobs in that period required long execution times, so job schedules optimized use of the scarcest resource: the computer. Such schedules were largely time-driven. Since the 1960s the costs of non-IT tools and services have increased tenfold while costs of IT have dropped by many orders of magnitude. So, optimum scheduling to maximize effective usage of computers has given way to patterns of interaction that optimize performance of people and their non-IT tools and services. This has resulted in more usage of event- and request-driven interactions that serve people's needs with greater celerity.

All-hands company meetings can be efficient at small startups but are inefficient for companies with hundreds of thousands of employees. Many IT systems have thousands of sensors, responders, and processors, and synchronized operations of large numbers of devices are inefficient. Even within a single microchip, synchronized scheduling of operations across a billion or more transistors is less efficient than executing multiple local asynchronous operations. Time-driven interactions won't disappear, because they are very useful, but system-wide centralized interactions are being replaced by multiple local interactions among fewer agents.

Certain activities—such as the government's reports on unemployment, or company quarterly reports—are time-driven, and the IT operations that monitor these activities are, perforce, time-driven too. Likewise, markets open and close at fixed times and so analyses of complex financial instruments are often carried out in a time-driven fashion: after the market closes each day and before the market reopens the next day. But 24/7 trading venues and the competitive advantages of celerity are incentives for event-driven computations. For instance, instead of running a batch application to check for medical insurance fraud once a day, an EDA application can detect anomalous behavior as possibly fraudulent claims are submitted, and the application can immediately schedule execution of more compute-intensive tasks to investigate anomalous claims and determine whether they are truly instances of fraud.

There are many advantages to time-driven interactions, including the following:

▶ Scheduled interactions among groups of agents allow a piece of information to be shared efficiently among all participants.

▶ Scheduled interactions serve as a "heartbeat" mechanism. If an agent who is expected to participate in a scheduled interaction does not appear at the expected time, then the other participants infer that there is something wrong with the missing agent. For example, heartbeat mechanisms are used in sensor networks to monitor sensor health.

▶ Measurements made at regular intervals produce time series that are readily analyzed. Most digital control systems use periodic signals.

▶ Listening intently requires energy both for people and wireless devices. The time-driven pattern saves energy by enabling groups of agents to listen and interact at specified intervals. Agents become dormant or carry out other activities between scheduled interactions.

These and other benefits ensure that time-driven interactions, supplemented with request- and event-driven interactions, will continue to be used in human organizations and IT systems, but will be used at multiple local levels rather than at system-wide levels. You will see later in this chapter that the PC-cubed trends are engendering hybrid systems that combine time-, request-, and event-driven interactions with predictive and proactive computational patterns.

Evaluation of Request-Driven Interactions

This section looks at how the PC-cubed trends impact usage of request-driven interactions. Consider, for example, the ratio of the cost of having a baby in a hospital to the cost of a standard IT operation, such as searching a repository of text documents, in 2010 and in 1960. The value of an hour of an obstetrician's time, measured in terms of number of IT operations that can be executed for the same price, has increased by many orders of magnitude in 50 years. Economics tells us that we should be as profligate in using IT to improve the performance and efficiency of obstetricians (and indeed of all people) today as we were cautious 50 years ago.

A critical and increasingly scarce resource is uninterrupted time. Request-driven interactions can help to husband this precious resource because agents choose the times of interactions and the services with which they interact. On the other hand, the demand for celerity requires people to respond to events rapidly; celerity argues for people to be interrupted when important events occur. You will see later in this chapter that the tension between having to respond rapidly to events and needing uninterrupted time can be managed by combining request- and event-driven interactions into proactive computations.

Evaluation of Event-Driven Interactions

This section looks at how the PC-cubed trends drive demand for event-driven interactions. Celerity requires rapid response to events and therefore favors event- or time-driven interactions. Increasing connectivity also favors event-driven interactions. It is more efficient for information about the outbreak of a factory fire to be proactively pushed across management layers to the CEO than for the CEO to request each person in the organization to report whether anything important has occurred. Task complexity can also be managed by event-driven interactions by sensing when results from complex tasks are required and responding by executing those tasks proactively. Trends in pricing, pervasiveness, and performance, likewise, drive demand for event-processing interactions as IT becomes the central nervous system that enables the enterprise to sense and respond to the business environment.

Contracts: Formalization of Shared Expectations

This section analyzes different types of interaction in the context of the PC-cubed trends and the expectations people have about components in different interactions. The expectations are manifested as contracts, so contracts for components in different types of interaction are the focus.

Contracts for Event-Driven Interactions

A parent on a business trip expects to receive a message if an emergency occurs at home. If the parent hasn't received such a message, he or she assumes that no emergency has occurred. This commonplace situation illustrates a characteristic of event-driven applications: *The absence of messages conveys information.*

The parent has a model of how the home functions and the parent expects to be notified when reality deviates significantly from this model. A parent can function only because he or she can estimate characteristics of the state of the home without monitoring the home continuously. In software engineering terms, the parent's expectation is a contract between the parent and a support system: family, friends, and others. Their joint expectation of what is, and what is not, normal in the home is based on an informal model of the home.

Note: In event-driven interactions, the absence of messages conveys information.

People function only because (possibly informal) contracts enable them to be aware of their environments without constant, continuous monitoring (refer to Figure 2-8). Likewise, designs of components of EDA systems are based on contracts that enable designers to conclude that the absence of messages to components conveys information. Event-driven interactions are fundamental to the operation of families, enterprises, governments, and EDA systems; organizations and event-based IT systems function only because people and components depend on others to detect and respond to events.

Let's look at contracts in event-driven interactions in more detail:

▶ A contract is for an interval of time. It may have a termination time or it may be open-ended. A parent on a trip has an informal contract with the support system for at least the duration of the trip.

▶ A contract is between an agent and the rest of the system. The agent has expectations of the rest of the system, and the system has expectations of the agent. A parent on a business trip expects the system to notify the parent accurately and in a timely fashion when a critical situation occurs at home; it doesn't matter whether the parent is notified by a son or a daughter, and it doesn't matter whether the notification is delivered by a hotel operator or a colleague at the office. The contract deals with the response to a situation and not with the identities of agents executing the action or the mechanism by which information is disseminated. Contracts that specify *what* must be done but don't specify *how* it must be done allow components of an EDA system to be modified without impacting other components in the system, provided the contracts remain unchanged.

▶ A contract is a collection of *when-then* rules: *when* certain situations arise, *then* respond in the following ways. For example, when a kitchen fire occurs, then call emergency services (such as 911) and attempt to put out the fire. Sometimes a when-then rule is broken down further into an event-condition-action rule; that is, when an event occurs, determine if a condition holds, and carry out the specified action if it does.

▶ The actions in when-then rules may be required to be executed in a timely fashion (though the specifications about time may be informal rather than quantitative). A parent on a business trip expects to be informed soon—say, within an hour—after a critical event at home. This timeliness gives the parent confidence that nothing unusual has happened in the last hour if he or she hasn't heard anything. A system does not help parents respond effectively if it informs them about emergencies only months after they occur. Timeliness enables an agent to deduce that nothing untoward has happened in a small time interval if the agent hasn't received a message to the contrary.

Contracts for Request-Driven Interactions

A contract in a request-driven interaction is between the client and server participating in the interaction. The server's contract specifies that if it receives a request in the schema specified by the server, then the server will execute the specified service and return results to the client in a specified schema. For example, a service that receives requests containing lengths in feet and then converts these lengths to meters may require requests to be positive decimal numbers. This server's contract is that it will accurately convert the value, given in feet, in the client's request to meters and reply with the value in meters.

The differences between contracts for event- and request-driven interactions are a consequence of the different goals of these interactions. A contract for a request-driven interaction has the following features:

▶ The contract between the client and server is for an interaction that begins with a request and ends with a reply; unlike event-driven interactions, the contract does not specify a time horizon nor is it open-ended. Compare expectations that users have about search engines (request-driven interactions) and alerts engines (event-driven interactions). A user who executes a search waits for a single reply; the interaction ends when the user receives the reply. By contrast, a user who enters a request to an alerts engine expects to get periodic notifications; the interaction ends only when the user cancels the alert service.

▶ A contract is between a client and a server, not between a client and the rest of the system.

▶ A contract is a relation between a request, the reply, and the state of the server when the request was received by the server.

▶ Contracts in request-driven interactions may include response time constraints in service level agreements; these contracts specify how quickly a server must respond to a client's request. *Generally, there are no constraints on when a client must invoke a server.* A client may invoke a server frequently or not at all. Servers cannot infer the states of clients from the absence of requests.

▶ A contract may specify that a request-reply interaction is transactional: it is either completed successfully or not done at all.

Contracts for Time-Driven Interactions

Consider a meeting of an engineering manager and an offshore development team. Each person comes to the meeting with some knowledge; during the meeting some of this knowledge is exchanged with others; and each person leaves with additional knowledge. The meeting changes the states of the participants. The contract for a time-driven interaction can be specified as a relation between the states of the agents immediately before and immediately after the interaction.

A contract for a time-driven interaction is different from contracts for event- or request-driven interactions. A contract for a time-driven interaction is a relation between pre- and post-interaction states of all agents participating in the interaction; the contract for a request-driven interaction is a relation between a request by a client and a reply by a server; and the contract for an event-driven interaction is described in terms of when-then rules.

Hybrid Systems: Combinations of Interaction Types

You saw that each of the basic types of interaction has strengths and some weaknesses. Hybrid systems exploit the strengths of each of the interaction types by using combinations of the basic types. The PC-cubed trends suggest that hybrid systems with composite types of interaction will become more widespread in the future. Humans are hybrid, composite systems in the sense that people have used event-, request-, and time-driven interactions since the dawn of history. IT systems that are optimized to support human activity will, likewise, be hybrid systems.

....

Note: Hybrid systems that combine different interaction types will become widespread.

Let's start by looking at the price trend: the exponential growth over the last half century in the ratio of the cost of an hour of a person's time—whether the person is a medical doctor, manager, lawyer, or engineer—to the cost of a standard IT operation such as the addition of two numbers on a computer. This trend tells you that computational patterns will evolve in the following directions:

▶ **Proactive**—People are getting expensive compared to information processing operations at an exponential rate; so an economical strategy is to carry out computational tasks proactively—do tasks even before they are requested. The results of these tasks may turn out to be not needed; but saving you time on some occasions, while discarding unneeded results on other occasions, is cost effective. Costs of carrying out computations, whether needed or wasted, will decrease over the years, while the benefits of reduced delay will increase. Carrying out tasks proactively requires systems to predict or speculate about results users will need. This, in turn, requires systems to learn each user's behavior pattern. The more the system knows about you, the quicker it will be able to tell you what you need to know, even before you ask. (Issues of privacy are discussed in Chapter 4.) Proactive computations are often event-driven. For example, a web-services company may proactively determine restaurants that will interest you based on your current location, the current time, when you last ate, your habits, and your food preferences; this analysis is event-driven because it depends on your location—and where you are at a point in time depends, in large part, on events.

▶ **Personal information manager**—An interruption can be a distraction at one point in time and valuable at another depending on the receiver's context. What is required is an application that manages your information—all the notifications pushed to an agent and all the information pulled proactively by an agent operating on your behalf. This application estimates your current context based on information it has about you—such as your location, the searches you are doing, and the IT applications that you are using—and determines whether a piece of new information is important enough to merit interrupting you. Heads of states and CEOs of large corporations have chiefs of staff who acquire information proactively, who know the current contexts of their bosses, and who determine whether their bosses should be interrupted to receive new information. The PC-cubed trends make software chiefs of staff both necessary and possible for the rest of us. A personal information manager is a hybrid system with a substantial event-driven component—it manages events that it detects and information pushed to you.

Ideas of speculative computation and dynamic settings of interrupt statuses have been discussed in the IT literature on parallel computing and operating systems. The driver behind these ideas is the increasing ratio of the costs of delay to the costs of IT resources. The same driver is applicable to people. Next, let's look at a few examples of hybrid systems that combine different types of interaction, carry out proactive computations, and use personal information managers in normal office activities and in EDA systems.

....

Note: Proactive, speculative computing is cost effective.

Capture of Event Information in Folders

A problem with proactively pushing event-driven information to a user—by visual or auditory alerts on computers or phones—is that the user may not be interested in that particular information *at that time*. Though a person going on a trip wants to know about the hotels in which he will be staying, he doesn't want an important meeting to be interrupted by alerts about hotels. The fundamental problem here is one of *context*. A user interested in information from multiple domains may want to focus on a specific domain at a specific time.

Consider a sales manager who has to deal with multiple contexts such as sales processes in her different territories, marketing campaigns, and travel schedule. When her administrative assistant receives an event object—say, a notification that a hotel booking has been confirmed—the assistant does not interrupt the manager when the assistant knows that the manager is in an important meeting. So, the assistant places the information in a travel folder. The manager requests information about her trip when her context shifts to planning trips, and the assistant replies to the request with information pulled from the travel folder. If, however, the assistant receives a notification that the assistant realizes requires immediate attention from the manager, then the assistant may interrupt the manager. Thus, the assistant plays the role of personal information manager.

The assistant has an event-driven role when the assistant receives event objects, such as notifications of hotel bookings from a travel agent. The assistant also plays the role of a server, with the manager as a client, in a request-driven interaction that gives the manager the data she requests by pulling data from folders. Thus, the assistant is an adaptor that consumes event objects in event-driven interactions and serves event objects in request-driven interactions. You will see adaptors from one kind of interaction type to another—such as from event-driven to request-driven, from request-driven to event-driven, or from event-driven to time-driven—in most applications (see Figure 2-12). This is analogous to the adaptors that you use every day: the power cord in your computer receives high-voltage alternating current from the plug point and supplies low-voltage direct current to your computer.

Note: Adaptors that convert one type of interaction to another are important components of event-processing applications.

An application in which a personal information manager acquires and organizes information, and interrupts you only when information arrives that is critical to your current context, has the benefits of both event- and request-driven interactions. The application has the benefit of celerity because you will be interrupted if an event is important, enabling you to handle the event immediately. On the other hand, the application optimizes a precious asset: your uninterrupted time. This application is an example of a hybrid system that derives strength by combining different types of interaction.

E-mail with filters is another example of a composition of event- and request-driven interactions. E-mail is sent on an event-driven basis. (The actual underlying protocol by which e-mail is obtained by a receiver may be request-reply, but in essence the delivery of e-mail is triggered by the event of the sender sending a message.) Received e-mail is placed in folders by filtering algorithms. You request mail from the folder appropriate to your current context. The e-mail server acts as an adaptor that consumes event objects in event-driven interactions and serves event objects in request-driven interactions. The e-mail server acts as a simple personal information manager, receiving mail and organizing it in folders for you.

Search engines are examples of hybrid systems that combine time-, request-, and event-driven interactions. Search engines crawl websites periodically and organize information in repositories. You execute a search by using a request-reply interaction and obtain alerts by event-driven interactions.

Figure 2-12: Adaptors between interaction types.

Location-based services will become increasingly proactive. Internet services companies will know where you are and where your friends and colleagues are (and possibly even know where the people you would rather avoid are). The services will predict where you are going and the activities you are about to do, and then download results of searches and other computations, based on these predictions, to your mobile phone.

Predictive systems that warn about forthcoming events are, as one might expect, primarily event-driven. The detection of past events leads to predictions of more serious events. For example, a hurricane far out at sea may not cause much immediate damage; however, the detection of a distant storm may result in a prediction that a hurricane will hit populated areas later. A drop in stock prices in foreign stock markets overnight may lead to a prediction that prices in domestic stock markets will drop in the next trading day. Increases in click-through activity in a marketing campaign website may lead to predictions of greater call volume and sales. Predictions enable proactive computations to be executed and other steps to be taken in preparation for future events. Predictive systems are often hybrid systems that are triggered by events, (such as a change in your location) and carry out proactive calculations (such as what you are likely to want in your new location) but then wait for a request from you before giving you results of the calculation.

Data Acquisition

Many data-acquisition systems are hybrid systems that combine time-, request-, and event-driven interaction patterns. Consider, for example, applications that help traders of electric power and other volatile commodities. These applications monitor several sources of information such as electronic markets, websites that offer weather predictions, news sources, and sensors that estimate power on transmission lines. The process of collecting data from websites outside the enterprise is often done through request-driven interactions: an agent in the enterprise requests a server outside the enterprise for data and waits for a reply. Agents in the enterprise poll external sources of data according to some time schedule, with a polling interval large enough to ensure that the external sites aren't overloaded and small enough to ensure that events are detected quickly. Thus, the acquisition of external data often combines time- and request-driven interactions.

The agent within the enterprise that acquires external data periodically may send this data on to other agents in the enterprise only when the data changes significantly. Repeatedly sending identical messages can be inefficient; therefore, the agent sends notifications in an event-driven way—that is, only when relevant changes take place in external data. Thus, the acquisition and dissemination of external data often combines time-, request-, and event-driven interactions.

Responses to Events

Many responders interact using the time-driven pattern; for example, systems send periodic digital signals to devices that control thrust in engines. When you turn on cruise control in your car, you are, in effect, establishing a contract with the car to keep the car's speed at the specified level until you either step on the brake or turn off cruise control. The cruise control system detects events when you turn the control on and when you brake. The system controls fuel flow into the engine by sending periodic signals in a time-driven manner. Thus, the cruise control's interactions with you are event-driven whereas its interactions with the engine are time-driven.

Some agents receive event objects and react by executing request-driven interactions such as invoking a web service or updating a database. These agents are event-driven on one side and request-driven on the other. Detections of rare threats, such as tsunamis, are carried out using event-driven interactions, but the responses—such as assigning first responders to different threat regions—are often executed using request-driven interactions.

Summary

The pattern of interactions and decision-making among people in an enterprise is similar to the interaction patterns among components in IT systems. Basic types of interaction include time-driven, request-driven, and event-driven interactions. Each of the basic types has advantages and therefore many applications are hybrid systems that employ combinations of these types.

The business trends, described in Chapter 1, that drive demand for event processing impact how IT systems use different types of interaction. These business trends are summarized in Figure 2-1. Business needs for agility, timeliness, and information availability have resulted in greater reliance on event-driven interactions. The combination of the trends of technology producer push and consumer pull, summarized in the PC-cubed trends—price, pervasiveness, performance, connectedness, celerity, and complexity—impact the ways in which interaction types are combined in applications.

Different types of interaction between components evolved at different points in the history of IT for good reasons; a study of these reasons helps us to estimate how software will continue to evolve. Even in the 1950s some IT components were request-driven and some were event-driven; the relative prevalence of request-driven interactions increased over time with widespread use of client-server interactions; and now technology and business needs are leading to increasing use of event-driven interactions.

Informal expectations about component behavior, or formal contracts about components, help in designing systems and clarify the utility of different types of interaction in different settings. IT applications have combinations of the basic interaction types, and therefore adaptors that convert from one type of interaction to another are useful in most applications. Proactive, predictive systems that use combinations of the basic interaction types will get more common as IT costs continue to drop relative to the costs of workers' time and costs of non-IT devices.

When discussing the relative merits of EDA, SOA, event-driven SOA (EDSOA), asynchrony, synchrony, or other concepts, it is helpful to cut through to the basics and ask "What is going on at the most basic level?" And the answer is this: interactions among people and among software components.

3

Using Event Processing in Business Applications

This chapter explores the business implications of the two seminal aspects of event processing: event-driven architecture (EDA) and complex event processing (CEP). Each is valuable by itself, but they're even more interesting when used together as event-driven CEP. Event-driven CEP is the underlying technology for continuous intelligence systems in which computers analyze events as they occur instead of after-the-fact. The main reason for the recent upsurge of interest in event processing is that continuous intelligence has become practical to use in a wide variety of business situations. This chapter explains the nature of EDA and CEP and describes how they are applied separately and together to improve the timeliness, agility, and information availability in business.

Event-Driven Architecture

"EDA" refers to a particular style of event processing; it is not an umbrella term for every activity related to events. Progressing from the general to the specific (see Figure 3-1), EDA fits this way into the overall scheme of event processing:

1. **Events**—Things that happen or, viewed another way, changes in the state of anything. Broadly speaking, everything in the world participates in events, so the concept is too general to help in designing business processes or IT systems.

2. **Business events**—Events that are meaningful in a business context. Other events occur in our personal lives, politics, science, sports, the weather, and other realms but they're not directly relevant to business computing. Every application system used in business during the past 50 years has processed business events in a sense, so it's still a very broad area.

3. **Event objects**—Discrete reports of events. An address change on a paper form is an event object that a person can use. Computers, of course, use electronic, machine-readable event objects, such as XML documents. When people say "event processing" in an IT context, they usually imply event *object* processing. Intent is essential to the definition of event object—it is intended to convey information, not just store information. As one wag put it, "An event (*object*) is

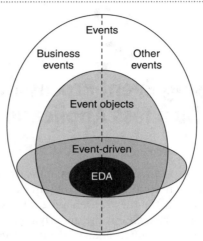

Figure 3-1: Positioning EDA in an event-filled world.

a message with an attitude." An amorphous set of data scattered about in various databases, files, electronic documents, and sections of memory doesn't constitute an event object even if it is all related to a real-world business event. That's data about an event, but it isn't a discrete report that can be used to notify another software component. Event objects don't need to convey everything known about the event; they may be only a simple electronic signal. Chapter 7 drills down deeper into the design of event objects for business applications.

4. **Event-driven**—The behavior of an entity that acts when it recognizes an event. A person is event-driven when he or she reacts immediately upon finding out that something has happened, perhaps by seeing it or hearing about it. A person can be event-driven without receiving a tangible event object. When software is event-driven, however, it is event *object*–driven, meaning it has received news about an event in a discrete, intentional, electronic form. The notion of being "event-driven" is implemented in many different ways in computer systems (see Chapter 7). Something can be event driven without using EDA, just as something can be service oriented (see Chapter 9) without using service-oriented architecture (SOA).

5. **EDA**—An architectural style in which one or more of the components in a software system are event-driven and minimally coupled. "Minimally coupled" means that the only relationship between the event producer component and the event consumer component is the one-way transfer of event objects.

A business application implements EDA if it complies with five principles:

▶ **Reports current events**—A notification reports a discrete occurrence as it happens.

▶ **Pushes notifications**—Notifications are "pushed" by the event producer, not "pulled" by the event consumer. The producer decides when to send the notification because it knows about the event before the consumer does.

▶ **Responds immediately**—The consumer does something in response immediately after it recognizes an event.

▶ **Communicates one-way**—Notification is a "fire-and-forget" type of communication. The producer emits the notification and goes on to do other work, or it may end processing and shut down. It does not get a reply from the consumer.

▶ **Is free of commands**—A notification is a report, not a specific request or command. It does not prescribe the action the event consumer will perform.

The first three of these principles describe what it means to be "event-driven." The last two specify the meaning of "minimally coupled." If an event producer tells the event consumer what action to perform, the consumer is event-driven but the application is not using EDA because the two parties had to explicitly agree on the function of the consumer. If an event consumer sends a reply back to the producer, it is event-driven but not EDA because the producer is dependent on the consumer. Software engineers have used EDA for years, although they were more likely to call it "continuous processing," "message-driven processing," "data-driven," or "document-driven." An EDA system always adheres to these principles at a conceptual level but the implementation details are more complex, as we'll explore in Chapter 6.

The next four sections of this chapter explore how the EDA principles are used to improve timeliness, agility, data consistency, and information dissemination in business scenarios. Following that, the latter half of the chapter describes CEP and explains how event-driven CEP enables situation awareness.

Timeliness

Business processes that need to be completed in a short amount of time are automated by continuous-processing, event-driven systems rather than batch-oriented, time-driven systems.

Consider the limitations of classical batch-based processes, such as the order-to-cash process summarized in the upper diagram in Figure 3-2. The first step, order capture, is request-driven because a person can submit an order at any time and the interactions between the person and the application involve a sequence of requests and replies. The person engages in a conversation with the application to look up product information, enter and validate the order, correct any input errors, and receive confirmation that the order was submitted. The order-entry application could be either an internal application operated by a salesperson or an externally facing, web-based ordering system used directly by a customer. The application puts the orders in a database or file, where they accumulate throughout the day.

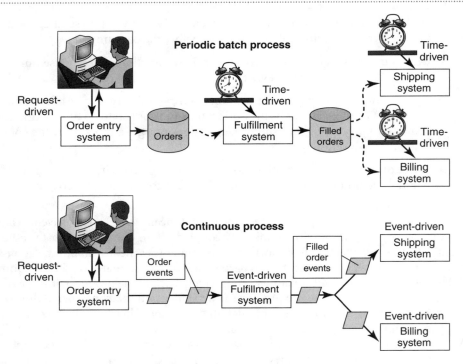

Figure 3-2: EDA reduces elapsed time of multistep processes.

Note: A time-driven system is inherently a batch system if more than one transaction has accumulated while waiting for the work to commence.

After the initial step, the remainder of the process is time-driven. At a designated time, typically once a day (at night), a batch of orders is sent to an order-fulfillment system in an operations department. The next day, the operations department picks items from shelves, packs them for shipment, and relays the goods and related data to the next functional areas, such as the billing and shipping departments, generally through other time-based batch file transfers. The IT applications that support this multistep process literally do event processing, because they're processing event objects—each order is an event in a general sense—but the work is instigated on a time-driven schedule, not by the arrival of the event objects (orders).

The process can be accelerated by redesigning it as a continuous-processing system. The customer's order is still captured through a request-driven, conversational interaction, but the order-capture application immediately sends a notification message to the next step in the process, the operations department (see lower diagram in Figure 3-2). The order-fulfillment, shipping, and billing systems run all day (and in many cases, around the clock), ready to respond as soon as each new item of work is received. In event processing terminology, the order-entry application is an event (object) producer and the order-fulfillment system in the operations department is a consumer of order events and a producer of filled-order events. A growing number of web-based and other sales systems operate continuously, so it is becoming common for orders to be dispatched within hours of receiving them.

Continuous-processing systems also have the benefit of distributing the work more evenly to eliminate bottlenecks, peaks, and troughs. Companies are having an increasingly difficult time squeezing growing batch workloads into the traditional overnight slow periods. "Batch windows" are shrinking because business hours are expanding and global operations often force some applications to remain online for more hours—sometimes 24 hours, 7 days a week.

Before the 1970s, even the first step, order capture, would typically have been done manually. Transactions were written on paper and typed into a data entry system as a separate step. Transaction data was made available to the first IT system in the process in an offline, time-driven, batch mode. Companies migrated most of the initial transaction-capture steps in business processes to request-driven online systems by the end of the 1980s, but most of the subsequent steps in processes remained batch-based, as shown in the top diagram in Figure 3-2. Since the 1990s, companies have been gradually reimplementing those subsequent steps in some multistep processes as continuous, event-driven systems, although a surprising amount of work is still done in batch. This is not necessarily a problem. Some batch systems are still perfectly sensible because the business would derive no benefit by accomplishing the work more quickly, and in a few circumstances, the business may actually gain by deferring the work.

Some companies have gone partway to continuous processing by running batch jobs more frequently. For example, they may process a small batch every hour rather than waiting for a whole day's worth of work to accumulate. Depending on the business requirements, this may be fast enough to harvest most of the benefits of continuous-processing systems. Moreover, this sometimes allows the company to maintain its investment in legacy batch-based applications rather than redesigning them as continuous-processing systems. However, unforeseen side effects on other applications often crop up, so it's not as easy as it sounds to run batch jobs more often. Ultimately, the notion of frequent batch jobs is appropriate and valuable in some circumstances where the absence of truly immediate processing doesn't matter.

Note: As a rule of thumb, new systems should use continuous processing as the default choice. However, if you're trying to retain batch programs that are otherwise sound, running frequent small batches may be a good alternative until the system needs to be replaced for other reasons.

The choice between continuous or batch processes has important implications outside of the IT department. This is a business architecture issue, not just an application architecture issue. The flow of raw materials and finished goods, job descriptions, customer interactions, policies and procedures, the organizational chart, and even product makeup and prices may be affected by the style of processing. However, further analysis of organizational and business architecture issues are outside of the scope of this book.

Note: Analysts should work with operations managers and other businesspeople to re-engineer the business process before designing the IT systems to avoid "paving cow paths" (automating obsolete process models).

If fast process execution is a goal, analysts re-engineering the business should eliminate unnecessary steps, combine steps, perform steps in parallel, and accelerate activities within each step as the first phase of designing the new application systems. This is sometimes described as "taking the air out of business processes." In most situations, it leverages EDA to achieve continuous processing. Chapter 10 has more discussion of the overlap between business process management and event processing.

Continuous processes can be a mix of human- and machine-based automated activities, or they can be fully automated from end-to-end as straight-through processes. The term straight-through processing (STP) originally came from the financial industry, where it is a key objective for payment systems and other applications. STP is also increasingly popular in most other industries, sometimes under the label of "flow-through provisioning" (in telecommunications), "paperless acquisition" (in the military), "lights-out processing" (in manufacturing), or "no touch" or "hands-free processing" (in insurance and other industries). STP reduces the duration of a process and eliminates the need to enter data manually. The most obvious benefit of STP is eliminating the delays that occur when people rather than computers perform the work. However, eliminating clerical error is usually more important. Wherever people re-enter data, some mistakes will be made. If errors are undetected, the wrong goods may be shipped, the wrong amount of goods may be shipped, or the customer may be overcharged or undercharged. Recovering from clerical errors can add substantial time and cost and reduce customer satisfaction.

However, many processes can't be made entirely straight through because machines can't handle exceptional situations or make certain kinds of complex decisions. Processes that require human participation can't run as fast as STP processes, but they can still use EDA and be relatively continuous, therefore demonstrating shorter elapsed times than time-driven processes. The human steps in a continuous process can be event-driven by using workflow software to manage task lists and "push" new work items to people as soon as they appear.

Agility

It's fairly obvious why EDA-based, continuous-processing systems demonstrate better timeliness than batch systems, but it is less obvious why EDA systems have advantages over request-driven systems. Request-driven applications operate in an immediate, message-at-a-time fashion, just like event-driven systems, so they often match the timeliness of EDA systems. However, EDA is minimally coupled, so it has an inherent advantage over request-driven interactions with respect to agility, as explained next.

In Chapter 2, you saw that an agent in a request-driven interaction is dependent on the response that is returned by a server. The agent can't finish its task if the server is not running or if the network is down. The team that designs and builds the requesting software agent must know a lot about what the server is going to do and the team that builds the server must know a lot about the requesting agent. If the requester or server is modified in a way that affects the request or response messages, the other agent must also be changed. This *logic coupling* makes the overall system more brittle and difficult to modify.

By contrast, the contract in an EDA relationship is minimally coupled. Agents have fewer expectations regarding each other's behavior and communicate in only one direction. An event producer emits the notification message in a "fire and forget" manner, and goes on to do other work or ends its work and shuts down. It does not get a reply or any other returning message from the event consumer. Fewer things can go wrong and it is easier to change or add one component without changing another.

....

Note: EDA systems are more agile than request-driven systems because they are minimally coupled. Developers can change one EDA component without having to change another component as long as the event notifications don't change.

For example, a company might want to add a step to its order-fulfillment process to check the credit rating of the buyer before an order is filled. This activity could be added to the order-capture step using a request-driven design pattern (see top diagram in Figure 3-3), but this approach introduces unnecessary dependencies among the components. The order-entry application would be modified to invoke a credit-checking service, wait for a reply, and send an approved-order notification or a rejected-order notification for further processing. Developers would have to modify the order-entry application, including recompiling, retesting, and redeploying the software to implement this new step.

Alternatively, the new function could be added to the business process using EDA without changing the initial order-entry application (see lower diagram in Figure 3-3). The order-entry system would capture the order in a request-driven conversational mode and emit the new order object as it did before credit checking was added. A new, event-driven credit-checking software service would be inserted into the business process after the order-entry step. It would consume the order event in place of the order-fulfillment system, verify the credit of the customer, and send an approved-order notification to the order-fulfillment system or a rejected-order notification to a component that handles problem cases. Adding the credit-checking step is nondisruptive because the order-entry and order-fulfillment applications don't have to change. EDA makes this kind of "pluggability" possible because a notification

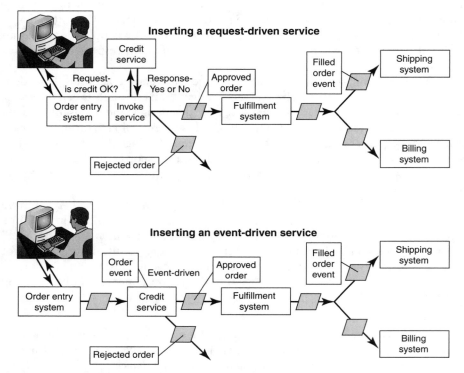

Figure 3-3: EDA facilitates process modifications and agility.

message comes with "no strings attached." The order-entry application doesn't specify the action that a subsequent step would execute, so analysts and developers are free to change the business process with minimal effort.

EDA systems are agile and can accommodate piecemeal, incremental changes more quickly and at lower cost than request-driven systems. So why aren't all functions designed this way? Chapter 2 introduced the answer—EDA comes with inherent limitations that affect the behavior of the application in ways that are sometimes undesirable. Our example of an event-driven credit-checking step assumed that the business would implement an asynchronous "rejected order" step to handle orders that failed the credit verification test. A rejected-order notification triggers a person or software agent to inform the customer that their order has been rejected; or the customer might be asked for payment or payment guarantees to put the order back into the system. However, if the company wanted to handle credit problems synchronously as part of the initial order-entry conversation, the EDA approach would not have worked. The credit-checking step would have had to be implemented as a request-driven interaction with a software service (top diagram in Figure 3-3).

Note: One size does not fit all. When business requirements can be supported by either EDA or request-driven approaches, analysts and architects should use EDA to leverage its minimal coupling and superior agility. However, when a reply to the transaction originator is required, a request-driven approach should be used.

Request-driven interactions will remain more common than EDA relationships in business systems, although the trend is to use EDA more often than in the past.

Data Consistency

The case for EDA in data-consistency scenarios is compelling. For the same reasons that EDA improves the timeliness of multistep processes, it also improves the timeliness of data-consistency work compared to time-driven, batch approaches.

The most common method of synchronizing the contents of two or more databases is still to create a file containing updates in the application that has the most recent information and then transfer the file to other interested applications in a time-driven batch job. This is typically done using a combination of custom programs, an extract-transform-load (ETL) utility, File Transfer Protocol (FTP), or managed file-transfer utilities. Batch synchronization is simple, easy to develop, and slow. The downstream applications and their databases operate with obsolete data until the synchronization job runs. This is increasingly unacceptable in a connected world where customers and customer-facing service agents need to have current information to ensure customer satisfaction and avoid making errors.

If a customer places an order, requests a service call, changes her address, or makes a financial transaction, she expects the new information to be visible almost immediately through any system owned by the same company. An EDA approach to data consistency meets that requirement. For example, a company may have 11 or more application systems (A through K) that maintain copies of customer address data (see the left side of Figure 3-4). When application A captures an address-change event from a web page, it updates its local database and immediately publishes the event to a messaging infrastructure that delivers it to all applications that have registered an interest in receiving that type of data. The fire-and-forget nature of EDA is inherently suited for one-to-many communication mechanisms that deliver an event to multiple recipients. Every authorized customer and user in every business unit using systems A through K will have the most-current information within a few seconds.

In theory, it would also be possible to implement a near-real-time data-consistency solution using a request-driven approach, but it would be intolerably clumsy and impractical. Request-driven systems are almost always one-to-one—that is, a requester interacts with one server at a time. In this case, the original application A would have to invoke an address-change function in each of the other systems in succession (see the right side of Figure 3-4). Application A would send a request containing the new address to system B, which would update its customer database and return an acknowledgment. A then would call C with a similar request, and so forth. After ten request-driven interactions, systems B through K would have posted the change to

Ways to achieve data consistency

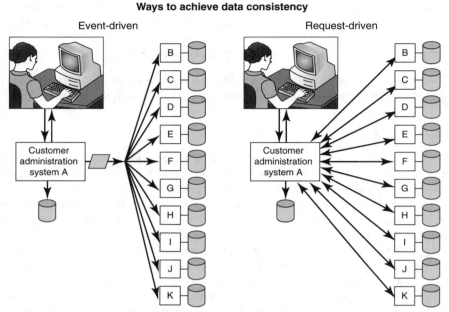

Figure 3-4: EDA supports immediate data synchronization.

their respective databases. However, if a communication problem occurs, or if any system isn't running, A won't get an expected response. Developers would have to implement complex logic in system A so that it can keep working if it doesn't get a response back from one of the other systems that are supposed to do an update. Moreover, application A would have to be changed, recompiled, and redeployed to add another application, L, that needs the new data.

This business problem cries out for EDA-style continuous processing and a fire-and-forget communication pattern. Nothing in the business logic in application A really needs to get information back from any of the other systems. The only role of a reply is to confirm that the update was delivered, but application A should not be in the business of verifying delivery. That function should be delegated to an intermediary, such as a publish-and-subscribe middleware agent, that distributes the updates, retries the message if a consuming application is temporarily unavailable, or puts a report in a "dead letter" file for subsequent, asynchronous follow-up if the update can't be conveyed successfully. The use of an intermediary insulates application A from changes in the other systems (we'll explore how this is accomplished in more detail in Chapter 6).

Information Dissemination

EDA is the obvious choice of interaction pattern for mass-notification situations where the information must be conveyed quickly and the timing of the event cannot

be predicted. The one-to-many, fire-and-forget nature of EDA makes it fast and efficient for this purpose. The point of mass e-mail distribution lists, "reverse 911" systems, Really Simple Syndication (RSS) feeds, and other kinds of alerting systems is to
convey the data to many recipients as quickly as the communication channel will
allow. Time-driven systems have too much latency and request-driven systems are
too inflexible and inefficient for the majority of dissemination problems.

However, time- and request-driven patterns are appropriate in some dissemination
scenarios. If the timing of the notification is not urgent, or if the timing of the event
can be accurately predicted, then a time-driven notification would work fine. Time-
driven notifications can be fire-and-forget and one-to-many because they are variations on event-driven interactions. A request-driven notification is appropriate when
the number of recipients is low and the recipients change infrequently because it is
then practical to build their identity and address into the sending agent. A request-
driven pattern is also appropriate when the sender needs some information in
response to perform some subsequent task.

Complex Event Processing

Much of the growing interest in events is focused on the second aspect of event processing, CEP. CEP is a way of distilling the information value from a number of simple business events into a few more-useful, summary-level "complex" events. CEP
helps companies make better and faster decisions in scenarios that range from simple decision support to robust situation awareness.

CEP isn't new, but the way computer systems are used to implement CEP is new.
For most of history, people did CEP in their heads, and even today computers are
used in a minority of CEP calculations. However, some critical, high-value business
processes depend on automated CEP, and it is spreading steadily out to other parts of
the business world. In this section, we'll present three ways to perform CEP: manual
CEP (without computers), partially automated CEP (a blend of machine and human
intelligence), and fully automated sense-and-respond enabled by CEP. All three
approaches to event processing involve three phases: event capture, analysis, and
response, but they are handled differently in each approach.

Manual CEP

Figure 3-5 shows how CEP works when people are at the center of the process.

1. **Event capture**—People find out about events by observing or interacting with
   the world. They talk to other people, receive phone calls, use IT systems, read
   thermometers and other sensor devices, get text messages, navigate the Web,
   subscribe to RSS feeds, watch television, listen to the radio, and read business
   reports, mail, newspapers, e-mail messages, and other documents.

2. **Analysis**—Each person analyzes the available event data and puts it into context. Part of what they do is "connect the dots"—that is, they make connec-

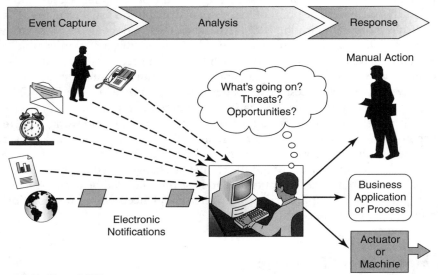

Figure 3-5: Manual CEP.

tions between simple events to develop big-picture insights ("complex events") that represent emerging threats or opportunities. This is the heart of CEP.

3. **Response**—The person initiates a response to threats and opportunities that have been identified in the analysis phase. They may undertake some action personally, send a message to another person or other people, kick off a transaction in an IT system, or start up a machine or other device.

....

Note: Although the label "complex" may initially seem off-putting, complex events actually simplify data by summarizing and abstracting what is happening.

For example, suppose the district sales manager at a power equipment distributor receives weekly sales reports from the 20 stores in his region. Think of each sales report as an event object that records the store identifier, date, and the quantity of snow blowers, chain saws, and other equipment sold. Every Thursday, the sales manager looks through the reports, calculates the total sales for the district for certain key items, and compares the results with historical data. In event-processing terms, the fact that "the district sold 193 snow blowers this week" is a complex event that reflects the collective significance of the *base events*, the 20 individual sales reports. No sales report was important by itself, but when analyzed together, they revealed a meaningful insight about what is happening on the district level. The sales manager enriches this complex event by comparing it to historical data to produce another, yet-more-complex event, "snow blower sales volume was 30 percent above average this week." He combines this with another type of event data—the weather forecast for next week predicting more snow—to synthesize a further complex event that "this is an opportunity situation to sell more snow blowers." This complex event is said to be an *abstraction* because it is several steps removed from the original input data, but it is now in a form that is directly usable for decision making or for communicating with his boss. The sales manager might respond by ordering a rush shipment of additional snow blowers.

Note: A complex event is an abstraction because it is one or more steps removed from a physical world event. However, it is more usable for decision-making purposes because it summarizes the collective significance of multiple events.

This example should sound familiar to anyone who makes operational decisions or who builds operational intelligence applications for use by others. We've described a routine decision-making scenario using event-processing terms as a way of demonstrating the commonsense nature of CEP. Strictly speaking, this actually involves CEP although no one would call it that. The application that generated the sales reports is an event (object) producer. The sales manager who synthesized the series of complex events ("the district sold 193 snow blowers," "snow blower sales volume was 30 percent above average," and "this is an opportunity situation to sell more snow blowers") was performing a kind of manual CEP.

This style of "CEP" is unremarkable partly because it is time-driven (the reports and the sales manager's analysis happen every Thursday) and partly because most of it is performed manually. Companies have been operating this way for decades. It's reasonably effective as long as the volume of data is low, people are available to do the analysis, and decisions don't have to be made very quickly. When the business requirements are more demanding, however, automated CEP becomes appropriate.

Partially Automated CEP

Most partially or fully automated CEP systems involve many more than 20 base event objects, and they come in much faster—every few seconds, or even a few milliseconds apart. Nevertheless, automated CEP follows the same three general phases as manual CEP (see Figure 3-6):

1. **Event capture**—An increasing amount of business event data is available in digital form through a company's network or the Internet:

   ▶ Web-based RSS news feeds convey reports that used to come from newspapers, television, and radios.

   ▶ New types of market data are distributed from exchanges and clearing-houses.

   ▶ More of a company's internal functions are automated in application systems that can be tapped to provide near-real-time data about what is happening in sales, manufacturing, transportation, accounting, and other departments.

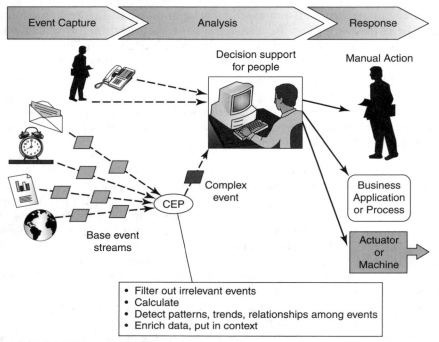

Figure 3-6: Partially automated CEP.

▶ Bar code and radio frequency identification (RFID) readers and Global Positioning System (GPS) devices pump out reports on the location of specific items.

▶ Web page scrapers can poll a competitor's website every 10 minutes to see if the company's prices have changed.

Some of this data wasn't generated in the past. Other data was available to people but computers couldn't read it. Now, however, more data is produced and most of it is electronic so it can be handled by automated CEP systems.

2. Analysis—CEP software can be used to handle some or all of the analysis phase. CEP software is any computer program that can generate, read, discard, or perform calculations on complex event objects. It can be packaged as a stand-alone CEP agent running on its own; it can be implemented as a section of code intertwined in a larger application program; or it can be built into a software framework or business event processing (BEP) platform that can be extended by a software developer to construct a complete application. CEP software is technically a type of *rule engine*. (See Chapter 10 for an explanation of how CEP relates to other kinds of rule engines.)

CEP software may do the following:

▶ Read through all the incoming base events and discard those that are irrelevant to the task at hand (called filtering, or screening, the data)

▶ Calculate totals, averages, maximums, minimums, and other figures

▶ Use predefined rules to look for patterns in the base events, such as trends, relative timing (the order in which events took place), or causal relationships (an event that led to another event)

▶ Enrich the event data by comparing it to historical data or adding data from other kinds of databases

CEP computation produces one or more new complex events that summarize the significance of the available data. This is connecting the dots in a high-performance, sophisticated fashion (Chapter 7 explains this process in more detail). Most key performance indicators (KPIs) are actually complex events (but not all complex events are KPIs). Complex events may be reactive, summarizing past events, or predictive, identifying things that are likely to happen based on what has occurred recently compared to historical patterns.

3. **Response**—In the majority of cases, CEP software is used for decision support. It can't do the whole job of analyzing the situation by itself, so it does some of the preliminary calculations and turns the complex events over to people who determine what to do next. The single most common way of delivering complex events is through a business dashboard in a web browser, although many other channels are also utilized depending on the circumstances. In a growing number of situations, CEP can trigger a response without human involvement (it is an STP model of operation). We'll describe this further in the section "Fully Automated Sense-and-Respond."

Event-Driven CEP

A traditional partly automated IT solution for the power equipment distributor (in the example presented in the "Manual CEP" section) would be time-driven and its computation limited in scope. It would be CEP but only in the broadest and weakest sense of the term. An application would generate sales reports from the 20 stores, calculate totals, and produce a summary report that says "the district sold 193 snow blowers this week." A well-designed system would go further by comparing the results to historical data and highlighting the fact that "snow blower sales volume was 30 percent above average this week." The sales manager would need to take the initiative to check the report, notice that the sales volume was out of the ordinary, and check the weather forecast.

This scenario becomes more novel and the solution more helpful if automated as event-driven CEP. The sales manager can specify that he wants to be proactively alerted whenever the sales of an item are outside of an expected range, such as more than 20 percent above or below the average. The software could be *context aware* in the sense that it could adjust its behavior according to the season—comparing results to a different weekly average depending on the time of the year or whether the season for that equipment was beginning or ending. A sophisticated system could base its decision to send an alert partly by parsing an RSS feed of weather information to see if the word "snow" appears in the forecast for the next five days. The resulting complex event, "this may be an opportunity situation to sell more snow blowers," would be transmitted to the sales manager through a web-based business dashboard, e-mail message, SMS message, automated phone call, or some other notification channel.

In this event-driven CEP solution, the sales manager doesn't have to remember to look at the weekly sales reports. The system notifies him only when there is something that needs attention, which frees him up to focus on other things (it's using "management by exception"). The CEP software helps him get to a faster or better understanding of whether a threat or opportunity exists by offloading the mechanical aspects of event computation. This scenario would probably not be designed using STP. The manager probably wants to remain in the loop and, in many cases, will want to drill down into the underlying data to understand why the alert was sent before he places the order for more snow blowers.

Event-driven CEP would be marginally useful in the power equipment distributor scenario, but timeliness is of limited value because orders for additional goods are only placed weekly and at a predictable time (Thursdays). It's more useful in scenarios that need continuous intelligence.

Note: Event-driven CEP is most important in business situations with a lot of event data and short decision cycles.

For example, customer contact centers generate records throughout the day for all customer interactions, including the wait time for phone calls, number of times the call is transferred, dropped calls, call duration, whether the issue was resolved in the first contact, and the service agent's name or identifier. These operational metrics are generally reported on a time-driven basis through hourly or daily reports. This supports service-level reporting, issue identification, root-cause analysis, and problem resolution of systemic weaknesses.

Increasingly, however, contact centers are moving to an event-driven, continuous-intelligence view of operations. This enables immediate detection and correction of problems as they appear rather than after the fact. For example, an agent dealing with a customer who has been transferred several times or has been on hold for more than 5 minutes can be prompted (and allowed) to give additional compensation for the negative experience. The contact center software may also generate "screen pops" to prompt agents to ask customer-specific questions to drive up-selling or cross-selling. If feedback indicates that an agent was irate, a supervisor may be alerted to give the agent an early break to recover. These immediate interventions require the use of event-driven design patterns for low latency and CEP intelligence to connect the dots. Commercial software that supports these capabilities for a contact center is available today and in use in a growing number of companies. The products are categorized as customer relationship management (CRM) analytic suites.

Note: Event-driven CEP provides continuous intelligence. Problems can be detected and opportunities can be pursued as they appear.

Fully Automated Sense-and-Respond

Some event processing scenarios can be fully automated because both the event analysis and the response to the situation can be done without direct human involvement. This involves the same three general phases found in manual and partially automated CEP.

1. **Event capture**—All of the input event data must be available in electronic form if the process is to be fully automated (see Figure 3-7). If any of the data requires human interpretation, the process must be done manually or with a partially automated approach.

2. **Analysis**—If the analysis phase is to be fully automated, the event processing logic and business rules must be expressed in explicit algorithms that CEP software is capable of executing. This works only if the factors that go into the decision are well understood and business decision makers, business analysts, and software engineers have worked together to articulate the processing rules. Chapter 7 explains how people specify event processing logic to CEP software in more detail.

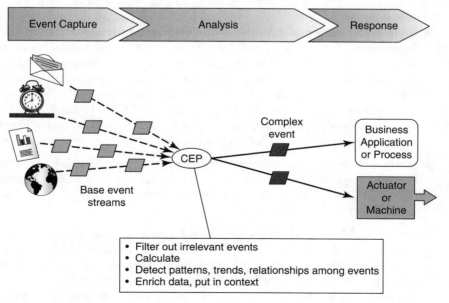

Figure 3-7: Fully automated CEP system.

3. **Response**—After the CEP software determines the appropriate response to a situation, it kicks off a transaction or SOA service in an IT system, initiates a business process through a software orchestration engine, or sends a signal to an actuator to start a machine, lock a door, increase the heat, or perform some other action.

Full automation of both the analysis and response phases is especially important in scenarios that call for an ultra-low-latency response. For example, sophisticated, event-driven CEP systems are widely used in capital markets trading operations. Algorithmic trading systems can calculate and issue buy and sell orders for stocks or foreign currency in less than 5 milliseconds without human involvement. A person cannot think that fast or even type one character on a keyboard in 5 milliseconds, so people must be left out of the process. Systems for smart order routing, market surveillance, fraud detection, anti–money laundering, and various kinds of risk management also use event-driven CEP-based technology. Some aspects of businesses have become similar to an "arms race," in which small differences in response time can lead to major financial gains or losses. Much of what is known about ultra-low-latency CEP came from research done for real arms races where CEP is used to control weapons and defense systems.

Benefits of Automated CEP over Manual CEP

Partially or fully automated event-driven CEP improves a company's situation awareness and its ability to behave in an intelligent sense-and-respond manner. As the examples in this chapter have demonstrated, automated CEP offers four key benefits:

▶ **Improved quality of decisions**—Computers extract the information value from dozens, thousands, or millions of base events (as long as the events are simple). By contrast, a person can assimilate only a few events per second and thus cannot consider nearly as many factors when making a decision. Moreover, computers don't succumb to boredom, so they make fewer mistakes in simple computations. Computer calculations are consistent and repeatable because they always implement the same algorithms the same way, as defined by knowledge workers, analysts, and software developers.

▶ **Faster response**—Partially automated decision-support CEP systems save time because people don't have to perform manual calculations. Fully automated CEP systems are even faster because they don't have to wait for people to digest and respond to the information.

▶ **Preventing data overload**—CEP systems reduce the volume of unwanted, unnecessary data ("information glut") presented to people. In some cases, a CEP system may run for hours or days, turning millions of base events into thousands of complex events before detecting a complex event that must be brought to the attention of a person. CEP systems are often used to implement management-by-exception strategies. People are disturbed less often, so they can reserve their attention for the few situations in which their involvement is important.

▶ **Reduced cost**—CEP systems offload the drudgery of repetitive calculations and pattern detection comparisons from people to computers. This reduces the amount of human labor needed to analyze the data. For example, the spread of algorithmic-based program trading in capital markets has reduced the number of human traders operating on certain categories of investments.

The amount of decision making that should be offloaded to CEP systems varies depending on the business problem. Managers and knowledge workers can delegate as little or as much as they want to the software.

CEP in Perspective

Most of the discussion of event processing in the remainder of this book—and in the industry in general—refers to event-driven CEP because it's new and different. Traditional management reports and business intelligence (BI) have always done time- and request-driven CEP (although it wasn't called CEP), both of which are discussed a bit later in this section. They are *retrospective*, presenting information after the fact, or *passive*, requiring the recipient to initiate the activity. Technology has recently made event-driven CEP, and thus continuous intelligence, attainable in many areas where it was previously impractical. However, it's only appropriate in business situations that have particular characteristics.

Event-Driven CEP

Automated and partially automated event-driven CEP systems are applied in diverse ways. They help monitor, manage, and enrich continuous operations, such as supply chains, transportation operations, factory floors, casinos, hospital emergency rooms, web-based gaming systems, and the customer contact center in this chapter's example. Many of the most sophisticated, high-volume CEP applications are found in capital markets trading operations. Other companies may have their first experience with event-driven CEP when they implement a business activity monitoring (BAM) dashboard that they acquire with a business process management suite (BPMS) (see Chapter 10 for more details).

Most of the examples in this book can be categorized as *business event processing (BEP)* applications because they deal with business events rather than personal, political, scientific, sports-related, weather, or other events. Event-driven CEP was used in military, scientific, and system and network management applications before its use became common in business applications. However, the term CEP was not widely recognized until the publication of David Luckham's book *The Power of Events* in 2002. BEP is now the fastest-growing type of event processing because more companies are starting to recognize its commercial advantages. Some people use the term BEP to mean applications that don't require low latency—computation in a second or two may be fast enough. Others use the term to refer to applications in which a business person has input the event processing rules directly into the system without involving an IT expert. However, we use the term to mean any CEP in a business context.

Event-driven CEP is sometimes called *event-stream processing (ESP)*. An *event stream* is technically a sequence of event objects arranged in some order, usually the order of arrival. Some people use the term ESP to connote applications that involve only one or a few event streams, each of which has a high volume of events (thousands or hundreds of thousands of notifications per second) and the events must be processed very quickly (for example, in a few milliseconds each). Other experts use the term to mean CEP systems that can't readily deal with events that arrive out of order. In view of the ambiguity of the term, it is best to get a detailed description of the usage scenario or software product before drawing any conclusions about anything that is described as ESP. All software that can perform event-driven CEP can handle event streams as input.

One way to describe event-driven CEP is that the query (the search for a particular subset or pattern in the data) is more or less permanent, and the data is ephemeral, continuously arriving and then disappearing as it becomes out of date. This contrasts with traditional database applications, in which the data is more or less permanently stored, and the query is ephemeral (it is instigated in a request-driven manner).

Time-Driven CEP

Time-driven CEP applications do the same kinds of computation as event-driven CEP applications: they filter events, calculate totals and other figures, enrich the data using other data sources, and detect patterns. However, they deal with event objects "at rest" in a file or database table, rather than event objects "in motion" in the form of arriving messages. Time-driven CEP is used when the business situation does not require an immediate response or when processing has to wait for event data to accumulate. For example, an update to a dashboard could be generated every 15 minutes, or a batch report could be prepared every night at 8:00 P.M. Offline, batch-oriented CEP is ubiquitous in many traditional applications where the term CEP is unknown and unnecessary.

The sophisticated, modern tools used for event-driven CEP (or "ESP") are sometimes used in an offline mode by replaying a log of an event stream from the previous day or some other time frame. These applications are time-driven although they are pseudo-event-driven in their structure. Examples of this are found in market-surveillance, fraud-detection, and regulatory applications, such as payment card industry (PCI) compliance.

Request-Driven CEP

As with time-driven CEP, request-driven CEP deals with the event data at rest in memory, a file, or a database. A person can issue an ad hoc query using a BI tool or some other interactive application, or an application can make a programmatic request for data. The time of the processing is determined by the person or application making the request, unrelated to when the event notifications arrived. This is a useful type of CEP, although it is not EDA. Most traditional analytical BI applications deal with event data and thus conform to a literal definition of "request-driven CEP," but there's no clear benefit to applying event-processing terminology to traditional BI. (See Chapter 10 for more discussion on the overlap of CEP and BI.)

Summary

When people say "event processing" in an IT context, they mean event-object processing. The contemporary discipline of event processing is based on two big ideas. The first is EDA—sensing and responding to individual events as soon as possible. The second is CEP—developing insight into what is happening by combining multiple individual data points (event objects) into higher-level complex events that summarize and abstract the collective significance of the input data. EDA and CEP are important, useful, and well worth pursuing in their own right, but they're nothing new when considered apart. Used together as event-driven CEP, however, they enable new kinds of responsive and intelligent business processes that were impractical until recently. In the next chapter, we'll take a closer look at the costs and benefits of applying event processing to business problems.

4

Costs and Benefits of Event-Processing Applications

This chapter describes methods for evaluating the costs and benefits of event-processing applications. This evaluation helps identify the range of applications for which event-processing approaches are suitable.

The costs and benefits of event-processing applications are related directly to business, because they visibly impact businesspeople as well as customers and suppliers. Therefore, costs and benefits should be evaluated by, or in conjunction with, business users. Applications that help businesspeople respond to events may change the way people work. For example, an application that detects risks and opportunities for traders in a company enables them to exploit these events and increase profits; however, a side effect of the application could be that trading patterns of different traders become increasingly similar and, as a consequence, correlations among trades increase. These types of influences are more likely to be apparent to people in the business than to IT experts.

Exploiting Events for Business Value

Millions of events are generated in enterprises every day, and many events are recorded in logs of various types. Enterprises can detect and record torrents of information generated by customers, suppliers, competitors, government agencies, and academic organizations. A study evaluating event-processing applications for a business has the benefit of identifying valuable, but unexploited, event sources inside and outside the enterprise. The study will also identify technology trends, such as decreasing costs of sensors, that allow the business to exploit entirely new sources of events. You will learn best practices for evaluating opportunities for using EDA to solve business problems in Chapter 11. In this chapter you will learn the key categories of costs and benefits of event-processing approaches and this will provide a foundation for analyzing the appropriateness of EDA methods to help solve your business problems.

We organize the cost/benefit metrics into a collection of categories with the acronym REACTS, which stands for the following (see Figure 4-1):

> ▶ Relevance of information to a user
>
> ▶ Effort in tailoring a user's interest profile to ensure that the user gets the information needed

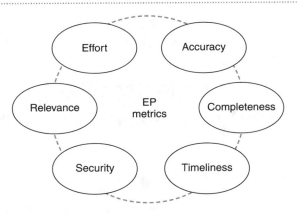

Figure 4-1: Cost-benefit metrics for event-processing systems.

▶ Accuracy of detected events

▶ Completeness of detected events

▶ Timeliness of responses

▶ Security, safety, privacy, and provenance of information, and system reliability

We first discuss each of these measures and show how designers trade off one measure against another in developing different applications.

Relevance

Information can be accurate but irrelevant. The relevance of information to a person depends, in part, on the person's context. Information about road congestion due to an accident on a freeway in Los Angeles is relevant to people in the Los Angeles area but irrelevant to most people elsewhere. People pay attention to different issues at different times, so the relevance of information to a person changes over time.

Attention Amplification and Distraction

A benefit of a well-designed event-driven architecture (EDA) application is *attention amplification*: by filtering out irrelevant information and prioritizing relevant information, the application enables users to gain uninterrupted time to concentrate on important issues. Stephen R. Covey, in his popular book *The 7 Habits of Highly Effective People*, emphasizes the importance of prioritizing tasks so that you carry out activities that are important before those that appear urgent but are actually unimportant. A well-designed EDA application helps you do important tasks first: it acquires data from varied data sources, processes the data, identifies the information that deserves the most attention at the current time, and computes data that helps in executing responses. A poorly designed EDA application, on the other hand, is an attention distracter: it distracts agents from important activities by interrupting agents frequently to handle apparently urgent, but often irrelevant, events. Attention distracters are best turned off.

Note: A well-designed EDA application is an attention amplifier.

A precious, and increasingly scarce, resource is uninterrupted time during which you can give your undivided attention to the issues that truly matter to you. Applications that interrupt agents frequently, forcing them to pay attention to irrelevant data, create organizational attention deficit disorders with their concomitant huge costs. Critical information may not be seen if it is surrounded by irrelevant information, and systems that deliver too much irrelevant information are turned off or ignored.

The meanings of attention amplification and deficit are obvious when applied to human users of event-processing systems but they also apply to software agents. Communication of irrelevant data uses communication bandwidth and processing power unnecessarily. An important aspect of designing an event-processing application is determining what information obtained from data sources should be sent on for further processing and what should be discarded immediately.

Relevance is one of the metrics that businesses use when evaluating EDA technology. A question that you should ask when embarking on a smart systems application in general, and an EDA application in particular, is this: Will better relevance be obtained by continuing current business practices or by developing a new EDA application? The answer depends critically on how well the application is designed. Business as usual, without new technology, is better than a new system that interrupts your concentration by demanding your immediate attention for every piece of spam mail and irrelevant phone call. Well-designed EDA applications learn or can be told about your current context so that only relevant information is pushed to you.

Note: More irrelevant information, more quickly, is unproductive. An increasingly scarce resource is uninterrupted time to focus on what is important. A well-designed application enhances that precious commodity while a poorly designed one destroys it.

Enable Business Users to Tailor Systems to Their Needs

It is a best practice to allow end users (operations personnel or other business people) to control or modify the types of event notifications sent to them by the application. End users best understand tradeoffs between missing occasional critical information on the one hand and notification fatigue—weariness from getting too much irrelevant information—on the other. If an IT person or a top business executive decides which events will be pushed to the end user, their concern about costs of missing relevant events may make them configure applications to push more data, including more irrelevant data, to operations personnel. Furthermore, IT staff members and senior executives cannot predict the changing contexts of the people who use

EDA applications; so, they may choose modalities of event notification—such as audible alarms—that are inappropriate for the current contexts of users.

Note: Enable end users to control the types of event notifications they receive.

Effort

This measure is the cost of the effort required to develop an EDA application that meets the individual needs of each user. Greater relevance is obtained by applications that are tailored by end users for their own specific needs; but, this requires investment in mechanisms that enable business users to tailor IT systems and also requires each user's time in configuring and reconfiguring systems to meet his or her individual needs. The overall effort in configuring systems falls into two broad categories: the IT and systems-development effort in implementing the initial application, and each user's effort in tuning the application to match that user's needs. Business and user needs change, so the effort in reconfiguring the application to suit each user will continue long after the initial design.

Effort Required to Tailor Systems for Different Business Users

Different users within an enterprise have different needs: a one-size-fits-all specification of events and responses doesn't work. People in many roles participate in tailoring a system to fit the needs of each user: professional services consultants provided by systems integrators and vendors tailor software to fit business needs. Technical staff have to do a great deal of background work and application integration to develop event-processing applications: they install sensors, tap into networks and data logs, and output events from business processes to capture events. IT staff in the enterprise learn event specification notations provided by vendors and set up business-oriented templates for end users; power business users create their own macros; and, finally, each business user spends time learning how to use tools to tailor the system to that user's individual needs. This effort takes time because the fundamental issue is not technology but rather understanding how to carry out business activities better. *Don't rush this part of application development.*

Business Users Need to Tailor Event-Processing Applications Themselves

Business environments change and the needs of business users of event-processing applications change too. Business users must be able to tailor event-processing applications to meet their changing needs. For example, financial traders use strategies that they want to keep private, and when they change trading strategies they need to be able to reconfigure their applications themselves. Central IT organizations cannot easily tailor applications to meet each business user's changing needs and role. This implies that traders and other business users must have notations or user interfaces that allow them to change applications to meet their needs. This implies, in turn, that business users must spend the time to learn the notation and become skilled in working with a user interface, but time spent by business users away from their businesses is expensive.

Business Dialects for Tailoring Event-Processing Applications

One way of dealing with the tradeoff between generality and ease of use is to give business users a library of specification templates that they can combine in simple ways to obtain more-complex specifications. The templates are specific to the business; thus the template library and template composition mechanisms are, in effect, a dialect for specifying event-processing applications for a particular business. Mashups in web development are an example of a technology that enables combination of data from multiple tools easily. Integrated vertical applications for specific business problems, such as stock trading, logistics, or intrusion detection, reduce the amount of professional services and IT effort required to obtain an effective application for the business user. Nevertheless, business users need to participate in tuning the business-specific vertical application to their unique needs.

....

Note: The time and effort required to tailor EDA applications to the needs of business users is significant; nevertheless, this time and effort pays off in the long run.

Event Design Is as Important as Database Design

Event design is as important, and requires as much skill, as database design for several reasons including the following.

▶ Event processing will be used to repurpose "hard" infrastructure (steel pylons, wooden electric poles, transformers, and roads) for new applications. Hard infrastructure may last for 20 to 100 years, but the ways in which the infrastructure is used may need to be changed several times in that period. For example, society demands that utilities obtain energy for the electric grid from renewable—but volatile—sources, such as solar and wind power; this demand was not a factor when the hard infrastructure was set up. Event processing will enable hard infrastructure to be repurposed in cost-effective ways to satisfy changing needs provided events and event-processing systems are designed well. Designers of event-processing applications require deep business and technology skills: *they must be familiar with existing business infrastructure and must be able to estimate how it is likely to be repurposed in the future.*

▶ Many EDA applications will be layered on top of existing applications. Deciding what event objects to store and what to discard requires knowledge of the business because an event object may prove to be valuable for an application that isn't even on the drawing boards. Event objects generated by one division of an enterprise may prove to be very valuable for another division, and this inter-divisional value may not have been recognized. Recording everything—because the records may be useful to somebody at some time—is not a viable option because that requires too much storage. Designers of event-processing applications need business skill to identify business events in underlying applications that can be exploited across the enterprise at the current or future time, and they need technical skill to determine event schemas and storage mechanisms.

An Example: The Smart Grid

Let's look at the smart grid to understand the tradeoffs in the costs of configuring systems to meet each user's specific needs. An important aspect of the smart electric grid is demand-response—a mechanism by which businesses and residents adapt demand to the availability of power in general and renewable power in particular. To understand better the importance of design and configuration effort, consider two (of the many) options that utilities can offer consumers:

▶ **Simple option**—Each year consumers select from a small number of options offered by the utility. For instance, consumers get rebates if they allow the utility to turn off some of their appliances, such as air conditioners, for a few hours a year. Consumers who sign up for rebates may override control by utilities—for example, they may override the utility's signal to turn off an air conditioner on a hot day; but, in this case consumers are charged penalties and rebates may no longer apply. Alternatively, consumers may elect to pay a higher price and not give the utility any control over the consumer's consumption of power.

▶ **Sophisticated option**—Homeowners and businesses buy and sell power to utilities, from instant to instant, depending on the price of power, the rate-payer's needs for power, and the rate-payer's ability to supply power. Homeowners and businesses may generate power using distributed energy resources such as solar and wind or by drawing power from batteries in plug-in hybrid electric vehicles or other devices. With this option, utilities or Independent Systems Operators (ISOs) will manage real-time markets for millions of small customers, many of whom will be both producers and consumers of power.

The effort required to enable users to customize the system to meet their requirements in the first option is minimal: customers merely check off a box on a form received by surface mail. Even for this simple situation, customers need to be educated about the penalties incurred by overriding control commands from the utility after customers sign up for rebates. The second, sophisticated option exploits smart technology more fully: it uses prices to obtain dynamic adjustment of supply and demand. The investment required in configuration technology, user interfaces, economics, psychology, and training of consumers is, however, much greater in the second option than in the first.

Note: Carefully analyze tradeoffs between the desired sophistication of a system and the effort required by business users to exploit the system effectively.

Accuracy

EDA applications are beneficial when they generate accurate responses and display accurate data. Some degree of inaccuracy is, however, likely. One type of inaccuracy is a *false positive*, the incorrect reporting of an event that does not actually occur. An example of a false positive is a false prediction that a tsunami will strike a beach at a specific time. An example of inaccuracy in an event parameter is a prediction that a destructive, category-five hurricane will hit a city when the actual storm that hits is only a minor tropical depression. Inappropriate decisions are made when an EDA application generates inaccurate data. A false tsunami warning results in beaches being evacuated unnecessarily, and an inaccurate prediction of a surge in the price of the stock of a company results in traders incurring losses.

Accuracy is different from relevance: information can be accurate and irrelevant. Likewise, information about a hurricane that is about to strike your home is relevant to you but can be inaccurate. Accuracy refers both to the accurate detection of an event and the execution of an appropriate response.

Costs of Inaccuracy

The costs of inaccuracy over the lifetime of an application depend on the frequency of inaccuracies and the average cost of an inaccurate response. One of the costs of inaccuracy in a newly deployed EDA application is the cost of losing customer trust; the cost of regaining end-user trust after a negative news story about the accuracy of the application can be very high. In some applications, rare but massive losses are more costly over the lifetime of the application than frequent small losses. Société Générale reported in 2008 that it lost over $7 billion due to one of its traders, and Barings Bank collapsed in 1995 after a trader lost over $1 billion. Carefully designed event-driven applications could have detected anomalous trading patterns and reduced the losses. Steps can be taken to prevent massive losses by carrying out sanity checks of proposed actions: Unusual or high-risk responses are sent to another system for further approval while low-risk responses are executed directly. If an inappropriate high-cost response has been invoked, then compensatory activities are initiated.

Reducing Costs of Inaccuracy by Double Checking

For example, algorithmic trading systems are designed to reduce costs of "fat-finger" errors. A *fat-finger trade* is an erroneous trade in which the actual amount traded is greater than the amount that the trader intended. For example, a fat-finger error may result in a trade of a million shares of a stock when the desired trade was only a thousand shares. The name *fat finger* derives from possible errors caused by a person with a fat finger who accidentally types extra zeros in the amount to be traded or leaves his finger on a key for too long. Some systems automatically detect and block probable fat-finger errors and, if necessary, execute compensatory actions. Such systems are compositions of two event-driven subsystems: the first generates proposals for responses, and the second filters out suspicious responses and takes compensatory actions.

Note: Sanity checking reduces inaccuracy but slows down responses.

Costs of Inaccurate Predictions of Rare Events

The cost of inaccuracy is a fundamental problem in EDA applications that warn about rare events. When systems give alerts about rare events, the frequency of false alerts is likely to be higher, and sometimes much higher, than the frequency of the actual events. Alerts about huge trading opportunities are likely to be more frequent than actual opportunities, and alerts from sensors about emergencies in intensive care units are likely to be more frequent than actual emergencies. There is a solid business case for EDA applications that generate some amount of inaccurate data. The question for application designers is: what degree of inaccuracy is appropriate?

Note: There is a business case for EDA applications that generate some inaccurate data; the design question is: what degree of inaccuracy is appropriate?

Tradeoffs between Accuracy and Other Metrics

The tradeoff between accuracy and other cost/benefit metrics is a complex one. Too many false alerts results in EDA applications being ignored, and this has negative consequences: firstly, the investment in the EDA application is wasted, and secondly, organizations that depend on these applications may have a false sense of security. The costs of inaccuracy are nonlinear: when genuine alarms occur only once a year, the cost of ten false alarms a day is more than ten times the cost of a single false alarm a day. Designs of EDA systems with absolutely zero inaccuracy are likely to generate information so late that it has little value, or produce fewer genuine alerts, or cost too much. Design tradeoffs are discussed in Chapter 11 on best practices.

Completeness

A system that provides only accurate information but does not provide all the information required to make decisions can be very costly. An example of incomplete information is a *false negative*—a response that is not executed because an event was not detected. A false positive is an erroneous signal that claims that a particular state change took place when it really didn't, whereas a false negative is the absence of a signal that a particular state change took place when it really did take place. For example, in the smart electric grid example, a false positive is a signal that the grid is overloaded when it is not; and a false negative is the absence of a signal that the grid is overloaded when it truly is overloaded. A consequence of a false positive in this application is that demand for power may be reduced by turning off appliances forcibly and unnecessarily, whereas a consequence of a false negative is a possible brownout.

Relative Costs of False Negatives and False Positives

The costs of incomplete information are, in many cases, higher than the costs of inaccurate information. The cost of a false negative—no warning—when a tsunami strikes is measured in lives lost, property destroyed, and sea water inundating agricultural fields. The cost of a false warning of a tsunami includes the costs of clearing beaches unnecessarily, the negative impact on tourism, and possibly alarm fatigue from too many false warnings. In this and many other applications (see the smart grid example), the cost of a single false negative is much higher than the cost of a single false positive.

Since the cost of each false negative is often higher than the cost of each false positive, it is tempting to turn the tradeoff dial toward generating many more false positives with the goal of reducing the likelihood of false negatives by a small amount. Don't yield to this temptation. The total costs of false positives don't increase linearly with the frequency of false positives—doubling the frequency more than doubles the cost.

....

Note: The cost of a single false negative—absence of critical information—is usually much higher than the cost of a single false positive—the presence of inaccurate information; however, in many systems the frequency of false positives is much higher than the frequency of false negatives.

Sanity Checks Don't Work Well for False Negatives

The costs of false positives can be limited, in some cases, by double-checking data or sanity checking information for reasonability. A sell-off in United Airlines (UAL) shares occurred after a report about the company declaring bankruptcy appeared on a website on September 8, 2008, but shares bounced back after investors realized that the report was about the company's 2002 bankruptcy filing. Double-checking data reduces the likelihood of responding to inaccurate data. Generally, costs of false negatives cannot be controlled by double checking or sanity checking in the same way. Suppose a company has gone bankrupt, but a trader has received no information about the bankruptcy. Usually, the trader cannot deduce that the company is bankrupt from the absence of information about bankruptcy. In general, you cannot deduce the existence of a false negative from the absence of information.

Business Cases for Responding to Frequent Events and Rare Events

Business decisions are taken in the absence of complete information. Some degree of incompleteness is inevitable. An enterprise determines whether to adopt an event-processing application, in part, by evaluating the improvement in the quality of decisions due to more complete information engendered by EDA applications. Making the business case for more complete information offered by EDA applications is easier for applications that detect and respond to events frequently. RFID (radio frequency identification) applications for handling supplies detect events continuously in regular operations, and so the business case for better information is clear. Moreover, an enterprise can measure the benefits of such an application after it is deployed and justify the investment in a quantitative fashion. The business case is more nuanced when the application detects and responds to rare, but important, events. And quantitative justification of the investment, by making measurements before and after the application is deployed, is more difficult in these cases.

Timeliness

The effectiveness of a response depends on its timeliness. A tsunami warning issued after a tsunami strikes has little value. The value of a response to an event almost always decays with increased response time. The decrease in value of a response as response time increases is captured in a value-time function that plots response time on the X axis and response value on the Y axis, as shown in Figure 4-2. The value of a response drops significantly when response time increases by even a few milliseconds in some applications, while in other applications the value of a response may not decrease much even when response times increase by minutes. The costs of not dealing rapidly with threats and opportunities in milliseconds are huge in missile-defense and algorithmic-trading applications, whereas the costs of not responding in minutes, or even hours, are not high in some accounting applications. Even within a single application, such as the smart electric grid, the value of information as a function of delay varies from function to function—for instance, delays of fewer than 1 cycle (with 60 cycles per second) are beneficial for automatic circuit-switching functions, whereas delays of hours are acceptable for billing functions.

The Value of a Response Decreases with Delay

The rate at which the value of a response decays with response time depends on the maximum rate of change of the evolving threat or opportunity and the costs of not reacting to the threat or opportunity. Consider, for example, the Adverse Event Report-

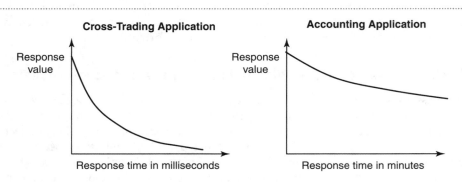

Figure 4-2: Value-time functions.

ing System (AERS) used by the Food and Drug Administration (FDA) to monitor side effects of prescription drugs. The cost of delivery of inappropriate drugs to patients is huge, but the rate of change of the evolving threat is small—few patients are likely to be injured by inappropriate prescriptions of the drug in the next few milliseconds. Detecting possible side effects may take hours. Responses in seconds are not expected in AERS because such responses aren't cost effective. Though faster is usually better, evaluate the costs and benefits of increased timeliness carefully before investing in faster systems.

Accuracy and completeness of event detections are critical in determining timeliness: detections based on less accurate and less complete information can be made quicker, leaving more time to respond to events.

....

Note: Faster detections of events leave more time to respond to them, but detections based on more accurate and complete information require more time for evaluation and less time for response.

Designers developing event-processing applications today have to consider the value-time function as it is today and *as it is likely to be in the future*. The value of rapid responses is likely to increase as business moves faster.

Tradeoffs between Timeliness and Accuracy

An analysis of the tradeoff between incremental costs of systems that deliver faster responses with incremental benefits accruing from greater speed shows that reducing response times by milliseconds does have benefits in many fully automated applications such as cross-trading. In cross-trading, an asset manager matches and then executes trades directly between client buyers and client sellers of an item without first sending the requests (bids and asks) to an exchange. Regulations prohibit an asset manager from holding buy or sell requests for more than a short time before passing the requests on to an exchange. Reducing delay between the initiation of a buy or sell order and the detection of the order by the cross-trading application by even a few milliseconds is valuable. If orders can be held by the application for a few milliseconds more, then the application can hold more orders before sending them to the exchange, and this gives the application both more time to detect matches and more orders to match.

An Example of the Timeliness-Accuracy Tradeoff from Seismology

The tradeoff between timeliness and other cost/benefit measures is illustrated by the following example from seismology. Networks of sensors and accelerometers detect shaking near geological fault lines and send data electronically to sites that analyze the data and issue alerts if appropriate. When a rupture occurs along a fault line, seismic waves emanate from the points of rupture; these waves can cause intense shaking many miles from the rupture. Seismic waves move along the earth's surface much slower than data sent electronically and so data from sensors can reach populated areas before intense shaking starts. Population centers, depending on where they are located, can receive warnings a few seconds to several hundreds of seconds before severe shaking starts. The responses to such warnings are to slow down trains, stop elevators at floors and open elevator doors, open fire station doors, and secure electric power and communication networks. The challenges in building the application include:

▶ **Completeness**—Identify areas where dangerous shaking is likely to take place.

▶ **Accuracy**—Issue warnings only for regions where dangerous shaking will take place.

▶ **Timeliness**—Issue warnings early enough that effective responses can be executed.

The system issues a warning based on sensor data accrued over a time interval after faults start to rupture. More sensor data can be obtained and more calculations can be carried out over longer time intervals. So, the accuracy and completeness of predictions improves with more time after the initial rupture. But, the longer the system waits to make a prediction, the less time there is to respond effectively. The tradeoff is between giving earlier, possibly erroneous warnings on the one hand, and giving later, more-accurate warnings on the other. This fundamental tradeoff has to be considered in relationship to tradeoffs among other measures such as total cost, effort, and security.

An Example of the Timeliness-Accuracy Tradeoff from Advertising

Advertisements, or sponsored links, shown with results of web searches and e-mail are selected in a timely manner. Users get impatient after waiting for more than a few seconds; so companies that offer services, such as web search, determine within those few seconds the appropriate sponsored links to show you. The companies execute complex algorithms to maximize their revenues based on the types of contracts they have with advertisers and their estimates of your behavior. They also have to deal with the tradeoff between timeliness and optimization—more time will help them show you ads that are most meaningful to you, but if the delay is too long, you will use an alternate system.

Better Timeliness from Predictive Systems

Systems that predict and respond to situations *before* they become critical give more time to respond. Many event-processing applications are predictive, which is why "the predictive enterprise" is one of the management aspirations that are specifically targeted by event processing. The benefits of prediction can also be captured by the value-time function, where zero time is the point at which the event starts; positive time is the time that elapses after the event starts; and negative time is the time before the event. Predictions of future events are, however, more likely to be inaccurate and incomplete than detections of the past.

Ways to Improve Timeliness

Timeliness of event-driven applications can be improved by improving any stage of the process: by receiving data more quickly, by responding more rapidly, by aggregating and analyzing data faster, or by predicting events farther into the future. For example, timeliness in algorithmic trading applications can be improved by obtaining trading data directly from exchanges rather than from slower, consolidated feeds. Timeliness can also be improved by using faster message oriented middleware (MOM) software, faster processors, and effective use of parallel systems such as networks of multiprocessor machines. Designers of event-processing systems make reasoned tradeoffs between timeliness and other parameters. This tradeoff must focus on the response time of the entire business application and not merely the time spent in a single component such as the event detector.

Security

Security is a concern for users of all software systems. It is, however, a particular concern for users of event-driven applications, because these applications are often critical to business. For example, electric power transmission companies that respond to possible brownouts by turning appliances on and off in homes via the smart electric grid must prevent hackers from orchestrating attacks that result in brownouts. The problem of cyber attack wasn't as acute for utilities not so long ago when the companies' IT networks didn't reach homes and expose more points to attackers. Security is becoming more important and more challenging with increasingly tight integration of critical infrastructure—electric power, gas, water, roads, and air traffic—with sensors, responders, and IT woven into the infrastructure.

....

Note: Security is one of the biggest hurdles to the widespread deployment of EDA applications.

Event-Processing Applications and Customer Privacy

The broad area of security includes protection of privacy. Many event-driven applications acquire and store a great deal of personal information. An application that detects and responds to a customer's location by monitoring mobile phones acquires information on where the customer has been. Cars equipped with GPS and tele-monitoring devices can inform remote vehicle management sites about speeds at which cars are driven. Car insurance rates may depend on estimates of driving habits gathered from sensor data on cars. Many people don't object to making some event types, such as car locations, public. Many people make videos public—and videos are event objects. Event objects, like diamonds, are forever. Event objects can be analyzed by everybody who can get access to them at any time—even long after the event. Business intelligence (BI) can be used to learn a great deal about a person by fusing event objects recorded over the years. Copyright laws can be used to prevent proliferation of copies of event objects, but finding and destroying all copies is an intractable task. Furthermore, copyright laws may not prevent people and companies from maintaining information deduced from analysis of event objects even if the objects themselves are protected by copyright.

Note: Protection of privacy is an increasing concern. But, event objects, like diamonds, can be forever. Event objects can be analyzed by everybody who can get access to them, even long after the event.

Smart systems are smart because they respond better to your needs and the needs of society and the environment; but responding better to your needs also requires that these systems know more about you. Consumers and regulatory agencies are already concerned with the potential invasion of privacy from smart systems. This issue will become even more critically important in the future.

Cyber-Security of Infrastructure

An attacker can find many ways to break into an EDA application. An attacker can *spoof* the enterprise, pretending to be a customer, and a hacker can spoof the customer, pretending to be the enterprise. In the case of the smart electric grid, a customer can attempt to change the signals sent from his home to the grid to reduce his bill. More dangerously, malicious hackers can attempt to cause brownouts by sending signals to turn on appliances in homes, thus overloading the system and possibly causing brownouts. Sensors and responders are becoming more widespread and more exposed; this gives malicious hackers more points at which to attack the system.

Preventing attackers from bringing down the system requires understanding the relationship between potential attacks and the underlying physical system; in the case of the electric power system, this requires understanding the effect of cyber-attack scenarios on the electromechanical system consisting of generator, transmission, distribution, and consumption systems. *Cyber-physical security—understanding and managing the relationship between attacks to the cyber-infrastructure and the underlying physical, biological, or social system—is becoming increasingly important as EDA becomes widespread.*

Event Processing for Detecting Attacks from Within

Not all attacks come from agents outside the enterprise; losses due to rogue traders at some major institutions (such as Société Générale and Barings Bank) were due to agents within the enterprise. Detection of insider attacks requires that EDA applications detect behavior that indicates attacks, and this is difficult when the attacker knows the detection algorithms. *As systems—roads, ports, oil fields, and banks—get smarter, with event processing carried out at every step, the consequences of insider attacks get ever more serious.*

The area of security includes forensics—understanding what went wrong when a system was attacked or when errors were made—and BI tools operating on event-object repositories help here. An aspect of forensics is event *provenance*—descriptions of data items used to generate an event object and the process by which the event object was generated. This highlights the importance of careful designs of event schemas and links between simple event objects and the complex event objects created from them.

System Resilience

Resilience and robustness are related to security and fall under the broad rubric of security costs and benefits. Systems with standby or surplus capacity are generally more robust. The electric grid is robust because the ISO that manages the grid can call upon spinning reserves to supply additional power the instant it is needed. A fender-bender on a freeway doesn't cause massive delays when traffic can flow along alternate lanes. A problem with an airplane doesn't cause hours or days of delays for passengers when there are spare parts and spare planes available immediately. We are now increasingly relying on EDA to make our systems smarter and more efficient; we are using more information technology so that we can use less steel, burn less fossil fuel, build fewer power plants, and reduce our impact on the ecosystem. But, this also means that we are operating critical systems closer to the edge, with less spare capacity. And that's why EDA applications must be reliable.

Impact of Interconnectedness on Security

The demand for event processing is driven, in part, by increasing global connectedness. Event-processing applications, in turn, drive increasing connectedness. EDA applications enable traders in New York and London to respond in seconds to changes in Shanghai. Electric power grids in Europe and North America are being consolidated. Increasing connectedness can lead to greater resilience: shortages at points in the network can be supplied from surpluses at other points. Tighter coupling across larger networks can also lead to rare, but catastrophic, events on a regional or even global scale. A problem in the power grid in Ohio caused a blackout for over 50 million people in the United States and Canada on August 14, 2003. Errors may propagate and failures can cascade across interconnected networks. EDA applications can monitor for errors and respond by taking action to prevent system failure. As EDA helps supply chains, stock exchanges, power grids, energy supplies, and water resources across regions become more interdependent, careful designs and alert operations are required to reduce the likelihood of rare but cataclysmic network-wide failures.

Security problems are not new; however, smart EDA applications woven into the fabric of daily life make security problems much more severe.

....

Note: The cost of ensuring security is a large part of the overall cost of EDA applications, but the cost of not ensuring security is much higher.

Summary

Since EDA applications have direct, visible impact on business, particular attention must be paid to business participation in evaluations of costs and benefits. The analysis of costs and benefits will help you determine whether to implement an EDA application for a business problem, or to use alternative technologies, or make no changes at all. The REACTS cost-benefit measures are more important in EDA applications than in other types of applications. Use the REACTS measures to help you design the best EDA application for your business problem.

All software systems have costs and benefits. The discussion in this chapter has restricted attention to features that are more typical of event-processing applications than other software applications. Be aware of another important cost since the discipline of business event processing is relatively new, finding people with expertise both in your business and in event-processing technologies will be difficult. Chapter 11 discusses how enterprises can deal with this issue.

5

Types of Event-Processing Applications

A list of business problems for which event processing is the preferred solution would help you to determine where it could be applied in your organization; however, such a list would be incomplete and out of date the instant it was compiled. The ever-increasing variety of business problems for which event processing is being used profitably will make any such list obsolete. A better approach is to use a systematic framework to evaluate whether event processing in general and event-driven architecture (EDA) and complex event processing (CEP) in particular are appropriate for a given problem. Let us look at a framework built upon the material presented in the preceding chapters. Let's use this framework in this chapter to evaluate the suitability of event processing for existing business problems, and in Chapter 12 to predict how event-processing technologies will evolve.

> Note: A list of business problems for which event processing is applicable will be incomplete and out of date the instant that it is compiled.

Features Driving Demand for Event Processing

This section discusses features of business problems that drive increasing demand for event-processing applications. The presence, or absence, of each of these features in a problem is one of the measures used to evaluate the appropriateness of event processing for the problem.

As you read in Chapter 1, the system drivers for event-processing applications are timeliness, agility, and information availability. The technology push and consumer pull drivers for event-driven interactions were summarized in Chapter 2 as the PC-cubed (price, pervasiveness, performance, connectedness, celerity, and complexity) trends. You also saw that the informal expectations people have about event-driven components, as well as the formal contracts that designers use to specify components of event-driven systems, are different from those for more traditional time- and request-driven systems. Chapter 3 showed how EDA and CEP help improve business. You explored different categories of benefits and costs in Chapter 4, organized under the REACTS (relevance, effort, accuracy, completeness, timeliness, and security) rubric. Now, you'll see how these concepts help you evaluate whether the best IT applications for a business problem should, or should not, include EDA components.

As you saw in Chapter 2, most IT systems are hybrid systems with components that are event-, time-, or request-driven. Good designs use components that are tuned to execute the functions they perform; even in event-processing applications, some functions are best carried out in a time- or request-driven manner. This chapter helps you determine whether EDA components are part of the best IT solutions to a given business problem. This chapter identifies the characteristics of business activities for which hybrid systems containing event-driven components are the best technology:

▶ Looking outside the virtual enterprise to detect critical events

▶ Responding to rapidly changing situations by keeping up with newly generated data

▶ Managing by exception

▶ Adaptability—adapting the behavior of business activities as needs change

▶ Instrumenting business activities in a virtual enterprise for purposes of business intelligence, application monitoring, and application integration

Looking Outside the Virtual Enterprise

Much of enterprise IT, from the 1950s through the 1980s, focused exclusively on services within the virtual enterprise. Things have changed: now IT is expected to help the enterprise respond rapidly to conditions outside the virtual enterprise, as depicted in Figure 5-1.

An enterprise can ensure that interactions among all agents within the virtual enterprise follow well-defined protocols and speak the same language—that is, use the

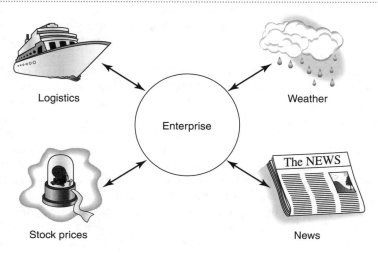

Logistics

Weather

Enterprise

Stock prices

News

Figure 5-1: "Looking outside the enterprise."

same schemas, the same meanings for phrases, and agreed-upon services. A supplier may be required to submit a quotation to a manufacturing company by making a request for a submit-quotation service provided by the manufacturer. The supplier's request must use the schemas and meanings specified by the manufacturer so that the service can process the request. The manufacturer, for example, may require a supplier of ball bearings to specify the size of a bearing in terms of diameters in millimeters as opposed to radii in inches. When you buy an item from an online retailer, you describe the item you want by filling out a form specified by the retailer; you are, in effect, using the retailer's language and the retailer's service. Agents within the virtual enterprise can interact with each other using services and languages approved by both parties.

Agents outside the virtual enterprise may be unwilling to interact with agents within it by using services and languages specified by the enterprise. An enterprise's competitor, for example, will not keep the enterprise informed about the competitor's actions by invoking the enterprise's services. Government agencies will not inform an enterprise about new regulations or unemployment figures by using schemas and services specified by the enterprise. The enterprise must actively acquire external information and make sense of it.

Agents within a virtual enterprise may collaborate with each other using time- or request-driven interactions. For example, a buyer in the enterprise may meet with a supplier at a specified time and place, or a business activity may invoke a service in a logistics company. Agents, such as competitors, outside the virtual enterprise do not carry out actions at the times of the enterprise's choosing. In a smart road management system, cars enter toll booths when drivers choose, not when the system determines that they should. In a smart electric grid system, customers turn on appliances when they want to. Patients fall ill and need medical care at unscheduled times. These actions are driven by external agents and are, therefore, inherently event-driven.

....

Note: Use event-processing technologies for applications that sense and respond to activity outside the virtual enterprise.

Responding to Changing Situations

Some situations change so rapidly that applications cannot keep up with the changes. For these business situations applications that keep up with arriving data, but drop items occasionally, are better than applications that never drop items but fall behind. Cross-trading is an example of such applications. Cross-trading applications make money by matching offers between buyers and sellers of a stock within a firm; however, not identifying a match isn't a catastrophe. Normally, buy and sell orders are matched in an open exchange, but a firm can match the buy order of one customer with the sell order of another within the same firm, provided the transaction is executed in accordance with regulations. If the firm cannot match buy and sell orders within specified times, the firm is required to send the orders on to an exchange. Regulatory agencies impose severe penalties if the application falls behind and the firm holds buy and sell offers for longer than the permitted time. Therefore, the firm passes a buy or sell offer to an exchange when the offer is held for a time near the regulation limit. The firm makes more money if it executes more matches, but the system does not incur severe penalties if it misses making a match. Event processing is more suitable than request-driven interactions for such applications that must keep up with arriving data in a best-effort fashion and that don't have to process every single item of data.

Online transaction processing (OLTP) applications, such as airline reservation systems, handle high data rates using request- or event-driven interactions. Ticket purchases are required to be transactions—that is, either the purchase is aborted (the customer doesn't pay for the ticket and the airline doesn't sell the ticket) or the purchase completes successfully. Many business interactions do not have to satisfy the stringent constraints of transactional processing, and EDA applications are particularly cost effective in these situations. Though EDA can be used for transactional systems, a more common view of transactional interactions is that they are request-reply interactions. EDA applications are often overlaid on top of request-driven applications where EDA applications capture and act on events generated by the request-driven substrate.

A commonplace illustration of event- and request-driven interactions is the way in which you pay the toll at a tollbooth. Fifty years ago, all tollbooth interactions were request-driven and transactional: the tollgate was closed when you got to the tollbooth, you paid cash, and then the tollgate opened, signaling the completion of the transaction. Now your car can be equipped with wireless payment mechanisms, such as *FasTrak*, that allow you to drive through. There are no gates that stop you. A toll system that lets people go through without stopping and later penalizes the few people who pass without payment is more efficient than a system that stops everybody and lets them through only after they pay the toll. Likewise, some applications that asynchronously send data items, as the items are generated, are more efficient than applications that send data items to their destinations in a synchronous request-reply fashion. In the smart electric grid, phasor measurement units are sent from multiple sensors several times per second to event-processing agents; a lost measurement is not a catastrophe, and so event-driven asynchronous messages are adequate and efficient. A synchronous request-reply transaction to transmit each phasor measurement is slow and unnecessary.

Note: Use EDA for applications that must respond quickly to situations that change rapidly and asynchronously, and where interactions do not have to be transactional.

Use EDA layered on top of transactional applications to capture and process events generated by transactions.

Managing by Exception

Colonel Alfred D'Amario, in his book *Hangar Flying* (AuthorHouse, 2008), describes flying an airplane as "hours and hours of sheer boredom punctuated by moments of stark panic." Like instrumentation systems that alert airplane crews about exceptional conditions, event-processing systems help organizations deal with atypical events. People aren't as effective as computers in remaining alert while monitoring the environment for signs of unusual events. Event-processing applications support management by exception (MBE)—the applications acquire and analyze large quantities of data, detect atypical situations, and initiate responses. This frees organizations from having to pay attention over long periods to multiple high-throughput data streams to detect and respond to uncommon conditions.

A seismic network for first responders that detects, locates, and identifies collapsed buildings, broken bridges, or buckled roads is a system that supports management by exception. Seismometers and accelerometers measure thousands of values each second, and many trillions of measurements may be made between the severe earthquakes that destroy buildings. The system provides a great deal of value when the unusual situation occurs.

The many examples of management by exception include applications that warn management about patterns of trading that indicate fraud, respond to overloading of the power grid, determine that peanut butter from a factory is contaminated with salmonella, detect mad cow disease, and identify drivers who run toll booths without paying. Management by exception enables systems to monitor huge volumes of activity efficiently because only a small fraction of the activity needs exceptional handling. Most stock transactions are not fraudulent, the power grid is rarely overloaded, most peanuts aren't contaminated, most cows don't suffer from mad-cow disease, and most drivers don't try to run through tollbooths without paying. Management by exception is an inherently event-driven activity since the occurrence of the exception is an event.

Smart infrastructure systems—smart bridges, smart water systems, and smart hospitals, for example—deal with high rates of events. Strain gauges on bridges, phasor measurements on the electric grid, and electronic monitors on patients measure many values each day. Only a few seconds in a day are critical and require extensive analysis; most of the time systems behave in their usual fashion. In normal periods smart systems monitor data for unusual situations and may log data, but otherwise do relatively little; when exceptions arise they carry out computations, communicate data, and actuate responders to deal with the exception. Our nervous systems work in the same way. Most of the time our bodies operate in normal mode, but when we detect threats we transition to fight or flight mode: adrenaline is released, heart rate increases, and blood is pumped into the major muscles. Smart people and smart systems often manage by exception.

....

Note: Use event-processing technologies for applications that support management by exception.

Let's compare the following two applications with respect to the variety of actions that the application must handle: (1) an application that customers use to configure and purchase computers online, and (2) an application that detects cybercrime. A customer specifies many parameters to configure a computer: the machine type (notebook, laptop, desktop, or tower), size of memory, number of hard drives and USB ports, and so on. Though the vendor does not anticipate each customer's specific request, the vendor does anticipate and restrict the types and ranges of requests. Unlike transactions used to configure computers, the cybercrime application must deal with more varied and unanticipated actions—not all criminal behaviors are foreseen. Criminals remain undetected by hiding evidence of criminality. Detecting criminal or non-compliant behavior often requires CEP.

Responses to anomalous behaviors are, perforce, less well defined and more fluid than responses to anticipated situations. Applications for configuring computers online can be request-driven because behaviors generally fall within anticipated ranges. Applications that detect cybercrime and other anomalous behaviors are largely event-driven because the detection and characterization of the behavior is a key part of the application.

Detection of anomalous events and management by exception are not exclusively event-driven; exceptions are also raised in request-reply interactions. When you fill a form on the Web that asks for your address and you leave the address field blank, the application will raise an exception and display a message such as "this field is mandatory." So, what makes EDA and CEP particularly better for detecting unusual patterns and management by exception?

An unfilled field in a web form is an exception in a single interaction whereas the detection of a pattern that indicates a significant anomaly, such as cybercrime, requires analysis of data from multiple sources over a period of time. Trading stock "ahead" and "interpositioning" of trades by trading specialists are violations of federal securities laws, and such trading violations are not detected from a single violation but rather from a time-series analysis of trades. Warnings of tsunamis are based on fusion of data obtained over time from many sensors. CEP is useful when characterizations of anomalies are complex and when detections of anomalies require analyses of data gathered from multiple agents across time.

Note: Use event-processing technologies for applications that must react rapidly to unusual situations.

Adaptability

EDA applications can be more agile, and more adaptable, than request-driven applications. As discussed in earlier chapters, an important difference between event-processing interactions and time- or request-driven interactions is that the creation of an event object is decoupled from its eventual use. The dissemination network is responsible for getting event objects from agents that produce them to the agents that need to act on them. The dissemination network also stores event objects for later use by consumers, and the network may have databases to facilitate dissemination. A common structure of event-processing networks (EPNs) is a "hub-and-spoke," with agents—including sensors, responders, and other types of event-processing agents—at the spokes and the dissemination network at the hub. The spokes produce, consume, and process event objects. The hub receives event objects from the spokes and sends (copies of) event objects to the spokes that need them. An alternate view of the hub-and-spoke structure is that of an event-object bus (the hub), with producers pushing data on to the bus and consumers pulling event objects from the bus. An EPN is flexible to the extent that event-object producers and consumers can be modified, attached, and detached from the bus easily; and the flow of event objects through the bus can be modified easily. Most implementations of EDA are, indeed, flexible.

EPNs don't always have bus structures. Indeed, the dissemination network can be hardwired, with each producer sending event objects in proprietary formats to specific ports of specific Internet Protocol (IP) addresses. Hardwired networks are, however, generally less flexible. The bus structure is a logical structure, not a physical one, and the bus may be implemented as a distributed system. The specifics of the implementation are not important at this stage; what is important is the logical separation between producers and consumers of event objects on the one hand and the dissemination network on the other.

An EDA application can grow by accretion with the addition of agents and event object types that were not planned for when the application was first designed. For example, a record of a credit card transaction is an event object. A credit card transaction is itself a request-reply interaction between a retailer and the bank that issued the card, but the record of the transaction is an event object that can be used by other agents at other times. Fraud-detection applications act upon the information recorded about the credit card transaction to evaluate the probability of fraud. Customer relationship management (CRM) applications act upon the same information to determine whether the customer should be offered promotions. Risk-management applications act upon the same information to evaluate lines of credit. Corporate performance management (CPM) applications use the information on an aggregate level to tell top management about the overall health of the business. (Chapter 10 discusses performance management in more detail.)

If an EPN is represented by a hub-and-spoke structure, then the spokes are agents in applications such as CRM, fraud detection, risk management, and performance management, while the hub is the dissemination network. New applications, new producers, and new consumers of event objects can be added after the system is in operation. Adding spokes to a hub-and-spoke structure is generally easier than changing an organizational chart or some other graph structure. The key to flexibility is the dissemination network, and many flexible networks are available today.

....

Note: The decoupling of production, consumption, and copying of event objects results in looser coupling between components of event-driven systems than request-driven systems. Use event-processing technologies when loose coupling and adaptability are key requirements.

Instrumenting the Virtual Enterprise

Instrumentation to sense and respond to events helps make enterprises more efficient. The events that are detected may be routine events—such as bags moving along a conveyor belt, patients moving from one hospital ward to another, or steps in a business process—or they may be unusual events such as patterns that indicate fraudulent activity. Now, let's look at the combined benefits of efficiencies gained from instrumenting routine business activity coupled with the benefits of timely responses to unusual high-value events.

The benefits of instrumentation and EDA applications for normal activity are tangible and measurable as part of routine business operations. The potential benefits from timely reactions to rare but huge opportunities or major threats become evident when the events occur and the business responds more effectively with EDA than without it. A business case can be made for instrumentation and EDA that provides immediate and continuing value in normal operations with the added advantages of massive gains from critical rare events. There are many examples of such business cases; let's start with an example in astronomy.

Astronomers use telescopes to study the cosmos in a time-driven, scheduled fashion and to detect important rare events. The Report of the National Science Foundation, Division of Astronomical Sciences, Senior Review Committee of October 22, 2006 states: "The rise of organized, transient astronomy, with its enormous demands for follow up observations of supernovae, gamma ray bursts, and microlensing events, requires telescope networks that respond to alerts by immediately interrupting the background programs."[1] Astronomers schedule time on telescopes well in advance based on the positions of objects in the sky. When an important transient event occurs in the sky, time-driven control of telescopes is interrupted and telescopes are reoriented to observe the event. Astronomical event objects are called VOEvents—these are documents encoded in XML. The scientific community is considering automatic triggering to event-driven control when a VOEvent arrives; the current control mechanism is manual. Telescopes are instruments that provide value to astronomers on an ongoing, regular basis, and also provide high value in responding to rare, significant events.

RFID (radio frequency identification) tags can help pharmaceutical companies institute flexible, demand-driven supply chains, and the benefits of this event-driven application are tangible and measurable on a day-to-day basis. In addition, the application helps to detect and respond to rare, critical events such as diversion of drugs and the addition of counterfeit drugs.

Summary of Features Favoring Event Processing

Event-processing technologies are also used to deal with applications that don't have the features discussed here; however, most event-driven applications do have one or more of these features. The key features were identified in Chapter 1: agility, information awareness, and timeliness. Let's add detail to these features to help us determine whether event-processing technologies are appropriate for a business application. We refer to the features of business applications that favor event processing as "problem features" or the "A-E-I-O-U features":

----

[1] *From the Ground Up: Balancing the NSF Astronomy Program*, www.nsf.gov/mps/ast/seniorreview/sr-report.pdf, p. 51.

▶ **A** Adaptability—adapting to changes in a system, the environment, or the user

▶ **E** Exception—management by exception; responding to exceptional events

▶ **I** Instrumentation—instrumenting a system to measure and record events so that the system can be improved

▶ **O** Outside—responding to events outside the virtual enterprise

▶ **U** Unanticipated—responding to unanticipated situations

Event processing also provides features such as greater efficiency that play critical roles in our analysis of whether event-processing technologies are appropriate for a business domain; however, this book does not explicitly highlight evaluation parameters, such as efficiency and total cost of ownership, because these parameters are used to analyze all systems.

A Framework for Analyzing Which Business Domains Are Suitable for Event Processing

In this section, we propose a framework, based on the material presented earlier, that helps you determine whether EDA is the best choice for a problem you face. We use the framework to identify business problems suitable for EDA in different domains. The framework is based on the following:

▶ The types of contracts, or expectations, of agents in different interactions

▶ The cost/benefit measures

▶ The features of problems, such as the A-E-I-O-U features, that favor different types of interactions

The framework focuses on how information flow impacts what the business does and not on information as an end in itself. As a consequence, the framework must explicitly consider uncertainty, the likelihood of error, the costs of mistakes, and the benefits of timeliness. We review, very briefly, the elements that go into the framework:

1. A problem that has any of the A-E-I-O-U features is a candidate for event-processing technology. The degree to which these features are pronounced in the problem determines whether event processing, often combined with other technologies, is the preferred choice.

2. We also compare the expectations we have about the proposed application with expectations we have about components in time-, request-, and event-driven applications; if the expectations are similar to those for event-driven applications, that's a clue that EDA is appropriate.

3. If we decide, based on the A-E-I-O-U features and comparison of expectations, to evaluate EDA solutions, we then compare the REACTS cost/benefit measures for an EDA solution with alternative approaches and choose the approach with the best cost/benefit ratio.

4. Event-processing technologies may not be the best solution for a business problem today but may be in the future. So, we'll also look at trends, such as the PC-cubed trends, to gauge how event processing may be used in the future.

Note: A systematic framework for analyzing which business domains are suitable for event processing is more useful than a list of domains.

Applying the Framework to Determine which Business Domains Are Suitable for Event Processing

Many business activities are suitable for event processing, and an exhaustive list is not instructive. Our focus here is on applying a framework that will help you evaluate the suitability of event processing for any problem. Next, we'll carry out the exercise of applying the framework to several domains. This brief exercise illustrates the use of the framework but is far too brief to be a complete analysis of different vertical markets.

Defense and Homeland Security

Problems in defense, security, and crisis management exhibit all the A-E-I-O-U features. Many of the devastating events handled by homeland security agencies, ranging from tsunamis to chemical spills, are rare exceptions to normality. Systems continuously monitor the environment for signs of these events and take action when the events are detected. These situations unfold rapidly, asynchronously, and unpredictably, and responses to events must be rapid as well. Agencies must respond to critical events that occur outside the agencies. And though agencies plan extensively for crisis situations, each crisis has unanticipated features.

The kinds of expectations we have for components in defense and homeland security applications are more typical of expectations for components in EDA than of expectations for components in request- or time-driven applications. We expect components to sense and respond to conditions continuously. For example, they must sense when contaminants are in the water supply and take remedial action, predict when and where a hurricane will make landfall and warn citizens, and detect intrusion into a network and then identify and shut out the intruder. We don't expect a server to tell a client the condition of the water supply, the location of a hurricane, or the presence of an intruder only when the client makes a request.

An analysis of each of the REACTS cost/benefit measures demonstrates the value of EDA in general and CEP in particular. Military applications are tuned so that only highly relevant information is pushed to soldiers on battlefields. Technology is helping soldiers communicate relevant information—such as their location, their health status, and the status of their equipment—with little or no effort. Event-driven applications and sensor technologies provide more accurate situation awareness; for example, remote-controlled unmanned aerial vehicles, such as the Predator, give soldiers views of the terrain. The benefits of event-driven applications in defense, when compared with time- or request-driven applications, in terms of accuracy, completeness, and timeliness, are self-evident. Security is a problem, however, as EDA applications are as vulnerable to attack as are other types of applications. Nevertheless, military, security, and crisis-management problem domains exemplify areas where EDA and CEP have great and obvious business value: these problems have all the A-E-I-O-U features and have excellent cost/benefit values for the REACTS measures. Defense and homeland security applications are examined in more detail in Chapter 12.

Track and Trace

Most shipping, trucking, railroad, and other logistics companies use track-and-trace applications that allow the company and its customers to track the location of an item and trace its path from shipment to destination. Concerns about mad-cow disease and bioterror attacks are leading toward a national farm identification system that tracks every farm animal with an identifier and possibly a tag or microchip from birth to death. Contaminations of milk products with melamine, peanut butter with salmonella, and spinach with *E. coli* have highlighted the importance of ensuring safety in food supply. Tracking food sources, both animal and vegetable, helps identify problems early and minimize risk.

Electronic pedigree systems record major events—location of manufacture, shipment, prior sales, and trades—that occurred over the lifetime of items such as pharmaceutical products. All of these applications track events in the items' histories—whether they are packages, cows, tomatoes, medicines, or data. Some applications send alerts when histories deviate from norms: for example, when a food shipment that should have been kept at temperatures below a specified threshold is exposed to higher temperatures for an extended period, or when a package that should have arrived at a trans-shipment station by a specified time doesn't arrive.

Expectations for track-and-trace applications and components are closer to expectations for EDA systems than to those for systems based on request-driven or time-driven interactions. We want to initiate the process of detecting a salmonella outbreak or tracing a lost package as soon as possible—not on a once-a-month or even a once-a-day basis. And we expect these components to be continuously active carrying out tasks; we don't expect them to remain passive, waiting for requests.

Most track-and-trace problems have some of the A-E-I-O-U features. The consequences of poor track-and-trace systems may be severe; in the food industry the consequences include deaths and loss of confidence in basic food staples such as milk and peanut butter. An analysis of the REACTS measures shows that CEP is an appropriate technology for many applications dealing with track and trace. The detection of a salmonella or *E. coli* outbreak, for instance, requires analysis of time-varying data from multiple sources in different organizations. Pinpointing the outbreak to a specific peanut factory or spinach plant requires a great deal of analysis. A study of the cost/benefit measures suggests that public health agencies, fast-food chains, agribusi-nesses, package-handling companies, and indeed all enterprises that need to track and trace items benefit from EDA. The PC-cubed trends tell us that event processing will be even more widely applied in the future for track-and-trace applications. As described next, a look at e-pedigree systems for tracking pharmaceutical products shows that event processing will be adopted more widely in the future.

The U.S. Food and Drug Administration (FDA), defines a drug pedigree[2] as follows:

A drug pedigree is a statement of origin that identifies each prior sale, purchase, or trade of a drug, including the date of those transactions and the names and addresses of all parties to them. Under the pedigree requirement, each person who is engaged in the wholesale distribution of a prescription drug in interstate commerce, who is not the manufacturer or an authorized distributor of record for that drug, must provide to the person who receives the drug a pedigree for that drug.

Electronic pedigrees (e-pedigrees) help combat counterfeit drugs and diversion. In the future, wholesalers will be required to have drug e-pedigrees to acquire or sell pre-scription drugs. California and other states have passed legislation requiring elec-tronic records of pharmaceutical drugs; these laws are planned to take effect at different times in different states. Let's analyze where track-and-trace technology is headed in the pharmaceutical industry from the vantage point of the PC-cubed trends. Trends in prices of RFID and bar-code technology, when compared to costs and errors of manual tracking, favor automation and event processing. The performance of busi-ness intelligence systems at ever-decreasing costs will allow many points along the supply chain to track the provenance of drugs. Increasing complexity of regulations in different countries, the global supply chain for pharmaceutical drugs, and the need for rapid detection of counterfeits all point to increasing use of event processing. All the trends—price, performance, pervasiveness, celerity, connectedness, complexity—in the context of greater enterprise agility and situation awareness tell us that IT in gen-eral and event processing in particular will play a greater role in the pharmaceutical supply chain.

Smart Infrastructure

Increasing amounts of funds in many countries are being allocated to public infra-structure such as roads, bridges, the electric power grid, and the water supply. Increas-ing power and decreasing costs of sensors, responders, and CEP agents makes "smart infrastructure"—a combination of traditional infrastructure with IT—more cost-effective than traditional infrastructure. The term "cyber-physical systems" has been coined to describe systems that conjoin information systems with physical systems to

---

[2] FDA Compliance Policy Guide 160.900: "Prescription Drug Marketing Act—Pedigree Require-ments under 21 CFR Part 203," available at www.fda.gov/ICECI/ComplianceManuals/Compliance PolicyGuidanceManual/ucm073857.htm.

provide powerful capabilities. Buildings with active controls that determine how the buildings respond to earthquakes are examples of cyber-physical systems; the building without controls may collapse, but the building with sensors, processing agents, and responders is expected to be more resilient. A *smart* infrastructure is an infrastructure integrated with EDA applications. Cyber-physical systems have EDA applications tightly woven into the design and implementations of physical systems.

Monitoring the Health of Civil Infrastructure

Infrastructures, such as bridges, have been traditionally inspected on a time-driven basis. As the infrastructure ages, the frequency of inspections has to increase because the mean time to failure decreases. EDA applications integrated with the infrastructure can improve reliability without requiring more frequent inspections. Buildings and bridges can be equipped with sensors such as accelerometers and strain gauges that transmit data to event-processing networks that detect potential problems. Analysis of sensor data from instrumented buildings under normal conditions, before and after an earthquake, can help determine if hidden trusses and welds in the building have been damaged. The possible failure of transformers in the electric power grid can be predicted using data from sensors that measure parameters such as temperature, gas dissolved in transformer oil, and transformer vibration. Work crews are sent to inspect those components that are identified by the EDA application as likely to fail. A combination of periodic inspections and sensor-based health monitoring of infrastructures reduces the likelihood that the public will be exposed to catastrophic failure.

The A-E-I-O-U Features

All the A-E-I-O-U features that favor event processing appear in smart infrastructures. The systems are required to be adaptable to deal with additions and replacement of components such as sensors and actuators. Early-warning mechanisms manage by exception: smart infrastructures—roads, ports, buildings—behave normally most of the time, but rapid response is required to deal with anomalous behavior. Instrumentation of civil infrastructure monitors its health. Applications must respond rapidly to situations outside the enterprise, and they must deal with unanticipated situations. The expectations we have about components of smart infrastructure are closer to expectations for EDA than expectations for request- or time-driven systems.

The REACTS Cost/Benefit Measures

The values of the REACTS cost/benefit measures depend on the specific application; however, an analysis of these measures for many businesses that manage access to fixed resources—roads, power grids, and bridges—shows that EDA applications are cost-effective in managing smart infrastructure. Consider, for example, a traffic-management system. The users of the system include commuters, security personnel, and transportation officers. The information that is relevant to each group of users is well known, and so ensuring high relevance of traffic information displayed on dashboards is not a problem. The displays that commuters and transportation officers need are well defined, and different users don't need extensive tailoring of displays to fit their specific needs. So, the effort required to customize an application to each user is small. The system is helpful even if it has some inaccuracy—for example, a commuter derives benefit from a system that warns that traffic ahead has been slowed down to 30 miles per hour even if that true speed of traffic is only 20 miles per hour. Commuters also benefit from a system with some degree of incompleteness; for example, the system may not warn about a traffic accident and consequent slowdown of traffic for some time; however, both false positives and false negatives can be corrected quickly. Traffic-monitoring applications benefit from "crowd-sourcing" sensors: commuters report problems or GPS devices on cars monitor speeds. Timeliness is not a major problem; commuters can benefit from the system and adjust their commutes even when information is several minutes late. Security is an issue—the system must be protected from attacks, but the number of points of attack is more limited than in applications such as the smart electric grid. The benefits from reasonably timely, accurate, and complete information are that commuters have shorter commutes that adapt to changing traffic conditions.

The PC-Cubed Trends

The PC-cubed trends tell you that event processing (and "smarts" in general) will play an increasing role in infrastructure upgrades and new designs. The ratio of costs of information systems to costs of raw material—oil, iron, and steel—and costs of building physical artifacts such as cars, electric power transmission lines, and dams continues to change in favor of information systems. The decreasing price, increasing pervasiveness, and greater power of sensors, actuators, and computing devices will result in traffic systems, cars, bridges, and buildings becoming smarter, with the capability to sense and respond to changing conditions. Demands for greater celerity, the increasing regional and global interconnectedness of transportation systems, and the complexity of interactions—with a traffic accident in one part of a freeway system impacting traffic many miles away—will also result in greater use of event processing in traffic systems and infrastructures generally.

A useful exercise is to apply the framework to evaluate the appropriateness of event-processing technologies in other parts of civic infrastructure such as ports, water distribution systems, and air-traffic control systems. The standard evaluation metrics such as efficiency and total cost of ownership; the key drivers of agility, information availability, and timeliness; the A-E-I-O-U features; what we expect from components of these systems; estimations of the REACTS cost/benefit measures; and the PC-cubed trends—these all tell us that event-processing technologies will play an increasing role in infrastructure.

Science

The framework tells us that EDA will play an increasing role in science experiments. You saw the importance of instrumentation for continuous measurement and response to high-value, rare events in the context of event-driven astronomy described earlier in this chapter. Science experiments, perforce, deal with events outside the virtual scientific enterprise—scientists cannot schedule times of occurrence of natural events. Expensive scientific instruments are retargeted to observe new phenomena when unexpected events are observed. Scientific experimentation has many of the A-E-I-O-U features. The increasing costs of scientific instruments and experts and the decreasing costs of IT tell us that scientific experiments of the future will have increasing amounts of software. Indeed, each of the PC-cubed features drives greater use of EDA in scientific applications such as illustrated by the Large Hadron Collider.

The Large Hadron Collider, near Geneva, Switzerland, is one of the most important instruments for high-energy physics experiments. One of its goals is to detect rare events that indicate the presence of the Higgs boson particle. Detectors in the collider generate data at rates of hundreds of gigabytes per second. This data stream is filtered to produce a stream of interesting events at rates of hundreds of megabytes per second. This stream of events is valuable to physicists around the world. Truly wonderful, and probably rare, events are those that demonstrate the presence of particles that are hypothesized to exist but for which there is no measured evidence. The instrument will provide ongoing, continuing benefits during normal operations and may also provide immeasurable value when critical, but possibly rare, events occur. Seismic monitoring, observations of glaciers, and space missions also depend increasingly on EDA.

Workforce of the 21st Century

The PC-cubed trends tell us that the workforce of this century will be supported by increasing amounts of IT in general and event-processing technologies in particular. The devices that the workforce manages and maintains are getting increasingly complex. The smart electric grid, healthcare instrumentation, airplanes, cars, water treatment and distribution, and finance will become more complex in the decades ahead. Workers in the field are increasingly connected by communication devices, such as mobile phones, with experts elsewhere; for example, an electric utility worker dealing with an overheated transformer in the field can get advice from experts at headquarters. Celerity is vitally important in managing critical infrastructure such as power and water distribution. Likewise, trends in price, pervasiveness, and power of IT drive greater use of EDA for the workforce.

The workforce manages tasks on a time-driven schedule as well as an event-driven basis. A tree falling on a high-tension line is an event; this event is detected by the utility, which responds by assigning work crews to the problem. GPS and communication connectivity with workers in the field enables enterprises to have situation awareness about its workforce—it knows which crews are where and how long they've been in operation. The enterprise can determine the tools and workforce crews needed to handle a situation at a given location based on crew experience, resources available nearby, and work regulations. Scheduling and managing crews for airlines and railroads requires global situation awareness and dynamic management of the workforce to deal with unscheduled events.

An electric utility worker dealing with an overheated transformer on a pole several meters off the ground needs both hands and total concentration to deal with the problem. The framework tells us that EDA will support the worker doing the task; for instance, the worker will get just-in-time information about the transformer from RFID tags, detailed information about the device—its type, the time that it was installed, its repair history—will be flashed to goggles worn by the crew, and if necessary expert advice will be transmitted from the utility company's home office or from the transformer manufacturer. The detection and diagnosis of the specific problem and the delivery of just-in-time information are implemented by EDA systems.

Healthcare

Healthcare applications are likely to remain hybrid systems with request-, time-, and event-driven components; however, applying the framework to different areas of healthcare suggests that event-driven processing technologies will play an increasing role in many domains. There is insufficient space in this chapter to apply the framework to applications such as helping aging populations to take care of themselves; use of sensors and RFID devices in hospitals and health-delivery systems; application integration of medical devices and technologies; public health and epidemiology; and telemedicine. Here we consider a few applications briefly.

Older people who want to take care of themselves at home can do so better in smart homes equipped with sensors that detect such things as whether doors are open or closed, whether gas ranges and other appliances are turned on or off, and where people are inside the home and whether they are moving. Smart shirts and other systems monitor heart rate, temperature, and other vital signs and send alerts to healthcare support systems. Smart homes generate thousands of events a day, only a small fraction of which results in alerts that demand nontrivial responses; thus these homes manage by exception. Events such as heart failure are not scheduled by the healthcare system; in terms of our framework, these events are outside the virtual enterprise. Smart homes adapt to changing behavior patterns of the elderly and changing seasons. These applications have many of the A-E-I-O-U features. Each of the PC-cubed trends demonstrates that homes will continue to become smarter over the next decades.

A similar analysis of hospitals shows that though hospital IT systems will remain hybrid systems with time-, request-, and event-driven components, the number of event-driven components will increase. An EDA application that monitors hospital assets and generates alerts illustrates management by exception in a medical setting. Blood, vaccines, and medication must be stored in stable conditions and controlled temperatures; when temperatures deviate from specified ranges, the system must respond by recording the problem and either fixing it or discarding the assets. Time-driven systems monitor assets at regular intervals, and alerts are generated when potential problems are discovered.

RFID tags on patients alert staff when patients enter restricted areas or leave hospitals without authorization. An analysis of the REACTS cost/benefit measures is instructive. For example, Code Pink alerts are issued in a hospital when an event is triggered that suggests that an infant is being abducted. False positives are generated when

Code Pinks are triggered by parents or caregivers carrying an infant across RFID reader stations. Hospital caregivers may suffer from "alarm fatigue"; they can get desensitized to frequent false positives. Though EDA applications are not without cost, an analysis of all the REACTS measures coupled with PC-cubed trends for medical applications tells us that EDA systems will become commonplace in hospitals.

The Medical Device Plug-and-Play (MD PnP) interoperability program illustrates hybrid systems with significant event-driven components. The program supports acquisition of measurements from vital-signs monitors, ventilators, imaging systems, and other devices. It also supports integration of distributed medical devices to improve delivery of medication and fluids. For example, doctors may need an X-ray of a patient on an operating table. The patient's ventilator is switched off to keep the patient's chest still while the X-ray image is being recorded. If the ventilator is not turned back on, the patient may die. Synchronizing the ventilator with the X-ray machine obviates the need to turn off the ventilator.

Unexpected reactions may occur when pain medications are administered intravenously, and in such cases physicians must respond quickly to mitigate the situation. Connecting intravenous pumps to sensors that monitor vital signs improves the likelihood that the system will detect unexpected reactions in time. This is another example of an EDA application that helps enterprises manage by exception—most intravenous administrations of pain medication don't result in life-threatening conditions, but EDA applications help to detect such conditions in the rare cases when they do occur.

The components of the MD PnP system are similar to components of EDA architectures described in Chapters 6 and 7. The components include a clinical rules engine, components to manage privacy and security, mechanisms to maintain audit trails and carry out forensic analysis, components that enforce security, and network managers. MD PnP systems provide significant benefits compared with current hospital practices and these benefits must be weighed against the costs of the REACTS features including the effort required from hospital staff to maintain these systems.

EDA applications and CEP are used in public health surveillance systems. Companies and nongovernmental organizations (NGOs) are exploiting widespread use of mobile phones in poorer countries to provide healthcare to underserved rural areas. Telemedicine systems are hybrid systems with time-, request-, and event-driven components, and an application of the framework suggests growing emphasis on event-driven interactions.

Finance

Finance is one of the "sweet spots" for applications of event-processing technologies. More has been written about applications of EDA in finance and defense than in most of the other business domains. There are many areas of finance where the use of event-processing technologies provides a competitive advantage; some of them require millisecond responses and some require complex analyses in seconds or minutes. Many applications in finance have most of the A-E-I-O-U features that favor event processing. Financial applications must be agile to deal with rapidly changing global conditions; they must detect and respond to exceptional conditions; they are required to respond instantly; they instrument, monitor, and record a great deal of data to build accurate models; they monitor activities outside the enterprise; and they must respond to unanticipated situations.

Our expectations of many financial applications match our expectations of EDA applications: for instance, users expect financial applications to monitor markets and respond when conditions indicate significant opportunities or threats. Analyses of cost/benefit measures show significant benefits from using event-processing applications in finance, particularly in trading capital markets, but also in credit card processing, retail banking, and CRM applications such as cross-selling and up-selling. Many interactions in finance are not required to be transactional; in these applications businesses make more profit by keeping up with current conditions even if they drop a few events. EDA and CEP are used in many aspects of trading, including cross-trading, reducing errors such as fat-finger trades, algorithmic trading, order routing, market surveillance, and fraud detection.

Applying the Framework to Other Business Domains

The business domains analyzed in this chapter certainly do not include all the domains for which event processing is suitable. Next, we discuss a few more domains but treat them very briefly. Here too, our point is not that the list is valuable in itself but that you can use the framework to identify business domains where EDA adds value. EDA plays a role in the central concerns of people—water, food, energy, health, housing, work, civil infrastructure, and entertainment.

▶ **Entertainment and leisure**—Online games process events triggered by actions that cannot be scheduled. Timeliness is critical in interactive games. Sensors such as haptic gloves that simulate tactile sensations of objects in gaming environments generate events at high volumes. The framework tells us that event-processing technologies will be used increasingly in online interactive games. RFID devices embedded in plastic bands are used in theme parks to keep track of customers' movements enabling them to be participants in games that span large areas of the park. The devices also help ensure that underage children can be located if they do get separated from parents.

▶ **Water management**—Sensors that monitor algae and other contaminants in water systems and alert water resources officials have been deployed in many countries. These sensors are also used in power plants and factories to monitor water temperature and aquatic life, such as schools of fish, and alert systems to respond appropriately if water temperatures are too high or aquatic life is approaching a power plant intake pipe. The growing shortages of clean water around the world and the PC-cubed trends tell us that EDA systems will be used increasingly in water management.

▶ **Energy**—Events on oil rigs, wind farms, and solar energy farms cannot be totally scheduled. Demand-response of the smart grid, where electrical appliances are turned off automatically when the grid gets to its capacity, is event-driven. EDA will become increasingly important in energy systems because these systems have to respond to events over which they have little control.

Summary

This chapter proposed a framework for determining whether a hybrid system with event-processing components is the best choice for a business domain. The framework is based on the A-E-I-O-U collection of features that favor event processing, the expectations (or specifications of contracts) of what components of applications do, a comparison of the REACTS cost/benefit measures, and an analysis of the PC-cubed trends. We used this framework to determine the appropriateness of event processing for a wide variety of business domains. Chapters 6 and 7 describe the architectures of event-processing systems, and Chapter 8 describes best practices in developing these applications.

6

Event-Processing Architecture

This chapter takes a deeper look at how event-processing application systems work. We'll summarize how the flow of event-driven interactions differs from the flow of time- and request-driven interactions. Next, we'll present a reference architecture for event-processing networks (EPNs) and show some common variations of EPNs used to implement different kinds of applications. Then we'll look at how an EPN helps support the five principles of EDA. Finally, we'll explain some of the architectural issues associated with publish-and-subscribe systems because of their growing popularity in EDA systems.

Application Flow

As you know, the flow of control in an event-driven interaction differs from the flow of control in time- and request-driven interactions in fundamental ways. This has a big impact on the way applications are constructed.

An event-driven software component (an event consumer) is triggered by the arrival of an event object (E_1 in the top diagram in Figure 6-1). A time-driven component (call it a time-driven agent for lack of any specific label) is triggered by a signal from a clock (see E_t in the middle diagram). A request-driven component (a software "server") is triggered by the arrival of a request message (bottom of diagram).

Event consumer, time-driven agent, and server are merely roles; they don't imply anything else about the nature of a software component. A component is an event consumer only because it receives and acts in response to an event object. A component is a server only because it receives and acts in response to a request message. A software component could be event-driven in one interaction and request- or time-driven in another interaction. Moreover, a component that is event-driven in one interaction could be an event producer or a client in a request-driven interaction a minute later, and so forth. This is reflected on the right side of Figure 6-1 by the gray arrows connecting to and from other agents elsewhere in the environment.

The flow of work can be compared to a bucket brigade: each instance of a process is analogous to a pail of water that is handed from one firefighter to the next. In the course of a day, thousands or more process instances may be passed from one step to the next. The component that first controls the process instance—the event producer, the clock, or the client—is the firefighter who has the bucket first (left column in Figure 6-1).

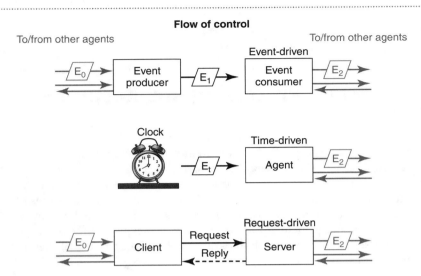

Figure 6-1: Flow of control in interactions.

Note: The terms event-driven, time-driven, and request-driven always refer to the second component in the interaction being studied—the firefighter who receives the bucket (right column in Figure 6-1).

Chapter 3 introduced a simple order-fulfillment process. Figure 6-2 shows the flow of the first part of that process in more detail. A new process instance comes into being when the order-entry component captures a particular customer order—for example, Fred Smith's order. The person designing the process must decide whether the second step, credit check, will be event-driven or request-driven. If the order-entry component passes an event object, it will be event-driven (top diagram in Figure 6-2); if it passes a request, the second step will obviously be request-driven (bottom diagram). The interaction that occurs between the first and second steps doesn't indicate how the first component, order entry, interacted with other agents further upstream. Order entry could capture the order through a conversation with a person entering the order through a web browser, in which case the order-entry component would itself be request-driven. Or it could accept incoming orders through an e-mail notification (E_0 on the left in Figure 6-2), in which case it would be event-driven. However, the nature of the order-entry component is not specified when the second component (credit service) is made event- or request-driven.

Chapter 2 explained that contracts are essential to the design of software systems. Contracts describe the expectations of component behavior with respect to other components in the system. The contracts for event-, time-, and request-driven roles differ in how the components behave regarding the flow of control:

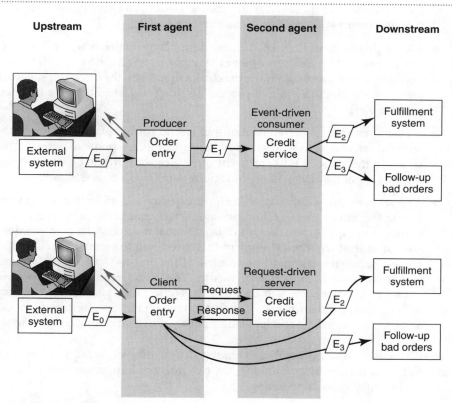

Figure 6-2: Order-fulfillment process.

▶ An event producer is expected to emit an event object whenever it detects that something happened. Order entry has a duty to emit a notification containing an order object every time it detects that someone has entered an order. The event consumer won't run correctly, and might not run at all, unless the event producer sends the notifications.

▶ An event consumer has no obligation to the event producer. It doesn't return control of the process instance back to the producer and it can even decide not to receive a notification (the order, E_1) in the first place. The event producer will run correctly in software terms even if the events it emits are not consumed. Of course, the process may not fulfill its business role if the consumer component doesn't do its job, so the event consumer has an obligation at a higher level, but not to the producer.

▶ A clock is expected to emit a signal (E_t) at a designated time. All computers have internal clocks. A clock is a highly constrained type of event producer because it emits only one kind of event and doesn't depend on anything from an external source. It simply increments a counter at regular intervals and emits the event when the appropriate time comes (clocks also can respond to requests if a component wants to know what the time or date is).

▶ A time-driven agent is an application component that runs when it receives the time event (E_t). Like any other event consumer, it has no obligation to do anything. It can choose to ignore the clock's signal, and the clock will still work properly, although the overall process wouldn't work right from a business point of view.

▶ A client in a request-driven relationship has no contractual obligation to the server. It can choose to send a request message or it can choose to never call the server. In this sense, it is like an event consumer—it is free to behave as it sees fit, although it may have other obligations to fulfill at a business level.

▶ A server in a request-driven relationship is expected to perform the action specified in the request message. In most cases, it will send to the client a reply containing some application data, a notification that it successfully performed the task, or at least an acknowledgment that it received the request. A client in a request-driven relationship lends control of the process to the server but usually doesn't give it control permanently. The client remembers the process instance (it retains some state data on Fred's order) that it uses in combination with the reply to do further work on that instance. If the server doesn't do its job, and in most cases that includes sending a reply, the client cannot finish its work.

We can now explain why event- and request-driven mindsets are sometimes compared to left- and right-brain thinking: the two interaction patterns reflect fundamentally dissimilar ways of operating.

Note: In event-driven relationships, the first agent helps the second agent by notifying it of the event. In request-driven relationships, the second agent helps the first agent by doing some work that the first agent wants to have done.

In an SOA system, a requesting client is called a "service consumer," demonstrating the similarity between it and an event consumer (see Chapter 9 for more discussion of the overlap of SOA and EDA concepts). However, the consumer in an event-driven relationship "consumes" event objects, whereas the consumer (client) in a request-driven relationship "consumes" a function or a service. The consumer in an event-driven relationship acts second in the interaction, but the consumer in a request-driven interaction acts first.

Reference Architecture for Event-Processing Networks

A reference architecture provides a formal template for system design in a particular domain. It describes the vocabulary, components, component interfaces, and the relationship among the components inside and outside of the system. In this section, we focus on the reference architecture for the EDA domain.

Note: Application systems or sections of application systems that process event objects using the EDA model are structured as EPNs.

The reference architecture for EPNs incorporates four kinds of components: event producers, channels, consumers, and intermediaries. Figure 6-3 shows the general structure of an EPN. Producers, consumers, and some intermediaries are *event-processing agents (EPAs)*.

Note: An EPA is an agent that creates, reads, discards, or performs calculations on event objects. A physical EPA is a software component. A conceptual EPA is an abstraction that performs logical functions on event obects.

A physical EPA doesn't have to be a separate module; it can be a section of code in an application, a database management system (DBMS), or any other program. Channels are not EPAs but they contribute to the EPN by providing communication capabilities.

Producers

EDA processing begins when a software component, the event producer, detects an event in its environment (see Figure 6-3, left column). A producer (sometimes called an "event source") is any EPA that emits event objects. For example, a radio frequency identification (RFID) reader may receive a message from an RFID tag indicating the presence of a package that was not within range a second earlier. The RFID reader recognizes this change in its environment as a business event, creates an event object, puts

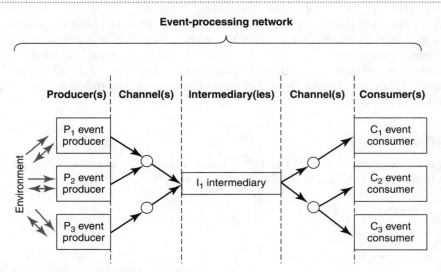

Figure 6-3: Reference architecture for EPNs.

it into a notification message, and emits it through an event channel. The event producer in this example is software embedded in the RFID reader. Event producers can be embedded in a device or run on a general-purpose computer as an autonomous software program or part of a larger software package.

Channels

An event channel is any means of conveying a notification from one EPA to another. The arrival of the notification signals the event occurrence. Channels work in any of three ways:

- ▶ By sending messages (the most obvious and common technique)
- ▶ By putting an event object in a shared location where the producer and consumer can both access it
- ▶ By the producer calling the event consumer

Later in this chapter, we'll explain how these options work in more detail.

Any technique for conveying a notification is a valid channel in the EPN reference architecture as long as the five principles of EDA outlined in Chapter 3 are observed. However, the EPN reference architecture doesn't apply to other types of event processing, such as time- or request-driven event processing. The event objects in those styles of computing are at rest in a file or database for an undetermined amount of time and the processing occurs at a time that is unrelated to the delivery of the event object. We don't present a reference architecture for time- and request-driven event-processing applications in this book.

A channel can carry events of multiple types. For example, "approved order" events can be sent over the same channel as "rejected order" events even though the types of data in the event objects are different, they may be received by different consumers, and they will be treated differently. Events conveyed by one channel may be delivered to multiple consumers (the channel is said to "fan out"). Events conveyed by one channel may originate in multiple producers and be delivered to one consumer (the channel is said to "fan in"). Figure 6-3 shows examples of fan out (on the right) and fan in (on the left).

Consumers

An event consumer is an EPA that receives event objects. The consumer evaluates the event and decides which of the following to do with it:

- ▶ Perform a response locally
- ▶ Invoke a service
- ▶ Trigger a business process
- ▶ Emit a message

▶ Save the event object to use in the future when additional events arrive

▶ Discard the event without doing anything

Consumers are sometimes called event handlers, sinks, listeners, or responders.

Intermediaries

All EPNs are intermediated because something is always interposed between the producer and consumer. EPNs may be intermediated by channels or by channels with EPAs.

Channels as Intermediaries

A channel is a low-level intermediary because its function is limited to communication-related tasks. A channel may itself be intermediated—a physical intermediary within an intermediary. For example, the circles in the channels in Figure 6-3 could be message servers in a message oriented middleware (MOM) channel. A message server is a software component that acts as a hub to relay messages from one computer or software component to another.

A message server or other channel intermediary is part of the channel; it's message-aware but not event-aware. For example, many MOM channels can selectively decide where to deliver messages based on the message topics or message properties. Topics are data that describe the subject of the message. Properties are data that describe other characteristics of the messages. Software developers design message topics and properties at development time. The producer agent typically puts this data into a message header—the "envelope" of a message—at run time. Channel intermediaries can use topic and property data to implement publish-and-subscribe messaging (we'll describe how this works in more detail later in this chapter). However, a channel intermediary is not an EPA, because it doesn't read or modify the event attributes, which are typically held in the message body—the contents of the "envelope."

Channels don't always have physical internal intermediaries. The software that implements a channel can be distributed to the endpoints of the network with no central hub.

EPAs as Intermediaries

Some EPNs also have higher-level intermediaries. A high-level intermediary that manipulates the event object within the message is an EPA (see I_1 in the center of Figure 6-3). It is an event consumer and an event producer because it receives notifications, interprets and processes them, and emits notifications. There are two kinds of intermediary EPAs: event routing and event generating.

Event-Routing Intermediaries

Routing EPAs don't alter the makeup of the event objects—every object that is emitted is identical to an object that was received. They read event objects, filter out (discard) those that are not needed by any consumer, and direct the remaining events to particular destinations depending on the contents of the event ("content-based routing"). This may be done using a high-level form of publish-and-subscribe that is more sophisticated than a channel's publish-and-subscribe because it is event-aware—able to deal with the event attributes in the message body. For example, a consumer agent could subscribe to all customer order events where the value of the order is more than $500 and the ship-to address is out of state.

Event-Generating Intermediaries

Event-generating EPAs do more than relay events; they actually terminate (receive and discard) the incoming "base" event objects and originate (create and send) new event objects that are created by performing calculations on the incoming events. An outgoing event may refer to the same real-world event as the base event, but the event object is different in one or more of its attributes. Event-generating intermediaries may

- ▶ Selectively copy data items from base events, change their format, reorder them, and put them into the outgoing event objects

- ▶ Enrich events by adding relevant data from databases or other sources

- ▶ Compute aggregate values such as totals, averages, minimums, and maximums from multiple events

- ▶ Perform other kinds of complex event processing (CEP) by applying rules to detect patterns in a set of base events (see Chapter 7 for more details)

Applying the Reference Architecture

As you know, EDA is based on the precept that producers are only minimally coupled to consumers. EPNs are used to implement EDA applications specifically because EPNs have channels and intermediary EPAs that insulate the EPAs from each other. A producer or consumer can be changed without requiring a change in other producers and consumers as long as the same types of event objects are transmitted through the channels.

....

Note: The combination of one or more channels and zero or more event-routing intermediary EPAs is a dissemination network. *An entire EPN consists of one or more event producers, one or more consumers, zero or more event-generating intermediaries, and the dissemination network between them.*

An EPN is not actually separate from the rest of a company's network, but rather is a conceptual description of how some parts of a company's network are being used. An EPN is physically implemented by some of the application programs, middleware subsystems, and messages that participate in the company's tangible network. The remaining programs, middleware subsystems, and messages are those that support request-driven applications (for example, web service calls), time-driven applications (for example, batch file transfers over FTP), e-mail, web interactions, IP phone traffic, and all the other aspects of a modern communication backbone. Chapter 8 includes more discussion of EPN implementation issues.

Architects who use reference architectures usually specialize or extend them, or combine them with other architectures to meet specific business requirements. The EPN reference architecture has several common variations that are employed depending on the circumstances.

EPN for Information Dissemination

An EPN that is used for simple information dissemination or data consistency often doesn't need an intermediary EPA. Its dissemination network may just consist of a channel (see Figure 6-4). A channel doesn't perform any logical operations on the contents of event objects, so the event received is the same as the event published (E_1). The software that implements the channel may be in multiple pieces that are physically collocated with the producer and consumer application endpoints. Or, especially if the channel is implemented using MOM, some of the functions may run in a channel intermediary such as a MOM message server (described previously). Examples of this simple EPN pattern include RSS feeds and real-time financial data feeds in capital markets trading activities implemented using publish-and-subscribe middleware. The producer publishes an event once and a copy may be delivered to thousands of consumers.

EPN for Situation Awareness

EPNs used for situation awareness typically need to gather events from multiple sources, process them internally to logically "connect the dots" and derive some com-

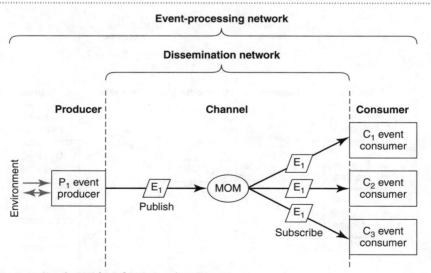

Figure 6-4: Simple EPN for information dissemination.

plex events, and then distribute alerts and other notifications to multiple people and systems. These EPNs have event-generating intermediary EPAs and multiple channels. The channels could be a diverse collection of basic network protocols, MOM products, and other middleware. Each channel may have a channel intermediary and be connected to multiple producer or consumer agents (see the channels in Figure 6-5). The higher-level intermediary EPA I_1 may be implemented by means of an enterprise service bus (ESB), integration broker, business process orchestration engine, CEP software agent, custom application code, or some combination of those. The intermediary terminates incoming events (E_1, E_2, and E_3), transforming them and performing some type of computation to produce events E_4 and E_5, which are distributed to the consumer agents.

EPN for Application Integration

In a large configuration, it sometimes helps to think about a set of channels and EPAs as a single entity for design purposes. In this case, architects treat an entire EPN as one conceptual EPA (see P_{21} in Figure 6-6).

Note: The reference architecture is recursive—it allows a conceptual EPA to be an EPN and vice versa.

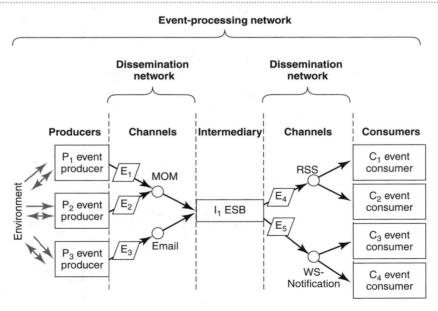

Figure 6-5: Complex EPN for situation awareness.

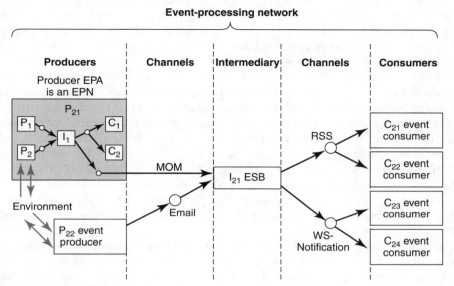

Figure 6-6: EPN as EPA in a larger EPN.

Implementing the Principles of EDA in an EPN

Chapter 3 outlined the principles of EDA at a conceptual level. Now we're ready to explore how developers apply those conceptual principles on a logical and physical level as they implement an event-processing application using software and an EPN. The five principles are listed again here and described in depth in the following sections:

► Reports current events

► Pushes notifications

► Responds immediately

► Communicates one-way

► Is free of commands

The most effective way of implementing these five principles is usually by means of a publish-and-subscribe communication model. We'll describe why after we examine the principles in more detail.

Reports Current Events

Principle: A notification reports a discrete occurrence as it happens.

Implementation details: An application component acting as a producer agent emits a notification as soon as an event is recognized. For example, when an RFID reader detects the presence of an RFID tag, it sends a notification message to report that event. However, developers may take some liberties with the way communication is actually handled by the software.

To reduce the number of messages going over a network, multiple notifications are sometimes bundled into one message. The system might send the message when it has accumulated five or ten readings, when a second or two has elapsed, or whichever comes first. On the receiving side, the message is unpacked and the notifications are separated and passed individually to the event consumers. A small increase in latency, typically less than a second or two, is incurred to get the benefit of reduced network overhead. This tradeoff is a quality-of-service (QoS) policy decision. An analyst identifies the business requirements and documents the willingness of the application owner to accept the slightly higher latency associated with bundling notifications or pay a bit more for the faster delivery of individual messages.

As long as the producer addresses each occurrence as it happens, the application style is EDA. The system would be time-driven if the producer postponed sending the notification to a prescheduled time, but that is not the case here. The clock plays only a minor role in constraining the time for sending the message.

Pushes Notifications

Principle: Notifications are "pushed" by the producer, not "pulled" by the consumer. The producer decides when to send the notification because it knows about the event before the consumer does.

Implementation details: The principle of push refers to the overall conceptual relationship between the producer and consumer agents, not the relationship between the agents and EPN channels. The producer-consumer relationship is always a push, but agent-channel relationships are more complex. The producer always pushes the notification to a channel. The channel may push the notification to the consumer or the consumer may pull the notification from the channel (the timing of a pull is determined by the consumer).

Channels work in any of three ways: by sending messages, by putting an event object in a shared location where the producer and consumer can both access it, or by the producer calling the event consumer.

Sending Messages

The most common kind of channel moves event objects between agents by sending them in messages. The producer may send the event object through MOM; put it in an e-mail; use a web-oriented communication protocol such as HTTP or RSS on HTTP; use a SOAP-based web services message; or use another kind of messaging.

If a channel is implemented by MOM, the consumer gets the notification from the MOM in one of three ways (see Figure 6-7):

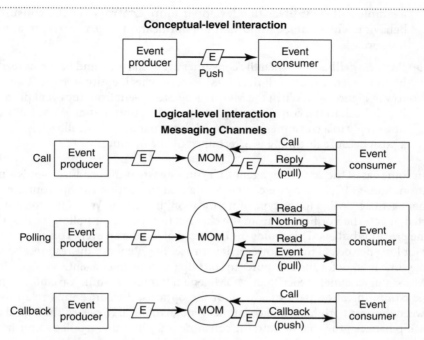

Figure 6-7: Implementing notification through messaging.

▶ **Direct pull (call)**—A consumer agent can call the MOM to ask for the next notification. It stops doing other work (it is "blocked") until the notification arrives in a reply (see the "Call" row in Figure 6-7). The MOM is an intermediary between the producer and consumer. When it gets the notification from the producer, it relays the notification to the consumer as a reply to the call. This is a request and a reply at a logical level. However, the timing of the reply is largely determined by the event producer, because it decides when to send the notification to the channel. If the producer sends two notifications very quickly, the MOM will temporarily hold the second one until the consumer issues another call to get it. However, if notifications are infrequent and far apart, the consumer may have to wait a long time. The consumer could potentially wait forever if a notification never comes. Sometimes the consumer is allowed to specify a timeout value, after which the MOM will return control back to the consumer even if a notification hasn't arrived.

▶ **Periodic pull (polling)**—The consumer can poll the MOM periodically (see the "Polling" row in Figure 6-7). In this case, the consumer calls the MOM at regular intervals, occasionally getting a notification in return. This is more complicated to program than a simple call to the MOM, but it means that the consumer doesn't sit idle for indeterminate periods of time, as it would with a simple call. This gives the developer more control over the consumer's behavior, which can be important if a notification doesn't arrive in a timely fashion.

▶ **Push via callback**—When the consumer agent starts up and becomes ready to listen to events, it can call the MOM to convey its identity (see the "Callback" row in Figure 6-7). When the MOM receives an event from the event producer, it calls back to the consumer to pass the notification message. The callback is not a reply to a consumer's request—it is a separate call. A callback is logically a push because its timing is determined by the producer.

In some cases, the consumer agent isn't running when the producer sends a notification. Some MOM software can be configured to start up the appropriate consumer agent according to the type of notification that is sent. When the consumer is started, it gets the notification from the channel using a call or polling, as described in the previous bullets. This avoids the overhead of having an event consumer sitting idle for long periods of time. However, it increases the latency of the response because of the time it takes for the computer to start up the consumer agent.

Messaging channels other than MOM generally support some variation of these three communication patterns. In all of the options, the conceptual relationship between the event producer and consumer remains a push. However, the logical relationship between the channel and the consumer may be either a pull or a push.

Data-Sharing Channel

In a data-sharing channel, the producer writes the event object to a file, database, shareable cache, or some other place in memory (see "temporary store" in the middle diagram in Figure 6-8). A write is essentially a push. The event consumer periodically polls the file, database, cache, or other place in memory to see if the data has changed. When new data (the event object) is found, the consumer knows that the event has occurred. A read is logically a pull because the timing is determined by the consumer and the command is a request (read) and reply (the data).

The event object can be a simple one-bit semaphore ("0" could mean no event yet, and "1" would then mean that the event has occurred). Often a semaphore is a number ("0" could mean no event yet, and "2" could mean that two events have occurred). Or, the event object can be a large data structure containing hundreds of data items that describe various aspects of the event in great detail.

The polling interval is a tradeoff between latency and overhead. If the polling interval is short, say, every 100 milliseconds, then the event object will be found almost as soon as it arrives and the latency of notification delivery will be low. However, this can place a heavy burden on the computer because the read may be done thousands or millions of times before the consumer finally gets an event. If the polling interval is long, say, every 10 minutes, the overhead is lower but the latency is higher (up to 10 minutes). The tradeoff is a QoS policy decision. An analyst and middleware specialist may need to confer with the application owner to determine the appropriate polling interval for each application.

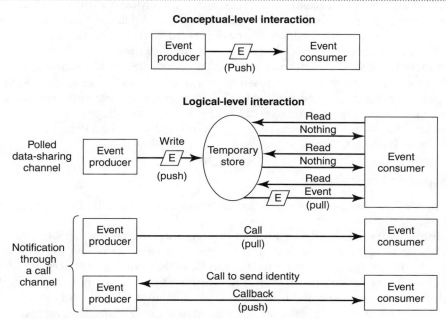

Figure 6-8: Notification through data sharing channels and call channels.

Notification Through a Call

A producer can notify a consumer by calling it through a procedure call, method invocation, remote procedure call (RPC), or remote method invocation (bottom section "Notification through a call channel" in Figure 6-8). Procedure calls and method invocations work within one computer, whereas RPCs and remote method invocations work across a network.

When a call is used in EDA, there is no reply message and the function to be performed by the consumer is not identified in the call (a nonspecific function name such as "event handler" is used). Request-driven systems use calls in a different way, always specifying the consumer's function and usually sending a reply.

In event-driven systems, the identity of the consumer agent is not built into a producer agent when it is compiled and deployed. The producer has to acquire this information when it runs so that it knows where to send the notification. One way of accomplishing this is to programmatically insert the consumer's identity into the producer at run time before the call occurs (For details, see *Event-Based Programming* by Ted Faison, listed in Appendix A). The other way for the producer to find out about the consumer is through the callback pattern described earlier (see the lower part of Figure 6-8). When it's ready to receive events, the consumer agent calls the producer to convey its identity. When an event occurs, the producer calls back to the identified event handler method to signal the event. A callback is logically a push because its timing is determined by the producer.

A call is a kind of messaging in the sense that it usually carries some event data as parameters or in an attached document. However, it is dissimilar to other kinds of messaging because the event producer also passes control of the application flow directly to a specific point (such as an event handler method) in the consumer agent. And a call doesn't have to pass event data. A call with no parameters or attachments still signals an event by the mere act of passing control of flow. In this case, it's a bit of a stretch to say that there is an event object—it is an imaginary or empty event object. We could compare this to a wakeup call at a hotel where the phone rings but no one says anything—a signal has been conveyed but no content beyond the act of ringing the phone is needed.

Responds Immediately

Principle: The consumer does something in response immediately after it recognizes an event.

Implementation details: In a simple EDA system, the consumer agent performs its function as soon as a notification arrives. In some cases, it may evaluate and discard the incoming event with no further action, so the evaluation is the extent of its function. In a CEP system, however, the consumer's reaction is more nuanced. Its only immediate response may be to make some calculations and discard the message or save the event object for later use when additional notifications have arrived.

For example, a customer contact center monitoring system could be designed to emit an alert if the average customer during a 15-minute window has to wait on hold for more than 2 minutes. The data to enable this alert comes from notifications that are created every time a customer call is received. The notifications report the customer's wait time along with other information such as the customer's phone number and the identity of the service agent who takes the call. The notifications don't trigger an alert directly. The continuously running monitoring system uses the notifications to recalculate the 15-minute average waiting time every time a new notification arrives. If the average waiting time is under the 2-minute threshold, the system just saves the data for future use. The system takes action—sends an alert—only when it reaches a "tipping point," that is, when it calculates an average waiting time greater than 2 minutes for any 15-minute window. The system is not reacting directly to the arrival of any input base event, but rather is responding to its own calculation of a complex event that reflects information from potentially hundreds of notifications.

Communicates One-Way

Principle: EDA notification is a "fire-and-forget" type of communication. The producer emits the notification and goes on to do other work, or it may end processing and shut down. It does not get a reply from the consumer.

Implementation details: Chapter 3 explained that the benefit of this principle is to free the producer from any dependency on the consumer at run time. If a producer needs a response from the consumer to complete its work on a particular process instance— for example, Fred's order—then the system isn't implementing the EDA design.

"Forget" means that the producer doesn't have to retain any data about that particular process instance. A producer could temporarily keep some data on Fred's order after sending a notication about the order to a consumer but this approach is rarely used. It would only be used if the producer has some additional work to do on the order before shutting down or moving on to work on the next process instance. Regardless, a producer never holds data about the process instance in anticipation of getting a reply back from the consumer or any other agent that later works on this process instance. In some business processes, the control of the process instance might actually come back to an agent that had been an event producer at an earlier time (the process would be "cyclical"). If the original event producer has forgotten that it worked on the process instance before, then it still complies with the principles of EDA. If it depends on a reply and has kept instance data in the expectation of getting a reply, then it is not implementing EDA.

However, "fire and forget" raises integrity concerns in some situations. How can a producer be sure that Fred's order isn't lost after it's sent? This concern doesn't arise in a request/reply architecture because the reply implicitly confirms that the consumer has received the message, but no reply occurs in fire-and-forget. Architects and developers can resolve this issue in fire-and-forget by using a channel that offers reliable delivery. For example, a producer sends the notification to a MOM facility that saves a copy on disk and sends back to the producer agent a confirmation that it has the message. The producer is then free to forget everything about Fred's order and move on to another task. It's conceptually a push, because the producer determined the timing and doesn't get a reply from the consumer, but the producer actually did get a technical reply from the MOM to verify that the message was accepted for transmission.

The MOM transports the notification to the consumer and doesn't delete the copy that it saved until the consumer has acknowledged (to the MOM) that it has received the notification. If the notification can't be delivered, the channel will generally try several more times. If it still can't deliver it to the consumer, it will send it to a "dead letter" agent for follow-up action. Analysts and developers determine what the dead-letter agent will do, just as they would design a recovery procedure for the original producer if a reply was not returned in a request/reply system.

If an event-driven system doesn't fire and forget, then it is not implementing an EDA pattern. It may be event-driven to the extent that it complies with the other four principles (Reports current events, Pushes notifications, Responds immediately, and Is free of commands) but the agents are coupled and mutually dependent in an important respect, making changes more complex to implement. The idea that an event-driven system is not always EDA can be disquieting to some architects, but event-driven systems with responses are not uncommon in real-world systems. They have more flexibility than request-driven systems, but they have less flexibility than full-blown, fire-and-forget EDA systems.

Is Free of Commands

Principle: A notification is a report, not a specific request or command. It does not prescribe the action the event consumer will perform.

Implementation details: This is the other aspect of minimal coupling. Chapter 3 explained that this is fundamentally different from a request-driven system, where both parties must agree on the function that the consumer will perform. In a request-driven system, the client might tell the server to "give me the data about Fred's order," "update Fred's order," or "delete Fred's order," for example. In an event-driven system by contrast, the message from producer to consumer is just "Fred has submitted an order (do what you will with this information)."

In rare cases, request-driven interactions are designed to have no reply—they fire-and-forget a "request" message. This makes the sender (the client) independent of the receiver (the server) at run time. However, they still are interdependent at development time, because the consumer's function is explicitly built into the sender and receiver. Both agents must be modified if a change in the business requirement dictates a change in function.

Although an EDA system is free of requests and commands at a conceptual level, the agents use commands at a logical and physical level to communicate with the channel. The event producer issues commands such as "write" to a shared location; or "open the channel," "send a message," and "close the channel." A consumer uses similar commands to "read" (poll) a shared location; or to "open," "get" a message, and "close" a message channel. These are different from commands in a request-driven system because they refer to the mechanics of communication instead of describing a function that is part of the business process. Even when a channel is implemented as a call directly from producer to consumer, no application-related request or command is built into the communication. A call to an "event handler" function in a consumer agent is unspecific—it doesn't tell the consumer what to do except "handle" the event as the consumer sees fit.

Publish-and-Subscribe

Publish-and-subscribe is a communication pattern that is well suited for implementing the five principles of EDA, although its use is not definitional to EDA. You can implement a successful event-processing application that conforms to all five EDA principles without using it. However, an increasing number of EPNs use channels that support publish-and-subscribe because it further enhances the flexibility of the application.

Many architects and analysts are initially drawn to publish-and-subscribe because one message can be delivered to zero, one, or millions of consumers without the producer having to send it multiple times. Publish-and-subscribe also allows multiple producers to send to one consumer, or multiple producers to send to multiple consumers (and it supports one-to-one communication too, of course). However, flexibility is arguably an even more important benefit of publish-and-subscribe.

....

Note: Publish-and-subscribe is a communication pattern in which the message delivery instructions are explicitly defined in an independent entity, the subscription, rather than being built into the producer or the channel.

A subscription describes the kind of messages that should be sent to each consumer. A subscriber agent sends subscriptions to a subscription manager that controls event delivery. In traditional publish-and-subscribe systems, each consumer is its own subscriber because it creates the subscription rules that describe the messages that it will receive. However, in some publish-and-subscribe systems, the subscription can originate in a third-party subscriber or in the producer rather than in the consumer.

A subscription manager applies the subscription rules to each message to determine which consumers, if any, should receive it. A subscription manager is typically implemented as part of a MOM subsystem or other channel, but in some systems, the event producer itself manages the subscriptions without the involvement of a third party.

Subscription rules can apply to data fields in the message header or message body. We pointed out earlier that channels implement publish-and-subscribe by looking at topic or property data in the message headers. EPA intermediaries can implement publish-and-subscribe by looking at any data fields in the body of the message. Publish-and-subscribe systems usually allow "wild-carding" using "*" qualifiers. For example, a message pertaining to currency trades might have three segments in its topic: From_Currency, To_Currency, and Date. A subscription rule could then specify "Give me all messages of the type 'From_Dollars.To_Yen.*,'" indicating that the consumer wants all trades related to those currencies regardless of the date. Or the rule could specify "Give me all messages of the type 'From_Dollars.*.June2010,'" indicating an interest in all dollar trades in June 2010 regardless of the destination currency. Subscriptions reduce the number of superfluous messages that are delivered; consumers receive only filtered information that is relevant to them.

Publish-and-subscribe is more flexible than other kinds of messaging or calling mechanisms because the delivery instructions are not statically defined. The subscription can be transmitted and applied when the agents start up, or even altered dynamically as the system runs. A new producer or consumer can be added at any time, or a producer or consumer can drop out at any time.

The task of moving the messages is logically separate from the task of managing subscriptions. Publish-and-subscribe systems use a wide range of communication protocols, some standard and some proprietary.

Summary

EDA applications can evolve gracefully because their components can be modified individually at different times. The flow of control in EDA is unidirectional and communication is generalized, unlike request-driven systems, in which agents depend more heavily on the behavior of other agents in the system. The reference architecture for EPNs describes the relationships among four kinds of software components found in EDA systems: event producers, channels, consumers, and intermediaries. The five fundamental principles of EDA refer to the relationship between producer and consumer agents at a conceptual level. However, analysts and architects designing EDA systems must understand the tradeoffs and other implementation considerations that arise at the logical and physical levels. Publish-and-subscribe communication enhances the agility of an EDA system because it routes notifications in a dynamically customizable manner.

7

Events and Complex Events

Events and event objects are the fundamental building blocks in event-processing application systems. Identifying and specifying the right events to use to address a particular business problem is an important and nontrivial activity. This chapter explores the issues involved in event object design. We'll start by taking a closer look at the nature of events and event data. Then we'll explain the characteristics of complex events, how they are computed, and their relationship to simple events.

Defining "Event" in Earnest

The experts in this field don't entirely agree on the best way to define events and event objects. We are aware of three major schools of thought (other good definitions may also exist):

▶ **State-change view**—An event is a change in the state of anything. An event object is a report of a state change.

These statements have clear technical meanings and are the most widely used definitions in the IT world. An event is the change reported by an event object, no more and no less.

▶ **Happening view**—An event is "anything that happens, or is contemplated as happening." An event (object) is "an object that represents, encodes, or records an event, generally for the purpose of computer processing."

These definitions are quoted from the Event Processing Technical Society's *Event Processing Glossary* (available in PDF format at www.ep-ts.com). The EPTS definitions draw largely from work done by Dr. David Luckham and presented in his book, *The Power of Events*, a seminal document in this field (see Appendix A for the full citation). His definition of event was based, in turn, on the Oxford English Dictionary. It's the definition assumed by people in everyday life. The notion of event object is the translation of that concept into the IT realm. An event (object) *signifies*, or is a record of, an activity that happened.

▶ **Detectable-condition view**—An event is "a detectable condition that can trigger a notification." A notification is "an event-triggered signal sent to a runtime-defined recipient."

Ted Faison uses these definitions in his thorough and well-regarded book, *Event-Based Programming* (see Appendix A for the full citation). These definitions apply primarily in a software development context. The precise description of a notification helps software engineers distinguish between a conventional procedure call to a server and a more dynamic procedure call that conveys an event signal to a run-time defined event consumer. Faison's notion of an event as a detectable condition can be applied within or outside the realm of computers.

The three sets of definitions largely overlap. Things that are considered events in one definition generally are also considered events in the other two. However, each represents a slightly different concept of events:

▶ The state-change view assumes a thing and a change in that thing from a before state to an after state. The event object represents the change, although it doesn't have to contain all of the details about the change.

▶ The happening view sees events as activities that occur. When activities occur, state changes, but the definition doesn't require anyone to specify how many things are involved or be able to document the before and after states.

▶ The detectable-condition view considers something to be an event only if it can be observed and give rise to a report about it (the notification). If a tree falls in the forest and no one is there to hear it, then it made no sound. Similarly, if something changed and nothing could detect it, it wasn't an event. Moreover, if a condition can be reported, it is an event even if nothing changed.

The happening view and the detectable-condition view are at opposite poles in some respects, representing the physical world and software world, respectively. The state-change view is roughly in the middle. Summarized in simplistic terms:

View	Thing(s) Change(s)	Observation Is Reported
State change	Yes	Yes
Happening	Yes	Optional
Detectable condition	Optional	Yes

Each view applies to some kinds of events more naturally than it applies to other kinds of events. The views also differ on the fundamental issue of whether an event happens at a point in time or has a finite duration. We'll illustrate the differences among the views by examining three examples of events and then look at the implications on the subject of event duration.

State-Change Example

Changes to a single thing or a few things are described well by the state-change definition. Our recurring example of an RFID tag reading is a quintessential state change.

The item was previously outside of the range of the RFID reader, and now it is within the range of the RFID reader. A computer-science state diagram can easily show this, and the state transition from "it's not here" to "it's here" can be reported by a notification message going from an RFID reader to a software agent elsewhere in the network. Because some activity occurred, the "happening" definition also applies nicely to this situation—the item showed up and the event (object) reports that happening. This is also a good detectable condition—the presence of the item is detected and a notification message can be created and sent.

Happening Example

Happening events are centered on an activity or work done as opposed to the object upon which the work was done. Complex software events and real-world events, such as buying a house, landing a plane, and World War II, are addressed well by the happening definition. People intuitively recognize these things as events. Various event objects that summarize such events can be easily designed, although they may not give a full accounting of what transpired. For example, here are three event objects that signify the activity of buying a house:

▶ A person sends an e-mail conveying the news to a friend.

▶ A notice is inserted into a newspaper to report the address, date, and sale price of the transaction.

▶ An application program in a local realtor's information system sends an XML document that summarizes the transaction to a real-estate clearinghouse.

None of these event objects tells the whole story. However, that's not a problem in the happening view of events because the observation and notification are not essential to the fact of the activity.

Buying a house is a complex event. It could entail a three-month process encompassing multiple house tours, dozens of phone calls and e-mails, many meetings, preparing and signing various legal documents, multiple bank transactions, a pest inspection, and other minor events. The state-change and detectable-condition definitions can be applied to complex, multifaceted events such as this, but the fit is more challenging. The state of the world, and hundreds of things in it, have changed, including legal title to the house; the bank accounts of the buyer, seller, two realtors, two lawyers, various tradespeople, and the government; and dozens of other things. Many state changes that occurred during the three-month process are not visible at the end of the process because they've been reversed or forgotten. No snapshot can capture the entire before and after state. World War II was more complex than a house purchase by many orders of magnitude—it changed the state of the world in countless ways. An expert can find plenty of detectable conditions and state changes in very complex events, but none of them captures the essence of the whole activity.

Detectable-Condition Example

Simple observations are well described by the detectable-condition definition. The term "detectable condition" reflects the fact that events and event objects can address things that aren't changing. For example, consider a truck with a GPS tracking device that emits a reading of its location every minute. When the truck is parked for 10 minutes, it emits ten readings with the same geospatial coordinates. The notifications differ only because they are generated at different times. The position of the truck is a detectable condition, so each reading is clearly an event notification according to our third definition.

Nothing has changed in the thing ostensibly being reported, the truck's location. Nevertheless, the state-change definition can be applied by thinking of the passing of time as the change. The state of the world, including the truck and the central monitoring system 200 miles away, has changed with respect to time for each notification. Similarly, the happening definition of "event" can be applied because the GPS device made an observation and emitted a notification—nothing happened to the truck but something happened in the GPS device.

Event Duration

Your chosen perspective on events affects whether events are instantaneous or have a measurable duration. Most "happening" events have a measurable duration (they are "interval events"). Buying the house took three months. A notification that describes that event may have three time stamps: one to record the start time, another to record the end time, and a third to record the time that the notification was created or emitted by the producer. A happening event can be of long duration (Hundred Years' War). However, some happening events are apparently instantaneous. Instantaneous means that the start time and end time are the same. If your clock can only measure time in one-second increments and the end time occurs less than one second after the start time, the measured duration can be literally zero seconds. When an event is instantaneous, the notification may only need one time stamp.

If an event is a state change, the duration of the event is the state transition time. This could be measured in years or it could be virtually instantaneous. However, those who believe that an event is always instantaneous would say that the end of the state transition is the point in time when the event occurs. In this interpretation, the house purchase event took place in the instant that the last signature was put on a certain document, or perhaps when the deed with the new owner's name was placed into the county hall of records.

The notion of event duration is less applicable in the "detectable condition" view because an event is a snapshot of the condition of something. A time stamp will generally reflect the point in time when the observation was taken.

Designing Events

Theoreticians have a lot more to say about the definition of events, but analysts and architects designing business applications probably don't need to drill any deeper into this subject. However, they do need to be aware of certain implications of these definitions.

General Guidelines

Regardless of which definition of event you use, the following guidelines apply:

▶ There is no limit on the number of event objects (or notifications) that can be designed to report a particular business event. It is up to the person who designs the system to determine what kind of notifications will be generated and what data items will be included in each.

▶ The term "event object" doesn't mean object in the object-oriented programming (OOP) sense. OOP objects include code as well as data whereas event objects are just data, or have methods restricted to getting data from the event object.

▶ An observation of something that isn't changing is a valid event under any of these definitions. Time is always changing, and an observer taking a reading is inherently something that happens.

▶ An event object is not just data about something; it is the record of a particular observation, according to all three definitions. The existence of data describing a state change or condition doesn't constitute an event object unless it is associated with an act of observation. A notification is an event object conveyed from an event producer to an event consumer (however, a notification can be stored in an event log in a database at an event consumer or a potential event producer—it's a notification if it was conveyed in the past or could be in the future).

▶ There is nothing special about the data in a notification—all application systems have always dealt with data about events. State changes are nothing new either—all applications involve state changes. The unique nature of notifications, and event processing in general, derives from the way in which agents exchange and process the event data. The five principles of EDA are special. Three of the principles ("Reports current events," "Pushes notifications," and "Responds immediately") facilitate timeliness, and the other two ("Communicates one-way" and "Is free of commands") facilitate flexibility through minimal coupling. Other kinds of interactions among software agents have some of these characteristics, but only EDA has all five of them.

▶ Some people think of an event as a thing that *causes* a change to occur. They're partly right—many events do cause a change. Others think of an event as a report of a change, happening, or condition. They're always right— all events report a change, happening, or condition. The confusion arises because there are two different kinds of notifications. We'll elaborate on this in the next chapter.

Event Types

In Chapter 6, we described the various ways that event producers notify event consumers. A notification can consist of any of the following:

▶ A message containing an event object sent from the producer to the consumer

▶ An event object in a shared file, database, cache, or some other place in memory where the producer and consumer can both access it

▶ A procedure call or method invocation from producer to consumer, usually containing event data as parameters or in an attached document

In most event processing, including all complex event processing (CEP), the event object is a set of data. The degenerate case, in which the event object is implicit (the event is signaled by a procedure call or method invocation without any data in parameters or attached documents), applies to certain event-based programming scenarios but is outside the scope of this discussion. Here, we are dealing with event objects that are composed of explicit data items (*fields* or *attributes*) that describe things about the event that occurred.

....

Note: All event objects are instances of an event type.

An XML document that represents Fred's order for a computer is an instance of the order event (object) type. Different kinds of event objects are of different types. An event type is sometimes called an event class, so Fred's order would be said to be an instance of the order event class. All of the event objects of the same type have the same structure—that is, they have the same kind of data items, and the data items are organized in the same way.

One of the fundamental tasks in developing an event-processing application is identifying the data items to include in the event object. Some of the kinds of data that may be included are

▶ A tag that indicates the type of event (for example, an order event, an RFID reading, a change-of-address event)

▶ A unique event identifier used to reference the event instance (Fred's order has a different identifier than Susan's order)

▶ A time stamp that indicates when the event object was created (it may include the date as well as the time of day)

▶ Time stamps for the start and end times (and dates) of an interval event

▶ The name, address, or a unique identifier of the producer software agent that generated the event

▶ Indicators of the urgency or priority of the event

▶ A small or large number of other data items that describe the event (any data of the sort that is typically handled in application programs and databases)

▶ The unique event identifiers for the base events that were used to generate this event, if this event is a complex event (these identifiers can be used by an event consumer to trace back the origins of a complex event—this is sometimes called the event's *pedigree* or *genetics*)

▶ A copy of the base events (and their data items) that were used to generate the event, if this event is a complex event (if a complex event contains all of its base events, then it is called a *composite* event)

Developers are free to include any or all of these data items, or anything else that they think would be useful for the purposes of the application that they are designing. This is like any kind of data modeling—there is no one right answer, although some choices will be better than others.

....

Note: In many cases, an event is reported by more than one type of event object because there are multiple event consumers (people or application programs) with different information needs.

The "Happening Example" section, earlier in the chapter, described three complex-event objects that described buying a house. Each would be used for different purposes:

▶ If the buyer wants to tell a friend what they did with their old house and how close the nearest park is to their new house, he or she would probably put that in an e-mail (the event notification listed first).

▶ If neighbors want to know when the property sold and the purchase price, they would probably look in the newspaper (the notification listed second).

▶ If someone is compiling statistics on average house prices, or investigating the quality of housing stock in a particular neighborhood, he or she would probably download a copy of XML documents from the real-estate clearinghouse (the third type of notification).

In many event-processing applications, developers work with event streams provided by another organization so the base event types are already defined before development of the new application begins.

Complex Events

As you know, the fundamental idea behind CEP is "connecting the dots." Event-driven CEP systems generate complex events by distilling the facts from multiple incoming base events into a few complex events. Complex events represent summary-level insights that are more meaningful and helpful for making decisions than are the base events. A complex event is abstract in the sense that it is one or more steps removed from the raw input data.

> Note: The EPTS Event Processing Glossary *(version 1) defines* complex event *as "an event that is an abstraction of other events called its* members."

In the physical world, house tours, e-mails, and bank transactions are "members" in the complex event called buying a house. In a computer system, member events are the base event objects that CEP software uses to compute a complex-event object.

Events that your application generates by performing some computation on base events are always complex events (they also can be called *derived* or *synthesized* events). When events come in from somewhere outside of your system, they may be simple or complex. We'll come back to this point after we discuss the nature of complex events.

Event Hierarchies

The relationship between a synthesized, complex event and its base events can be depicted as a hierarchy. A complex event is at a higher level in the hierarchy than the base events that were used to generate it. Consider the example introduced in Chapter 3 of a continuous monitoring system in a customer contact center. Each customer call is an event recorded in an event object. The event object contains information such as the time and date of the call, whether the call was inbound or outbound, length of time that the customer waited on hold, the number of times the customer was transferred, the duration of the call, whether the issue was resolved during the first call, the name or identifier of the agent who took the call, and perhaps some measure of customer satisfaction or other data items. The event objects record things that happen at the transaction, or operations, level in the call center (see the bottom level in Figure 7-1). Other events also happen at the operations level. For example, customer service agents log in to indicate that they are available to take calls and log out to indicate that they are taking a break or leaving for the day. Operations-level events are base events in an event hierarchy.

Team supervisors are interested in the volume of customer calls and the performance of the agents who work for them. They have a dashboard that reports metrics such as the call volume, the number of agents logged in as available, and the average time that customers spent waiting on hold. "Team A Average Wait Time$_1$" is a complex-event object that reports the average waiting time for the calls into team A between 10 A.M. and 10:15 A.M. (see the middle level in Figure 7-1). It is calculated from 70 event objects, the base events that signify the 70 calls to the team during that time window. The average wait time is an abstraction; it happened in the physical world but it's intangible—you can't see it or hear it, and it can't be directly measured and reported by the phone system. It's visible to the Team A supervisor because it's displayed on a dashboard that is refreshed every minute or every 5 minutes. "Team A Average Wait Time$_2$" could be calculated and displayed at 10:16 to reflect the average

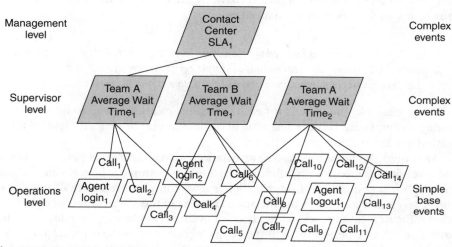

Figure 7-1: Event hierarchy in customer contact center.

wait time between 10:01 and 10:16. It will encompass many of the same base events (for example, $Call_4$) that were reflected in the previous calculation of average wait time, but some older call events will be dropped and new ones added. The dashboard for the team B supervisor reflects "Team B Average Wait Time$_1$," which was synthesized from the event objects of a different set of calls.

A higher level of complex events is relevant on the management level. For example, the contact center manager may have a dashboard that continuously monitors the overall performance of the contact center. "Contact Center SLA$_1$" is a complex event that is computed from the average wait times from all of the teams—its base events are complex events. The dashboard might represent this complex event in a "traffic signal" that turns yellow if the contact center wait times are beginning to deteriorate. It turns red if the average wait time has exceeded the threshold specified in the service-level agreement (SLA) that the contact center has with the marketing department. Missing an SLA is another abstract event—it's intangible but real. An alert could be generated just when an SLA is missed or an SLA event notification could be routinely sent to update a graphic on a dashboard every few seconds depending on the needs of the end user.

A manager who sees a yellow light warning that the customer wait times are becoming too long may want to drill down into the details to find which team is experiencing the problems. A dashboard generally has the capability to show the individual events that contributed to a higher-level event. If the manager sees a problem in Team A, he or she might consult the Team A supervisor and take remedial action, such as reassigning Team B from making outgoing calls to helping Team A with incoming calls. Remedial actions at the supervisory level are typically at a finer level of granularity than those at the management level. A supervisor who sees that the average customer wait time is too long may drill down into the average call duration for each of their agents. If a particular agent has had several unusually long calls, the supervisor may need to give the agent additional coaching on a new product or service procedure or respond in some other manner.

Note: The volume of events forwarded up an event hierarchy generally is sharply reduced at each level. In many cases, thousands of simple events are condensed into one or two complex events, depending on the nature of the data and the business situation.

In this example, the records for each individual call don't need to be sent to the manager's dashboard because a handful of complex events provides the level of information needed at the upper level.

We should also point out that the association between levels in an event hierarchy and levels in a company's organization chart in our example is largely coincidental. Although it is common to find that higher level complex events are of interest to higher levels in a company's organization chart, as in the contact center example, in other CEP applications, several levels of an event hierarchy may be relevant to the work done by one person or multiple people at one level in the organization chart. Event hierarchies reflect the degree of refinement and abstraction of the event data irrespective of the level of the person who uses the data.

Event-Processing Rules and Patterns

The logic to transform simple events into complex events is carried out in CEP software at run time. Chapter 3 summarized the role of CEP software at a high level. This section explores event computation in more detail.

Programming CEP Software

CEP software is any computer program that can generate, read, discard, or perform calculations on complex-event objects. In some cases, CEP computation is implemented by the code of a packaged or custom application. CEP logic can be written in any programming language, such as C++, C#, or Java. However, when the event processing is more complex or needs frequent modification to adjust to changing business requirements, using a software tool that is specially designed for CEP may be more practical (Chapter 11 discusses the build versus buy issue in more detail).

The core technology for CEP is also available in purpose-built commercial products such as event-processing suites, business activity monitoring (BAM) products, CEP-enabled DBMSs, or CEP-enabled industry- or application-specific frameworks. The core technology is capable of reading notifications from event channels and performing calculations on them, but it needs to be tailored to each business situation.

Note: The background understanding needed to design event-processing business systems comes from users and business analysts. Analysts, software developers, or, in some cases, technology-savvy users then turn the business understanding into instructions for the CEP software.

The language used to give instructions to a CEP system is called Event Processing Language (EPL). Every product uses a different EPL because there is no industry standard. The CEP product's development tool can use pull-down menus, a graphical interface with drag-and-drop icons, a scripting language, or a combination of these. The details of the language, development process, and nature of the development interface are different for every product. Developers typically specify the following things:

▶ The source of the incoming base events

▶ The data format and types of content in the base events

▶ The algorithms and functions to be applied to the base events and the patterns to be detected

▶ What to do with the complex events that are computed or detected (such as emitting alerts and other outgoing notifications, invoking a software agent, or controlling an actuator)

CEP Computation

The kinds of operations that can be applied to the base events typically include

▶ Filtering the incoming base events and discarding those that are irrelevant to the task at hand. To calculate "Team A Average Wait Time$_1$," only the event objects that pertain to customer calls to particular agents within a certain time window are used.

▶ Calculating aggregate figures such as totals and averages, counting the number of events, or sorting the events in order of ascending or descending value of some data item. The algorithm to compute average wait time in our example is trivial—the system adds the wait times and divides by the number of calls.

▶ Transforming the data in a base event to another format to be used in the outgoing complex event.

▶ Enriching the data by using the value of a data item to look up an entry in a table or database, and then inserting the data that is found in the table or database into the complex-event object that is being generated.

▶ Splitting an event stream, forwarding some event notifications to one destination and others to another destination.

▶ Looking for patterns in the base events by correlating events from different streams or within one stream.

Pattern Detection

Pattern detection warrants a more complete explanation because it is at the heart of "connecting the dots." Developers tell the CEP software what combination of things to look for in the base events—the event pattern. A simple event pattern could look like this:

```
NewsArticle(About Stock X) followed by
StockPriceRise(Stock X, > 5%) within 3 minutes.
```

This tells the CEP software to listen to the NewsArticle event stream for published articles that mention companies and also listen to the StockPriceRise event stream for reports of companies whose stock has increased more than 5 percent. When any company appears in a NewsArticle event object within 3 minutes of the time that the same company appears in a StockPriceRise event object with a price rise of greater than 5 percent, the CEP software has detected a complex event that is a pattern match (the pattern match is called a pattern *instance*).

This example demonstrates correlation between two event streams based on a match of company names (called a *join*). It also shows the importance of time in many CEP applications. The pattern requires that two events happen within 3 minutes of each other (a temporal constraint). It also requires a particular time order—the stock price change had to happen after the article was published, not before it.

Although it is not obvious, some additional continuous event processing had to take place to make this application possible because the StockPriceRise data is not directly available from any external event stream provider. The raw event data that is used to generate the StockPriceRise event stream comes from a stock exchange that publishes a basic trade data event stream. A continuous analytic function—coded in a separate section of event-processing language—is applied to the incoming trade data to calculate price change data that are published in a newly generated StockPriceRise event stream used in the example described above. Such value-added, CEP-based continuous analytic pre-processing is common in event-processing applications. Analytics may be used to calculate moving averages, discard outliers that are presumed to be bad data, or perform other tasks to improve the information quality of a raw event stream. In our example, the NewsArticle event stream may not require such preliminary analytics if high quality, tagged event data can be directly obtained from a third party information service.

Some event patterns refer to *causal* relationships between the events.

....

Note: An event A is said to have a causal relationship with event B if A had to happen first for B to happen.

Dr. Luckham identifies two kinds of causality, vertical and horizontal, in his book *The Power of Events. Vertical* causality is a causal relationship between events at two different levels in an event hierarchy. For example, a complex event called AvailableAgent$_2$ can be generated at the supervisory level to report that customer Agent$_2$ is available for calls. This event would be based on a pattern of simple base events from the operations level that indicates that the Agent Login$_2$ event has occurred and it has not been followed by a corresponding Agent Logout$_2$ event. Agent Login$_2$ at the operations level has a causal relationship with the AvailableAgent$_2$ event at the supervisory level.

Horizontal causality refers to relationships among events that are on the same level of an event hierarchy. Agent Login$_1$ is horizontally causal to Agent Logout$_1$ because they are on the same level and an agent can't log out unless he or she first logged in.

Note: Causality in event processing is not a cause-and-effect relationship in an ordinary sense. Rather, the term causality in this field implies that the causal event is necessary although it may not be sufficient to determine that the subsequent event will occur.

In our example, Agent Login$_1$ must have happened if Agent Logout$_1$ happened so it is said to be causal. However, Agent Login$_1$ can happen without Agent Logout$_1$ ever occurring because an agent might forget to log out.

How does the developer know what patterns to look for? This is the subject of event pattern discovery, an essential part of the CEP application development process. Analysts must study the business situation to identify patterns that reflect situations of interest. In some cases, analysts will replay copies of event logs from the past and try various combinations of rules to see which ones reveal the most meaningful connections. This is similar to the analysis performed in analytical business intelligence applications.

The vast majority of CEP applications today use patterns that are prepared by people using software tools to perform the event analytics. It is also possible to discover patterns with the assistance of machine learning, a kind of artificial intelligence. Academic research is actively underway in this area.

Note: Pattern discovery is done mostly by people. It happens before the application is deployed or when the application is being modified, as part of the application development process. Pattern matching to find instances of the pattern is done by CEP software at run time as incoming base events are processed.

Time Windows

CEP applications often are set up to work with time windows. In our earlier example, the average call wait time for a 15-minute window could be continuously sliding or jumping forward into the future, depending on how the developer has written the EPL. The window could jump once a minute by discarding everything that is more than 15 minutes old, adding everything that has occurred within the last minute, and recomputing the 15-minute total. Or the window could slide forward in time by discarding old notifications the second they are more than 15 minutes old, adding new notifications as soon as they arrive, and recalculating the total every time a new notification is added or an old notification expires. The choice of jumping or sliding window depends on whether very current (for example, up-to-the-second) information is significantly more valuable than almost current (for example, up-to-the-minute) information. A sliding window consumes more computer resources than a jumping window so it isn't warranted in many cases.

Commercial CEP software handles time windows more efficiently than conventional applications. A direct, conventional approach to computing an average call wait time would treat all of the relevant input data records at one time, summing the wait time and dividing by the number of calls. When the next time window was computed, the same operation would be repeated on a slightly different set of input records. Most CEP software can handle this with less overhead by only calculating the difference between the two time windows. It takes the results of the previous calculation, subtracts out the calls whose time had expired (those more than 15 minutes old), and adds in the new calls that had occurred since the previous calculation. If the volume of data is high, this algorithm can produce the updated result faster and with less computer overhead than the brute force calculation. Other aspects of CEP software are also optimized for its purpose—continuous intelligence.

Variations on Complex Events

An event-processing system is said to detect a *situation* if it finds a simple or complex event that a user of the system deems to be meaningful for any reason. A situation indicates that some event data item, combination of data items, or pattern instance has met some criterion that indicates a threat or an opportunity. For example, the system might calculate a complex event that reports an average on-hold waiting time for customers of 2 minutes and 10 seconds. If the developer had specified 2 minutes as the threshold for defining a threat situation, the event-processing system would act upon the rule it has been given for such situations. The rule might tell the system to turn a stop light on a dashboard yellow or send an e-mail alert to a manager.

Uncertain Events

In some cases, the meaning of a synthesized event can't be conclusively determined. So, a situation that is indicated by a CEP system may have a probability associated with it. For example, consider a CEP system that is designed to detect money laundering. It tracks streams of funds-transfer events and spots a person who has received $8,000, $9,000, and $8,000 on successive days. This set of events matches an event pattern that has been designed to identify suspicious activity. However, an analyst may have studied the historical event data and determined that this pattern indicates money laundering 40 percent of the time. The CEP system can be told to report the pattern match and the details of the transactions, along with an explicit indication of the probability that it is money laundering. Probabilities can apply to past events, as in this case. They are even more common for predictive events in which the pattern indicates something that will probably happen in the future. For example, a tsunami detection system might predict a 70 percent chance of a tsunami of certain magnitude hitting a particular location within a certain time interval.

Absent Events

Chapter 2 pointed out that the absence of a notification conveys information. A parent on a business trip expects to receive a message if an emergency occurs at home. If the parent hasn't received such a message, he or she assumes that no emergency has occurred. Sometimes the opposite protocol is used: the absence of a notification conveys information that there is a problem. A teenager is asked to call home by 11 P.M. to report that they are leaving a party to come home. If no call event occurs, the parent may call the teenager or go looking for them.

In our call center example, an inbound customer call ($Call_3$) could raise a question that can't be resolved during the initial call. An agent must call back with an answer at a later time. The lack of a return call event, such as $Call_9$, within 4 hours requires a supervisor's attention. An analyst defines an event pattern to detect when an initial call happens without a return call. This pattern will result in creating a complex event called $UnansweredQuestion_1$. The pattern is matched by the occurrence of $Call_3$ and a subsequent timer event T_n that occurs 4 hours after the time of $Call_3$ with the absence of a return call event. The pattern would not be matched by the combination of $Call_3$, $Call_9$, and T_n because the return call was made. You may note that $Call_3$ had to happen for $Call_9$ to happen, so it is horizontally causal. $Call_3$ also had to happen for the UnansweredQuestion1 event to occur at the supervisory level, so it is also vertically causal to $UnansweredQuestion_1$.

Complex Events Sometimes Are Relative

How can you reliably distinguish a complex event from a simple event? Any event that is generated (synthesized) by applying some processing logic to a set of base events is a complex event. If something is synthesized locally, you know that it is complex. However, you don't always know the nature of events coming from sensors, application systems, or other producers in the outside world.

You know that an incoming event is complex if the person who designed the event tells you that it is complex. He or she gives you a description (metadata) that describes the event type. If it includes data items that identify the base events that were used to compute the event, then you know that it is a complex event. If it is a composite event, the event object will even contain the actual base events that contributed to it.

You may also know that an incoming event is complex because you understand its inherent nature. It's obvious that buying a house and World War II are complex events, irrespective of what data items are in the event object or how a producer generates the event object.

However, incoming events with no information about their genetics may appear to you as simple events. For example, stock trade reports in financial data feeds from stock exchanges are difficult to categorize. The notifications are short and simple, often less than 100 bytes in length and containing only a few data items on the trade price and number of shares. They would seem to be the quintessential simple, base event. However, a trade report summarizes a transaction that is a complex event to the buyer, seller, and the traders who executed it. Before the trade occurred, the participants looked at the data from previous trades in that stock earlier in the day, and probably considered other market data, financial news, information from quarterly and annual reports, and various other sources. A trade is a complex event to those involved in its creation, but the trade report is a simple event object to those who receive it.

Almost any event is the result of prior events, arguably going back to the Big Bang that started the universe (perhaps that event had prior events too). This would seem to indicate that almost any event is complex if you know enough about it. The only possible exception would be purely random activity or noise that has no predecessors. These could be truly simple to all observers—but we'll leave that discussion for another venue.

Note: For those designing event-processing systems, the important implication is that complex and simple events are often in the eye of the beholder. If you have reason to be aware of the member or base events that contributed to event X, then event X is complex. If you don't care about the details, then X is a simple event.

When you develop a CEP application, most base events that come from outside of your system will be treated as simple events because you don't know or care what events led up to them. If a domino falls, you may only need to know about the domino that struck it, not the domino that struck the domino that struck it. An application that uses a stock trade report as input rarely needs to delve further into the origins of the trade. Only if the incoming event contains genetic information about its origins do you have the opportunity to treat it as other than a simple event.

Summary

Identifying business events and designing event objects are essential steps in the development of event-processing applications. In many cases, an event is reported by more than one type of event object because there are multiple event consumers (people or application programs) with different information needs. The fundamental principle of CEP is to generate one or a few high-level, meaningful complex events from multiple simpler base events. Analysts, software developers, or, in some cases, technology-savvy users turn their understanding of the business process and business requirements into instructions for the CEP software. The value of a complex event is only limited by the availability of event data and the creativity of people defining the patterns and algorithms to process it.

8

From Architecture to Application

A nalysts, application architects, and software engineers work in cooperation with businesspeople to design and build application systems that leverage event processing. They apply architectural concepts, such as those described in the previous chapters, to the requirements and conditions of particular business problems. The first part of this chapter explores how event data and notifications fit into business applications. The second part describes five very different styles of event-processing application.

Role of Notifications in Business Applications

Event-processing systems are an integral part of a company's IT fabric, not a separate or isolated activity. They tie into other business applications or are part of those application systems. The primary interface between event-processing components and other application components is through sending and receiving notifications.

Business event processing uses two kinds of notifications:

▶ **Transactional notifications**—Report an event and cause something else to change

▶ **Observational notifications**—Report an event but don't directly change anything

Transactional notifications are in the main flows of continuous-processing, event-driven architecture (EDA) applications. Observational notifications are outside of the main application flows (they're "out of band"), but they affect business decisions so they have an indirect impact on application systems and things in the physical world.

When we defined "event" in Chapter 7, we noted that some people think of an event as a thing that *causes* a change to occur. They're partially right—many events do cause a change. Others think of an event as a report of a change, happening, or condition. They're completely right—all events report a change, happening, or condition. If a domino in a row of dominos topples over and causes a second domino to fall over, it's analogous to a transactional notification. If a domino falls and doesn't cause another domino to fall, that's analogous to an observational notification. Many observational notifications are discarded by the recipient (the event consumer) without being used because the recipient isn't interested in that data.

The analogy holds reasonably well if you look at how complex events work. They are usually synthesized from multiple observational notifications. Observational notifications can have a big indirect effect on the business when combined into a complex event, but one observational notification can't directly cause a change. Similarly, if one domino leans into a larger domino, the larger domino won't fall. But if enough small dominos (observational notifications) lean on the big one (complex-event notification), it will fall.

Observational notifications and transactional notifications don't look different—they're just data. They differ only in how they are being used. Many business processes involve a mix of transactional and observational notifications. Consider the example of an equity trade. When an investor buys some stock, the deal is immediately captured and reflected in a handful of transactional notifications (TN_1 and TN_2 in Figure 8-1) at the stock exchange and in the middle office systems of the financial services companies that carried out the buy and sell sides of the transaction. In the hours and days after the trade, a series of additional transactional notifications (TN_3 and TN_4) or other kinds of records will be generated in back office and settlement systems, and in related accounting applications in the brokerage firms of the buyer and seller. These are the operational applications in the business transaction layer of a company's IT function (see middle band in Figure 8-1). Transactional notifications have financial

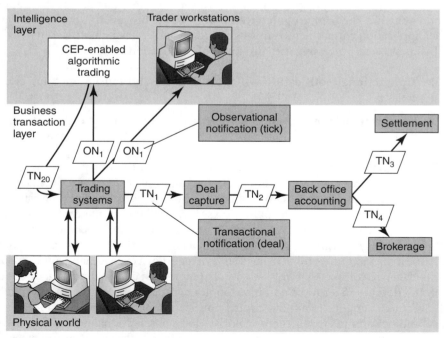

ON = Observational notification
TN = Transactional notification

Figure 8-1: Notifications in capital markets trading applications.

and legal implications, so they can't be lost. They contain many data items about the transactions and can be hundreds or thousands of bytes long. Some of the notifications indicate the identity of the buyer, his or her address, the amount of commission to be paid to the broker, and many other things.

The same transaction is also immediately reported in a "tick" (ON_1). A tick is a short trade-report message—an observational notification that contains the stock symbol, an identifier for the stock exchange, the trade price, the number of shares traded, an optional time stamp, and other optional fields. The whole message may be less than 100 bytes long. A stock exchange publishes ticks, quotes, and other notifications through its real-time market data network to tens of thousands of event consumers. If a copy of a tick is lost due to a network glitch or a problem at a recipient's site, generally no attempt will be made to recover it, because another trade in the same stock will come along soon reflecting a more-recent price. A tick doesn't directly cause an event to occur in the event consumers. However, a large set of trade reports combined together as a complex event can cause an algorithmic trading system at a consumer site to kick off a buy or sell transaction (transactional notification TN_{20}). The algorithmic trading system is in the intelligence layer of a company's IT function (see top band in Figure 8-1).

We'll look at the role of transactional and observational notifications in business applications more closely in the next two sections.

Transactional Notifications

Transactional notifications are the notifications in one-event-at-a-time EDA systems. In our recurring order-fulfillment example, the orders, approved orders, rejected orders, and filled orders are transactional notifications. Transactional notifications vary in size, ranging from a few dozen bytes to 100,000 bytes (100MB) or more. The single most common data format is XML but binary and other formats sometimes are still used.

....

Note: Transactional notifications are typically generated by business applications within the company or in its suppliers, customers, or outsourcers.

Each transactional notification is important. If one is lost, a customer won't get the goods they ordered, a bill may not be sent, the books may not balance, an insurance claim won't be paid, or some other problem will ensue. The need for data integrity affects the choice of channel that is used to convey transactional notifications. This kind of notification is often transmitted over a reliable messaging system that stores a copy on disk before sending it so that it can't be lost due to a problem in the network or another server. If a reliable channel is not used, software developers should build equivalent safeguards into the application components. The application programs and database management systems (DBMSs) that handle the notifications must also be implemented with careful attention to data integrity. Software developers use a set of rules to protect data integrity when writing programs that handle transactional data. The details go beyond the scope of this book, but if you're interested in knowing more, look up the ACID properties in Wikipedia (check for Atomicity, Consistency, Isolation, and Durability).

Ways Applications Communicate Business Events

We're calling these messages "transactional notifications" because we wear event-colored glasses and believe that this perspective brings some advantages in application design. However, analysts and software developers are already familiar with data in this form as plain old "messages." They know event data as orders, bills, purchase orders, equity trades, insurance claims, expense reports, deposit and withdrawal notices, payments, or some other term. They also know that messages aren't the only way to convey the information about a business event from one step to the next in a business process. If it's not conveyed in transactional notifications using the five principles of EDA (see Chapter 6), it's conveyed in some other manner, such as:

▶ In parameters or documents attached to a call or method invocation in a request-driven relationship

▶ By being temporarily stored in a file or database to be picked by the next activity in a time-driven relationship

The task is the same—transferring data about a business event from one agent to the next. In a request- or time-driven approach, the records would be called *transactions* or *business objects* rather than messages or transactional notifications.

Event Data, State Data, and Reference Data

Regardless of how it is conveyed, event data has a big impact on the application component that receives it. The data reports an event and also causes one or more events to occur in the recipient. The recipient interprets the event data, applies application-processing logic, likely sends messages to other agents, and generally updates some data in files or databases. The data in the application's files or databases before the event data arrives is *state data* or *reference data* (see Figure 8-2).

Developers sometimes find it useful to categorize all application data as event data, state data, or reference data:

▶ **Event data**—Data about a business event held in an event object or represented in some other manner, such as scattered among multiple documents, business forms, files, databases, web forms, or parameter lists.

▶ **State data**—Data in an application system that changes as a direct consequence of a routine activity related to the operational purpose of the application. Examples of state data include bank account balances, the number of items in a warehouse inventory, and airline seat reservations. A fundamental goal of a bank's demand deposit accounting system is to maintain a record of how much money a customer has in his or her account. A deposit or withdrawal event will change

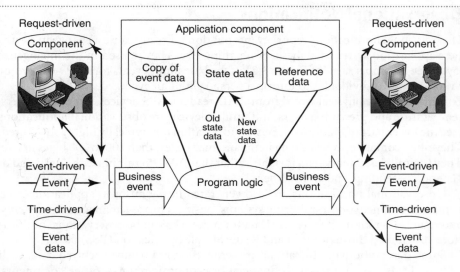

Figure 8-2: Business events cause change in application data.

the state of the account (that is, its balance). Similarly, the purpose of an airline reservation system is to keep track of who has made reservations and which passenger is assigned to which seat. In a sense, any application program's purpose in life is to take incoming event data and use it to modify its state data.

▶ **Reference data**—Data that describes the stable, more or less permanent attributes of a thing that are not being changed by the current event. Examples of reference data include a person's name and address, the address and size of a warehouse, a product description, the number of seats on an airplane, and an employee's demographic information. Reference data is actually a kind of state data. Event data can cause it to change, although it changes less often than state data does. Application programs refer to reference data (hence the name) without changing it. However, what is reference data to one application is state data to another application. The application that updates the product description, airplane seat count, or person's name considers those entities to be its state data. To the other applications that read but don't ever modify those data, it is reference data.

Note: The terms "state data" and "reference data" also have other meanings in computer science and information management so consider the context when using the terms.

Reference data is usually changed by discarding the old data and replacing it with new data. By contrast, state data is more likely to be recomputed incrementally—the new data is the old data plus or minus the event data. In a sense, all state data and reference data are just the accumulation of event data over time.

Observational Notifications

Observational notifications report events but don't directly cause a change in a business application system, database, or anything else. They're used in the intelligence layer (see the upper layer of Figure 8-3) as the base input events for CEP software, or in some cases, individually, to inform a person about an event.

Reports of the physical world from RFID readers, GPS devices, bar code readers, temperature and pressure sensors, and similar devices are observational notifications (see the lower part of Figure 8-3). Sensor notifications are typically highly structured. They often contain only a few data items and may be less than 100 to 200 bytes in size. They typically use binary data formats rather than XML to minimize the overhead of generating, sending, and storing them.

Observational notifications are also generated in the business application layer, computer and network monitoring systems, business process management systems, and many other kinds of software. Data from the Web can be observational notifications distributed through Atom and Really Simple Syndication (RSS) feeds.

Some observational notifications are semistructured or unstructured data, such as news feeds, e-mail messages, financial or economic reports, other documents, images, music, video, and other data. Observational notifications that contain text data are usually formatted using XML, which provides some inherent structure. Major

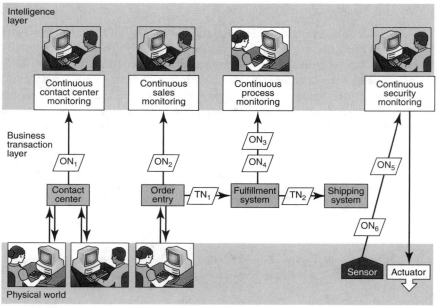

OE = Observational notification
TE = Transactional notification

Figure 8-3: Observational notifications enable continuous intelligence.

news services such as Dow Jones and Reuters provide news data streams in an "elementized" form where certain words and phrases are tagged so that they can be found more easily. CEP software can't interpret unstructured and semistructured notifications directly, so it must be preprocessed by adaptors. Adaptors parse the contents, extract the salient information, and generate more-structured observational events that can be manipulated for CEP.

Note: Observational notifications may be structured, semistructured, or unstructured data types.

Sources of Observational Notifications

Acquiring observational notifications, the "first mile" in a CEP system, can be relatively easy or quite difficult depending on the circumstances. There are six ways to get observational notifications, listed here in order from the most to the least invasive of the source:

1. From the physical world
2. From business applications that are designed to natively emit them
3. From business applications that emit transactional notifications that can be leveraged for observational purposes
4. From DBMS adaptors
5. From adaptors on request-driven interfaces
6. From external sources including the World Wide Web

The Physical World

Devices on the edge between the physical world and the IT world are usually easy to implement as event sources because they are intended for and dedicated to this purpose. This includes RFID readers, bar code readers, GPS devices, accelerometers, temperature and pressure sensors, and other types of sensors.

Natively Generated in Business Applications

Some application systems emit observational notifications because their developers foresaw the need for them when they originally designed the application systems. For example, trading systems in stock exchanges and other markets are designed from their inception to emit both transactional and observational notifications. However, most traditional business applications didn't emit observational notifications natively because no one saw a business requirement for them when the system was designed. They emitted transactional notifications only if they were using EDA. However, most newer packaged applications, including enterprise resource planning, sales force automation, and supply chain management systems, can be configured to generate outbound notifications for at least some business events. These may be used for transactional or observational purposes.

It's possible to modify an older application to add logic that will produce a notification, although this can be expensive and time consuming. Programs have to be analyzed, modified, compiled, tested, and moved back into production. It might be worth the investment, but in many cases, there are faster and cheaper alternatives, such as those discussed next.

The advantage of notifications that are deliberately generated by an application is that the developer can specify the precise nature of the notifications. However, this approach only works if the person or group that owns the application is willing to tailor the application for this purpose, so it isn't feasible in many circumstances.

Leveraging Transactional Notifications as Observational Notifications

A copy of a notification that is being used for transactional purposes can be sent to the intelligence layer for observational (CEP) purposes. For example, the record of a credit card purchase is inherently a transactional notification. A point-of-sale (POS) device or a business application generates the credit card transaction data when a consumer buys something. It is sent through a credit card network to a bank, where it ultimately will be used to bill the consumer. However, a second copy of the notification can also be delivered to a marketing system or a CEP-based fraud-detection system to see if a suspicious pattern of charges is emerging on this account number. This is sometimes done before the transaction is complete; elsewhere it happens after the fact, depending on the policy set by the company. Similarly, call-data records (CDRs) for phone calls are primarily intended for billing purposes but they can also be used as observational notifications for location-awareness, fraud-detection, and even marketing purposes. The proliferation of electronic transaction data is a rich and growing source of observational notifications.

If the available transactional notifications are large or not clearly structured, developers may use an adaptor to extract a few key data items from them to generate smaller, well-structured observational notifications. This is noninvasive with respect to the original system. The producer and consumer applications for the transactional notification don't have to be modified. The adaptor taps into the transactional notification when it is sent, delivered, or at some intermediate point in the network (for example, by getting a copy when the message goes through message oriented middleware or a router).

This approach works well if the source application uses EDA because EDA applications have transactional notifications that can be readily tapped. However, it doesn't work for applications or parts of applications that are request- or time-driven, because they have no transactional notifications.

DBMS Adaptors

Most business events cause an application system to add, modify, or delete some state data in an application database. That change is a database event, an event that is inherently detectable and available for capture without changing the application program. Database adaptors can use DBMS triggers or a DBMS log mechanism to take a copy of data that is being written to or deleted from a database. This can be implemented by custom coding or through a commercial, event-oriented, DBMS adaptor product.

This is a practical, noninvasive way of generating an observational notification for CEP without disrupting the business application. It works even if the source application is request- or time-driven. However, it assumes that the business unit that owns the database is willing to accept the introduction of a DBMS adaptor. If the application is owned by the same IT organization that wants the observational notifications, this will work fine. If it's owned by another organization, it's less likely to be palatable.

Adaptors on Request-Driven Interfaces

As a last resort, when none of the previous approaches is practical, a request-based adaptor can extract events from an application without affecting its application code or DBMS. A request-based adaptor is a software agent that runs outside of an application system, calling on a request/reply basis to detect and capture evidence of business events that occur within the application.

Acquiring notifications on a request-driven basis is difficult, because the source doesn't give any signal when an event has occurred. The event is hidden within the source application. The adaptor must discover the event by periodically requesting data and examining the response to see if anything is new. This is noninvasive—no change in the source application is required. The burden of detecting the change and transforming the returned data rests in the adaptor. Service-oriented architecture (SOA) applications that expose request-driven interfaces are a good target for this approach as long as the business unit that controls the SOA application allows access.

The quintessential modern request-driven adaptor is a *web scraper*, a time-driven agent that polls a website at regular intervals to see if something has changed within the target system. For example, a company might deploy a web scraper to monitor a competitor's website for changes in products or prices. When the agent discovers a change, it will send an alert to a person, application, or CEP engine. The antecedents to web scrapers were "screen scrapers" that spoof traditional applications by pretending to be people at dumb terminals, such as 3270s and VT100s. Screen scrapers only work if the adaptor is authorized to act as a client of the application, so it's usually only practical within a company. By contrast, web scrapers can operate on any application with a public website.

Events from the World Wide Web and Other External Sources

The Web is a rich source of event information. Some is available through event-driven mechanisms such as Atom and RSS. More of it requires adaptors because it is natively request-driven. Most of the data is free, although some of the more valuable sources are only available as fee-based, software-as-a-service (SAAS) resources. News feeds, economic data, trade association data, and weather information are already widely exploited in business, although direct links to deliver such data to CEP systems are just coming into use. Most of this data is funneled to human decision makers, just as much internal information about events is handled by people. The possibilities for collecting new kinds of observational notifications relevant for making business decisions are increasing rapidly. Some companies have installed agents that listen to Twitter, a micro-blogging website, to detect the frequency of use of certain keywords. Web cams provide video trails that can be mined to detect events.

Comparative Value of Event Sources

User requirements determine which sources of event data are most relevant for any particular application. Consider our familiar order-fulfillment process, repeated in Figure 8-4 with minor changes. If you're building a monitor for the marketing department, you might want to tap into the process at the point where the order is captured from a customer. An adaptor at point X can obtain a copy of order transactional noti-

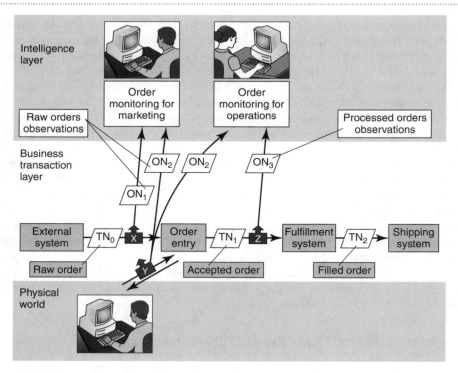

ON = Observational notification
TN = Transactional notification

Figure 8-4: Capture events at the point of greatest information value.

fication TN_0 as it comes in over a messaging link from a business partner. A full copy of TN_0 could be used as an observational notification, or the adaptor could generate a new, subset version (ON_1) of the notification to use for monitoring purposes.

If the order is captured in a web interaction rather than in a message, a different kind of adaptor can capture all of the communication between a customer and the web server at point Y to generate a set of observational notifications (ON_2). Commercial adaptors that listen to web traffic are available and some have been integrated with commercial CEP software. This configuration collects information about orders, but also much more: it can track which pages the customers viewed and which other products and options the customers considered. It can also get information about prospects who chose not to place an order. Some web monitors get their data from a web server–based application rather than intercepting the web page traffic on the way into the Web server, but the general approach is otherwise similar to other web monitors.

If you're building a business activity monitoring (BAM) dashboard for an operations manager in the order-fulfillment department, you might use the same observational notifications $(ON_1$ or $ON_2)$ used by the marketing monitoring system because that would give an advance warning of the orders that will eventually hit the fulfillment system. Or you might put an adaptor at point Z to capture only the accepted orders TN_1 because you don't want to burden the operations dashboard with information about all orders, some of which will never hit the fulfillment system because they won't make it through the order entry system. Again, you could use a full copy of the transactional notification TN_1 or generate a smaller version of the notification that contains only a few key data items to use as an observational notification ON_3. Accepted order notification TN_1 differs from the raw order notification TN_0 because the order entry application has validated the order and enriched it with information such as the customer's credit score, volume discount, and other information. They're both transactional notifications about the same order, but they're at different stages in the process instance's life. The kind of information available at each stage is different. User requirements will determine which notification is more appropriate.

As a rule of thumb, more information is available early in a process, especially as event data enters the company. This applies not only to our order-entry example, but also to many other applications, such as supply chain management. Raw documents, such as advance shipping notices (ASNs), that arrive via e-mail from external partners contain details and implications that are lost after an application takes the information from an ASN and puts it into an application database. In many kinds of business applications the transformation from raw input data to the data structure used internally within an application system is said to be *lossy* because some of the information value is lost. Companies are increasingly able to save and use raw event data (incoming notifications and web traffic logs) because of the decreasing costs of computers and storage. Nevertheless, observational notifications captured later in the process (downstream) can sometimes be preferable for some purposes if they have been enriched or combined with other events during the process.

Using Notifications

A notification is a notification. You can't tell an observational notification from a transactional notification by looking at its data items or how it is communicated, because all notifications look alike. As we have shown, many observational notifications are an exact copy of a transactional notification. The difference between transactional and observational notifications is only in how they are used.

Transactional notifications directly cause changes in the business transaction layer or in the physical world. Observational notifications are used, usually in sets, in CEP software in the intelligence layer to detect threat or opportunity situations. These indirectly cause events in the business application layer or the physical world. All CEP and BAM systems are closed-loop systems in the sense that they eventually result in something tangible happening to help the business in the business transaction layer or the physical world. A company wouldn't pay for a CEP system if it only produced information for entertainment. In some CEP systems, a person is in the loop to help make a decision or to conduct the response. In others, the decision and response are fully automated, so no person is in the loop. But there is always a loop back to the transactional or physical realms.

The output of CEP systems is used three ways:

▶ **Decision support**—Simple forms of decision support are provided through browser-based dashboards, e-mail alerts, SMS messages, other notification channels, or office productivity tools. Spreadsheets are one of the most common vehicles for monitoring business situations because they allow the end user to apply ad hoc analytics to data provided through CEP.

CEP software can also be tied into workflow systems for more-elaborate follow-up processes. Workflow systems manage the steps in a human response through a task list (or work list) mechanism (see Chapter 10 for more explanation of the links between CEP and workflow software). In other cases, the CEP software is integrated with a sophisticated notification management system (sometimes called "push" systems). These systems can deliver alerts to individuals, named groups, or roles (for example, all people with a certain job title or job description). They can also manage the response process—for example, by escalating the alert and delivering it to another person if the original target does not acknowledge receipt of the alert in a certain time interval. Such systems may also be used to implement multichannel, communication-enabled business processes (CEBPs). CEBP solutions may use a mix of web, SMS, phone, and other mechanisms to notify the appropriate people; automatically arrange joint conference calls to discuss the response; and integrate human and automated SOA services.

▶ **Driving business applications**—CEP software can trigger an automated response in a business application by invoking a web service, using some other kind of call or method invocation, or sending a transactional notification. Alternatively, the call or the notification can go to a business process management (BPM) engine that will, in turn, activate business applications.

▶ **Automating the physical world**—Finally, CEP software can drive an automated response in the physical world by controlling some kind of actuator to turn a machine on or off, increase the heat, open a valve, close a door, or perform any other action. The type of response is limited only by the capabilities of the development team.

Continuous Intelligence Compared to Periodic Intelligence

The intelligence layer has always been a part of a company's business operations rather than something that recently emerged through the introduction of CEP (see the top part in Figure 8-5). Virtually all application systems produce management reports at the intelligence layer to summarize what's happened at the transaction layer. Managers and analysts get regular reports on sales, accounting, inventory, financial controls, manufacturing, transaction volumes, service levels, and other metrics. Conventional reports give a fairly narrow view of business operations because they reflect the activ-

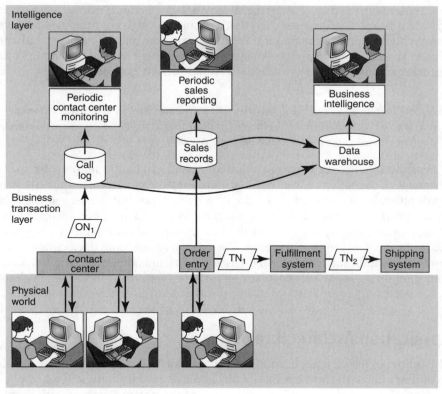

ON = Observational notification
TN = Transactional notification

Figure 8-5: Periodic intelligence—management reports and ad hoc analytics.

ity only within one application system or a set of related applications. However, a broader and deeper view is available through performance management and other business intelligence (BI) programs. BI programs pull together data from many applications and multiple business units. BI data is typically stored in data warehouses and data marts and made available to analysts and managers for a wide range of decision-making purposes (Chapter 10 explains the various kinds of BI).

CEP-based systems play approximately the same role as conventional management and analytics applications, with one big difference. CEP-based systems provide continuous intelligence because they're event-driven. Conventional management and analytics systems are periodic—they're either time-driven reports or request-driven queries that run upon user command. For conventional, periodic management systems, the data from the transactional systems is put into databases, where it rests until a batch report is generated or a query comes in. By contrast, observational notifications for CEP systems are processed as they arrive and sometimes are never put out to a database.

Aside from the timing, periodic management systems can provide all of the key performance indicators (KPIs) and other metrics available through continuous intelligence systems. In practice, some of the information that periodic management systems provide is broader and deeper than that available through continuous intelligence systems because periodic management systems are more mature and have the luxury of more time to compute things. Analysts can experiment with ad hoc inquiries and perform "what if" kinds of operations in request-driven systems.

....

Note: Companies will increase their use of continuous intelligence systems dramatically during 2010 through 2020, but will continue to rely on periodic management and analytical systems for conventional intelligence needs.

Periodic intelligence is reasonably mature but will continue to evolve to take advantage of technology advances. Continuous intelligence is still in the early stages of adoption. Most companies practice it in a few areas, but its fast growth is just beginning. In many cases it will complement conventional forms of intelligence, but in some cases it will replace it. We've used the example of continuous intelligence in a customer contact center in this book. Most contact centers still track customer calls and SLAs periodically, through time-based reports and ad hoc queries, but continuous monitoring is partially supplanting periodic monitoring in leading-edge contact centers.

Application Architecture Styles

CEP is used in business applications in multiple ways. Each way can be categorized according to how the application obtains and uses notifications, and whether and how the CEP aspects are tied into other parts of the system. The applications differ in the amount of effort that is needed to capture the events, process them, and respond to the situations that are detected (see Figure 8-6).

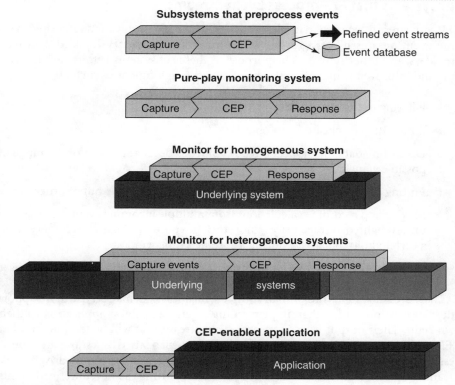

Figure 8-6: Five styles of CEP applications.

Five styles of CEP usage are:

▶ **Subsystems that pre-process event streams**—CEP platforms that listen to high-volume event streams to filter and condition event data for subsequent periodic analytical applications or near-real-time continuous monitors to use.

▶ **Pure-play monitoring systems**—Gather observational events from sensors and have little or no integration with other applications. The monitor is the application.

▶ **Monitors for homogeneous systems**—CEP-based facilities that help users manage an application system, network, IT subsystem, factory, or some other system.

▶ **Monitors for heterogeneous systems**—CEP-based applications that monitor two or more autonomous systems.

▶ **CEP-enabled applications**—Primarily transactional applications that are triggered by complex events or use complex events as input.

Subsystems that Pre-process Event Streams

CEP software is often used to implement subsystems that capture and refine high-volume event data as it arrives from web applications, industry-focused data feed providers, and other sources. The purpose of these subsystems is to reduce the volume and improve the quality of the event data through functions such as:

▶ Filtering out irrelevant data

▶ Eliminating duplicate event objects

▶ Discarding data that appears to be erroneous because it is out of the range of possible values

▶ Putting the events in some meaningful order if they arrive out of order

▶ Making and recording calculations from multiple incoming events, such as volume-weighted average prices for a stock or counting the number of events of a certain kind that arrive during a specified time window

▶ Enriching the events by looking up data from a table in memory or a database

These are subsystems rather than complete business systems because they support other applications rather than implementing an entire business application in their own right. Their output is an improved event stream that will be fed into another CEP application or stored in an event database that will be used by a subsequent business intelligence or other analytical systems on a time-driven or request-driven basis. Cleaning up the event data as it arrives rather than putting the raw, unrefined events directly into an event log allows subsequent applications that use the data to concentrate on analytic functions instead of data quality issues. Reducing the amount of useless event data that is stored in an event database is a major benefit, particularly when dealing with very-high volume event streams.

The need to perform several stages of continuous CEP in sequence—cascading the output event streams from one stage to use as input for the next stage—appears in many kinds of CEP applications. Examples include:

▶ The pattern detection application in the section "Event-Processing Rules and Patterns" of Chapter 7 is an example of cascading event processing. Incoming stock price events were the input to a CEP pre-processing stage that generated the StockPriceRise event stream for use in a subsequent CEP stage.

▶ Supply chain management applications that leverage RFID data are a type of multistage CEP because the RFID reader is a simple, purpose-built type of CEP pre-processor that eliminates duplicate tag readings before forwarding the events upstream to the supply chain application.

▶ A large bank uses a multistage CEP application to implement sophisticated trading strategies. The first stage is executed by a commercial CEP engine that listens to market data from stock exchanges and computes complex events that represent the current liquidity of particular financial instruments. These liquidity indicators are emitted as an event stream that goes into a second stage of CEP that runs in an older, custom-written, CEP-enabled trading platform. The trading platform also listens directly to market data events from stock exchanges to track current prices. The trading platform implements an automated trading strategy that reflects a combination of information from the liquidity indicator event stream and the raw market data.

Multistage CEP solutions will become more common as business analysts become more knowledgeable about CEP application design. CEP subsystems that pre-process event streams may be combined with the other CEP application styles described below to implement compound event-processing systems.

Pure-Play Monitoring Systems

Pure-play monitoring systems collect observational events from sensors, look for occurrences of patterns of interest, and send alerts and notifications to people or other systems (see the rightmost part of Figure 8-3). Examples include:

▶ Tsunami warning systems receive base notifications regarding the height of ocean waves from buoys stationed in multiple locations. They emit alerts that predict the time, place, and size of a tsunami that will hit the shore.

▶ Physical intrusion detection systems collect accelerometer sensor data on the magnitude and timing of the movement of fence sections. A CEP engine analyzes the patterns of movement to understand the nature of a disturbance. The challenge is to distinguish between a true positive, such as a person climbing over a fence, and false positives, such as the fence moving in the wind or being brushed by a small animal.

▶ Monitoring systems track the location of small children at amusement parks using RFID-tagged wrist bands. An alert is emitted when a child is more than 50 meters from a parent or guardian, or more than 10 meters apart if near an entrance, exit, or restricted location.

▶ Airport monitoring systems listen to notifications from check-in kiosks located in airport lobbies. If a kiosk has been unplugged or turned off by cleaning or maintenance personnel during the night, the monitoring system will notice the absence of activity in the early morning hours. It will send an alert to dispatch a person to start the kiosk up again.

The primary challenge when developing a pure-play monitoring system is in the pattern discovery—finding the event patterns that indicate the threat or opportunity situation. Analysts spend considerable time studying samples of event streams and defining the rules that will be applied at run time to filter and correlate the base events.

These are stand-alone systems with little or no integration with other systems. The input data are observational notifications from sensors that have been deployed just for the purpose of this application. Notifications are typically small—under a few hundred bytes and with relatively few data items. The response phase is generally straightforward, usually consisting only of alerting people through dashboards or some other notification channel.

Monitors for Homogeneous Systems

The most common kind of CEP application is a monitor that applies to one application system, physical plant, BPM facility, or other IT subsystem (see the middle level of Figure 8-6). Examples include:

▶ Network and computer system monitors report the health, throughput, performance, service levels, and other metrics of networks, computer systems, or parts of computer systems. They are an essential part of IT operations management tools and were among the earliest applications to use CEP concepts (they have used CEP since the 1990s, although it wasn't called CEP until the 2000s). Users are primarily IT network and system operations staff. Business service management (BSM) tools are a relatively new type of operations management tool. They track the health, throughput, and other metrics of SOA services.

▶ Operations monitors track the performance of factory production lines, power plants, and other process plants against targets and thresholds and help determine the causes of production problems and downtime. These products have event monitors that detect operating anomalies, mode changes such as whether equipment is running, and other situations that may need attention.

▶ Application-specific BAM dashboards and other alerting mechanisms are part of many Enterprise Resource Planning (ERP), accounting, and other packaged business applications. This is a relatively recent phenomenon—few applications offered these as standard features before about 2005 to 2008. BAM differs from IT operations management monitors because the user is a businessperson, not someone in the IT department. Most BAM capabilities are fairly limited in scope—they typically only monitor a small fraction of events and KPIs within one application or a suite of applications from one vendor.

▶ Most commercial BPM software products have a BAM dashboard facility for business process monitoring. The monitoring is generally limited to events that are under the control of the run-time BPM software (the orchestration and workflow engines). Chapter 10 describes process monitoring facilities in more detail.

The monitoring facility for a homogeneous system is generally developed by the same team that is building the underlying system, or by someone who is working closely with that team. The monitor is a relatively minor aspect of the project because most of the investment is going to develop and deploy the overall network, computer system, process plant, application, or BPM product. It's relatively easy to design and implement a monitor for a homogenous system because the underlying system can be designed to emit notifications from its inception. Developers know what events will occur and can format the notifications to provide exactly the kind of event data needed to support the monitor. The response phase usually consists of notifying people through dashboards or other alerting channels, although automated responses are implemented in some of these systems, particularly operations management systems. In this style of operation, the monitor directly affects the running of the system that it is monitoring.

Monitors for Heterogeneous Systems

CEP applications that monitor complex activities or end-to-end processes with multiple, heterogeneous event sources are relatively difficult to implement. Supply chain management (SCM) is a good example (see Figure 8-7).

A supply chain is a complex business activity with many autonomous participants such as suppliers, air carriers, express carriers, rail operators, freight consolidators, agents, warehouses, and, of course, customers. Each participant has its own application systems and makes its own decisions about what to do and when to do it. The

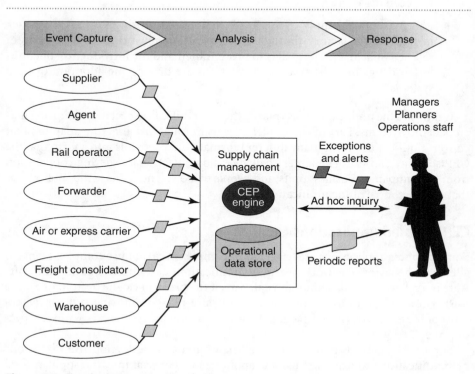

Figure 8-7: Supply chain management.

process cannot be predicted in advance because of unforeseeable events, such as factories running ahead or behind schedule, raw materials arriving late, labor issues, mechanical failures in trucks or planes, or weather changes. Shipments can be combined or split and sent separately. No process model or BPM engine applies to the whole supply chain from end to end.

Base events in an SCM system are a mix of observational events, such as ASNs, packing lists, and bills of lading, and transactional events, such as orders, purchase orders, invoices, and bills. Some of these are transmitted through e-mail, and others arrive through electronic data interchange (EDI) networks, web services, HTTP, messaging systems, or on paper. SCM systems have embedded CEP logic that consolidates notifications to derive complex events that make the goods pipeline more visible. SCM answers questions such as, "Where are the goods?" and "When will they arrive?"

Numerous other kinds of track-and-trace systems are emerging. They are similar to SCM systems because they involve multiple autonomous companies and their respective application systems, but they are specialized for particular types of problems. For example:

▶ The food industry is moving to track food items "from farm to fork" to safeguard the food and to be able to identify the source of bad food shortly after it has been discovered.

▶ Pharmaceutical supply chains are installing monitoring systems that track drugs from the factory, through the distribution network, and to the point of sale at a pharmacy. The goal is to prevent theft and the introduction of counterfeit drugs into the system. Regulations are driving the adoption of such systems.

Capturing the notifications is typically the most difficult aspect of monitoring heterogeneous systems. Part of the challenge is technical—installing the adaptors that convert notifications from many different formats and protocols into a form that the CEP software can use. The larger challenge is organizational—getting cooperation from the companies, business units, and people that own and manage the applications that are the source of the notifications.

CEP-Enabled Applications

Some business applications are triggered by complex events or use complex events to alter their behavior. The work to acquire notifications and implement the CEP software is a relatively small, although vital, part of the project (see the bottom of Figure 8-6). These applications are the opposite of pure-play monitoring systems, where most of the effort goes into detecting the situations and the response is a minor aspect of project.

Some CEP-enabled applications are all-new but many are developed as extensions or modifications to existing business applications. For example, the sophisticated "enterprise nervous systems" used in modern airline operations are event-enabled systems of systems that encompass many CEP-enabled applications. The essential business operations of major air carriers have been largely automated for 40 years. Transaction workloads that incorporate the central seat reservation systems can exceed 30,000 transactions per second. Other airline applications manage flight schedules, food catering services, flight crew schedules, fueling, aircraft maintenance, gate assignments, and report arrival and departure times (see the right side of Figure 8-8). These are separate applications, developed largely independently at different times and owned by different business units.

The ability of an airline to respond to change has always depended on the speed and effectiveness of the information transfer between the sources of data and the many business units and applications that depend on it. Airlines continuously track hundreds of flights, each at a different stage in its life cycle. Information about the location of each plane and status of each flight becomes outdated in seconds or minutes.

The observational notifications that drive an airline nervous system originate in hundreds of locations (see the left side of Figure 8-8). Event sources include telemetry devices on the planes, reports from the Federal Aviation Administration, application systems on the ground, and gate agents and other people. Notifications are sent through a variety of communication technologies to a virtual clearinghouse which maintains flight status information in operational databases. The clearinghouse publishes notifications and accepts inquiries from application systems and people to keep them informed of changing conditions for every flight worldwide.

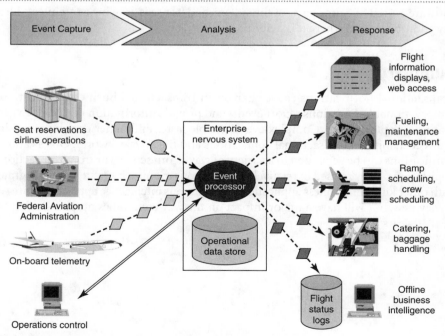

Figure 8-8: Events and complex events inform business applications.

An airline enterprise nervous system is all about situation awareness. Each business unit dynamically alters its plans when informed of schedule changes, weather, equipment failure, or other events. Planes and gates are reassigned as conditions change. If flights have become bunched together, there may not be enough available gates to serve all planes immediately. By having current information and predictions about likely future conditions, gate scheduling systems can make better decisions. Airlines pay penalties for flights that arrive after a night-time curfew, so flights that need an early departure are given priority over those that can afford to wait. The enterprise nervous system improves plane turnaround time because fuel, mechanics, food, crews, and baggage handlers are ready at the right moment. Fewer planes, gates, and employees can support the same number of flights. Passengers also have better access to information about the status of flights, and earlier warning of changes.

Airline networks are among the largest and most-complicated event-enabled systems. They combine the challenges of application integration with the challenges of high event volumes in the context of a highly competitive, cost-conscious industry. The underlying applications use a diverse set of operating systems, application servers, transaction-processing monitors, DBMSs, and network protocols. Many of the applications have been in place for years and are constantly being updated. Some applications were modified to accept notifications directly from the virtual clearinghouse. In other places, alerts are sent to people who intervene manually but use the underlying application systems to carry out the business functions. Most aspects of the airline nervous system don't use CEP software yet. They use simple events or minor sections of CEP logic coded directly into business applications. However, commercial CEP software is used for some parts of the system, and its use is growing as architects identify additional areas where it is helpful.

Summary

Transactional notifications cause changes in transactional business applications. Observational notifications report events and provide information that leads to generating complex events. Complex events enable faster and better decisions, causing indirect changes in transactional applications and the physical world. Observational notifications can be generated in a variety of ways from sensors or from transactional applications. They're used in relatively autonomous monitoring systems or integrated with other kinds of business applications. Continuous intelligence applications are relatively new, but will have a major impact on the way companies operate during the next 10 years.

9

The Role of Event Processing in SOA and Application Development

This chapter explores what it means to implement event processing in a commercial IT environment. We'll begin by looking at how service-oriented architecture (SOA) relates to event-driven architecture (EDA). Then, we'll discuss how projects that implement event processing differ from those that don't, and suggest six specific action items for achieving success in event processing.

Using Events in SOA

SOA is probably the most-talked-about architectural style for modern business applications. Unfortunately, the talk can be confusing because people use the term SOA to mean a variety of things. To some, SOA is a general term for any new distributed application. To others, it means an application that was built using web services technologies, specifically the Web Services Description Language (WSDL) and the SOAP communication protocol. Yet others have a concept of SOA that requires the use of the Web, representational state transfer (REST), or business process management (BPM). With this diversity of definitions, it is not surprising that some people think that SOA is obsolete or unimportant while others think that it will solve most of the world's problems. The reality is, of course, somewhere in between—SOA is a set of good ideas but it's not a panacea.

SOA and EDA are complementary notions. SOA applications, like other applications, can use request-driven or EDA interactions among their components. Conversely, many business applications that use EDA will also use SOA for some aspects of their construction. To clarify the overlap of SOA and EDA, we'll start by defining the nature of SOA.

SOA

SOA is based on the venerable concept of a service. One party, the service provider, performs a function to assist another party, the service consumer. Long before computers were invented, companies organized many parts of their operations as services. Today they use copy services, package and mail courier services, company cafeterias, shipping departments, accounting departments, human resources departments, legal services, security services, janitorial services, personnel recruiters, auditors, advertising agencies, and travel agencies. At a business level, a service provider is a department, workgroup, or some other business unit. For example, the HR department provides recruiting and other personnel-related services to other business units. Similarly, the IT department is a service provider to other departments. Some service providers are part of the company (they are internal departments) and others are part of another company (the work is contracted outside the company, or "outsourced").

In this context, a service consumer refers to a business unit that uses the service; it does not mean a private individual person acting as a customer. The "service" is technically the consumer's view of the provider's capabilities. A business unit can be a service consumer in some relationships and a service provider in others. The travel department is a consumer of the janitorial service every day, and it is a service provider to the accounting department when, for example, an accountant needs to travel.

Services are shared. All of the business units use the cafeteria, IT department, and enterprise network so that each group doesn't have to implement its own version of these functions. Moreover, a new company can start up more quickly by leveraging outsourced services from copy services, caterers, package and mail couriers, law firms, travel agencies, and other service providers.

The service structure improves a company's flexibility and efficiency. Each service provider is modular and largely autonomous. A company can replace its advertising agency without bringing in a new janitorial service because they are unrelated. It's relatively easy for each business unit to work with other service-providing business units because there is an informal or formal mutual understanding of the nature of the service. For example, the service provided by the company cafeteria is defined by a sign that lists the hours of operation, the menu, and the prices. If the cafeteria is outsourced, the service description will also be written into a legal contract between the company and the caterer.

Consumers generally don't have to know or care about the internals of a service provider's operation. The service is a "black box," so the consumer is relieved of the burden of understanding the details of the provider's operation. The provider benefits because it has the freedom to change its internal processes without telling the consumer, as long as the terms of the contract are not affected. For example, a mail and package courier can reroute its airplanes, build a new hub, or change the way it runs its sorting operations without needing permission from its customers as long as the service-level agreement (SLA) is not affected.

The characteristics that make the service concept helpful in organizing business units are translated into the software realm as SOA. SOA is defined as an architectural style for application software in which five principles are implemented:

▶ The application must be modular, so that software components (agents) can be added, replaced, or modified individually.

▶ The components must be distributable. They must be able to run on different computers and communicate with each other by sending messages over a network at run time.

▶ Component interfaces must be "discoverable" by another application developer. The interfaces and related externally visible characteristics of the software components must be clearly defined and documented in metadata. Metadata describes the input and output messages of each component and enough other information to enable developers to find and use the component as part of a new application. SOA metadata is almost always in a software form, such as in a file, web page, message, registry, or repository.

▶ A software component that provides an SOA service can be readily swapped out for another component that offers the same service as long as the new one uses the same interface as the old one. The interface design ("what to do") is separate from the internal service implementation ("how it is done").

▶ Service provider components must be shareable (or "reusable"). This means that they are designed and deployed in a manner that enables them to be invoked successively by disparate application systems or by multiple copies of the same application. The same code and data are available to users of any application that shares that component.

Any business application that implements these five principles is an SOA application. The combination of the first four principles implies that SOA components are "loosely coupled," a property that leads to flexibility. An SOA component can be added to the system or modified without causing unintended side effects or otherwise disrupting other components as long as the interface is constant. SOA systems can be developed, maintained, and expanded in small, easily understood increments, facilitating an "organic" approach to ever-changing business processes.

SOA emerged as a software architectural style during the 1990s as companies began implementing distributed applications on a large scale. The five principles of SOA represent what architects learned about best practices as they gained experience with component software. The term SOA first appeared in a 1996 Gartner report, but mainstream developers didn't use SOA routinely for another decade. It's now rare to build a new, distributed business application without adhering to the principles of SOA. The benefits of documenting the interface, making components replaceable, and making components shareable are clear. Modern software development tools make it easy to implement these characteristics. Experts differ on whether SOA is best implemented using REST or more-conventional interface styles, but few dispute the merits of SOA (using the definition given here).

Event-Driven SOA

The majority of the interactions in an SOA application are request-driven. It's natural for a service consumer to send a message to a service provider to request a service, and then get a reply containing some data or an acknowledgment that the service has been completed. However, most SOA application systems also have some aspects that are implemented using event-driven interactions.

Architectural styles are composable in the sense that multiple styles can apply simultaneously to one application system. SOA and EDA are composable—they are compatible and complementary. In Chapter 3, we explained the five principles of EDA:

▶ Notifications report a current event as it happens.

▶ Notifications are pushed not pulled.

▶ Consumers respond to events as soon as they are recognized.

▶ Notifications are one-way messages.

▶ Notifications are free of commands.

If an interaction conforms to the five principles of SOA and the five principles of EDA simultaneously, it is event-driven SOA. Virtually every SOA interaction, including request-driven SOA interactions, adheres to the first three principles of EDA. A request message is immediate, the request is pushed, and the service provider responds immediately. However, event-driven SOA diverges from request-driven SOA because of the last two principles. The notions of one-way, "fire and forget" messages and "free of commands" are what make event-driven SOA different from request-driven SOA. They are also what make EDA minimally coupled, whereas request-driven SOA is more coupled (despite the fact that it is loosely coupled compared to other kinds of request-driven interactions).

Conversely, most EDA interactions in business applications also qualify as SOA. EDA interactions are usually modular because of the separation of event producer and event consumer. They're also "swappable" because the producer or consumer can be replaced without modifying the other. Most EDA applications are also distributable (the event consumer can be on a different computer than the producer is on), discoverable (the event schema and other interface metadata are reasonably accessible to other developers), and shareable (an event consumer can receive notifications from multiple event producers and a notification from one producer can be delivered to multiple consumers). However, not all EDA systems qualify as SOA. Some EDA applications run entirely on one computer (the event producer and consumer are on the same platform). Developers can hide the interface metadata so that other developers can't send or receive notifications from an EDA component. The channel used between a producer and consumer can be closed to other components.

Event-driven SOA interactions should be used for those aspects of an SOA application for which the component that acts first doesn't need a response from the second component. Event-driven SOA is especially useful in data-consistency, information-dissemination, and situation-awareness scenarios. Conventional request-driven SOA interactions should be used for the aspects of an application that require a reply to the first component.

The process of developing an SOA application that includes both event-driven and request-driven services is similar to the process used for developing a request-driven-only SOA application with a few important differences. The next two sections of this report explore best practices for developing SOA applications that have both types of services. First we'll look at the communication and granularity issues that arise when specifying SOA services and events. Then we'll look at how the relatively new concept of "service components" can improve the quality of an SOA application.

Specifying SOA Services and Events

Many of the issues that arise when designing request-driven SOA services also arise when designing event notifications. In both cases, analysts and software engineers must document the contract or interface between the components. This includes defining the contents of the request, response, and notification messages (for example, XML documents). For request-driven services, the function of the service provider must also be specified: Will it GET certain documents, PUT some data in a database, LOOK_UP_CUSTOMER_CREDIT_RATING, or perform some other function? Event-driven interactions don't specify a function, but the developer must specify the message topic and sometimes other properties associated with the notification.

For both kinds of interface, developers must also resolve communication and service quality issues, such as:

▶ How will the sender obtain the address of the appropriate message recipient?

▶ What should be done to ensure security and privacy?

▶ Is the sender responsible for trying to send the message again if the first attempt fails, or will this be handled by the channel?

▶ Can the message be delivered twice or will this cause errors in the application logic? (Look up idempotence in Wikipedia if you're interested in pursuing this question further.)

▶ What should be done if the recipient isn't available?

▶ Is the message compressed?

▶ Is the message part of a group of related messages that must be handled together, or is it an individual message?

These issues aren't unique to SOA or EDA—they are inherent in the design of any distributed application. We won't address them here. However, the granularity of a service or event has emerged as an especially important consideration for all SOA interfaces, so it warrants some discussion.

Granularity for request-driven interfaces is the extent of the function that will be provided by the service provider. Granularity for an event notification is the extent or scope of the happening that is described by the event object. There is no simple formula for determining the proper granularity of an SOA interface. Analysts and architects must understand the business process and its data to identify the granularity of services and events for a particular business purpose.

As a rule, a well-designed SOA software service should usually map directly to a business task. Business managers, analysts, and software engineers can use the same service as a natural unit of composition on both a conceptual design level (describing a task in a business process) and an implementation level (describing the work of a software component that supports that task). For example, "Verify ZIP code for this address" is a narrowly focused task that is readily understood by business analysts and end users as part of a business process. It can (and should) also be implemented as an SOA service by a software component that can be shared by multiple applications.

Similarly, a well-designed business event object should usually map directly to a business document, part of a document, or something that could have been a document. A transactional notification is often modeled on a paper form in the same way that an SOA service interface is modeled on a business function. For example, a purchase order form, purchase order acknowledgment, and invoice can be used as starting points to design the respective transactional notifications.

A more complex task, such as "Give me this customer's profile information," also constitutes a potentially good request-driven service because it is meaningful to businesspeople and it represents a single, potentially shareable task. However, this broader, coarse-grained function would typically be a *composite* service because it involves multiple subordinate tasks. The service provider component for this service could invoke a series of other services to retrieve demographic information, account balances, transaction information (from mortgage, savings, checking, and credit card systems), and reports of recent customer activity on a website. A composite service coordinates the work of simpler services. It may be implemented in a regular programming language, such as C#, Java, or Visual Basic, or in a BPM tool using, for example, Business Process Execution Language (BPEL). In object-oriented programming, the component would be called a process object because it directs the work of other objects.

A complex event bears some similarities to a composite service. It is coarse grained in the sense that it represents the collective significance of a set of simpler entities (its base or member events). However, the complex event summarizes and abstracts multiple simpler event objects, which are data, whereas a composite service summarizes and abstracts multiple simpler services, which are functions. Functions may encapsulate data behind the scenes, but the component that sends the request doesn't see the data directly; it only sees the request and response messages. The fundamental distinction between requests and events makes the notion of granularity different.

Conventional wisdom holds that SOA services are coarse grained. However, that doesn't mean that SOA services are always broad in their scope. As you have seen, some good services are narrowly focused ("verify ZIP code"). A request-driven service should be narrow enough that its work is entirely directed at a single task (it is *functionally coherent*). That makes the service easier to implement and more likely to be useful in multiple different applications. Functions that are of potential use in multiple applications are good candidates to be services. If a function is unique to one application, it should probably be combined into the service consumer (requester) component to avoid the complexity and overhead of building a separate service provider component and sending messages over a network.

On the other hand, services should be broad enough to perform an entire task. This reduces the number of services that must be used to carry out a business transaction. Calls to invoke an SOA service are different from most procedure calls or method invocations because SOA is intended to work across a network. Most procedure calls and method invocations have relatively low overhead because they take place within one computer. By contrast, an SOA service provider is usually on a different computer than the service consumer (requester), so every request and reply message pair entails significant overhead and latency. Latency can grow to unacceptable levels if a service is invoked too many times in the course of one transaction. Therefore, services should be designed to encompass enough function to justify the overhead of communicating over a network (that is also true for remote procedures and remote methods). Developers and architects who are interested in understanding service design in more depth will benefit from reading Martin Fowler's *Patterns of Enterprise Application Architecture* (see Appendix A).

Note: Developers should design SOA services to minimize the number of messages that they receive and send, because they are invoked over a network. Service interactions should be less "chatty" (have fewer back and forth messages) than interactions with local (intra-computer) modules.

A similar set of considerations applies to event design. It's impractical to put a notification onto a company's network for every business event that occurs. Large companies capture 10,000 to 10 million business events per second in software through sensors, application systems, market data feeds, and other event sources. That's almost a billion events per day at the low end and almost a trillion in other companies.

The solution is to distribute event-processing logic to reduce the volume of notifications as close to the source as possible. Developers use event-processing agents (EPAs) to filter events at the source application, sensor, or adaptor that sits between the source and the network. In a few sophisticated systems, the filter can be adjusted dynamically at any time. EPA can get instructions from elsewhere in the event-processing network (EPN) to stop publishing notifications that no event consumers want to receive. In rare cases, the EPA may be able to stop the source sensor or application from generating the notifications entirely. More commonly, the EPA merely filters (discards) notifications that are not wanted, forwarding only those notifications for which there is an event consumer.

It doesn't make sense to flood the network with thousands or millions of simple notifications if multiple event consumers are really interested in the same, higher-level event notification. Distributed EPAs can aggregate simple notifications and find patterns so that a few complex-event notifications are published onto the network rather than thousands of simple events. Chapter 7 noted that the volume of events is typically sharply reduced at each level in an event hierarchy. Developers generally don't have much control over the type of raw event information that is available. They have to use whatever a sensor, application, or web source can produce. However, they can control the nature of the notifications that are published on the enterprise network through the use of CEP-capable adaptors.

A few commercial CEP platforms have been specifically designed to operate on a distributed basis. They filter events and synthesize complex events near or at the event sources to minimize the number of notifications that must be sent on the network and to reduce the need for multiple event consumers to recalculate the same complex events.

Note: Complex-event notifications should be shared ("reused") among event consumers for the same reasons that request-driven services should be shared wherever practical.

Service Components

Arguably the most important advance in SOA maturity in the past decade is the *service component* concept. The essence of a service component is to have more-complete metadata about the SOA service provider. Prior to service components, most SOA applications had a vulnerability found in procedure calls, most forms of object-oriented programming, and early Common Object Request Broker Architecture (CORBA). This vulnerability was that their metadata focused on documenting the interfaces through which they were invoked (their input and output parameters) but ignored their dependencies on the services that *they* invoked. There was no formal way to discover what services a service called unless you had the source code of the service. There also wasn't enough information about the local security and integrity characteristics of the service provider. By 1998, some architectural experts such as Clemens Szyperski (see Appendix A) had clearly described the problem and laid out the solution. An excellent explication of the service component concept can also be found in Zoran Stojanovic's *A Method for Component-Based and Service-Oriented Software Systems Engineering* (see Appendix A).

In a service component approach, the metadata for a service provider component covers the input and output messages, the identity of other services and remote modules that it invokes, the databases that it uses, its possible error conditions, and its security, performance, and availability policy characteristics. Vendors are moving to implement the service component concept, and some efforts are even being made to standardize it. The CORBA Component Model specification in CORBA v.3.0 outlined how to implement the service component concept as early as 1999, although the popularity of CORBA itself had already started to decline, so it did not achieve mainstream usage. The modern design model that underlies Microsoft's Windows Communication Foundation (WCF) represents a vendor-specific way to implement service components. Finally, the Organization for the Advancement of Structured Information Standards (OASIS), an international open standards consortium, formed six new technical committees in August 2007, under an umbrella called the OASIS Open Composite Services Architecture Member Section, to develop the Service Component Architecture (SCA) specification. Most of the early work on service components was directed at request-driven services, but recent efforts have been undertaken to extend it to improve its support for event-driven services.

Action Items for Successful Event Processing

There are no event-processing projects per se; there are only development projects that use event processing in some aspects of a new or modified application system. Almost all large or complex business processes have some aspects that should be implemented with EDA, CEP, or both. To succeed at event processing, an enterprise must do six things well:

▶ Acquire event-processing skills by either training its staff or hiring outside consultants

▶ Incorporate event processing into its IT architecture

▶ Use event-enabled packaged applications

▶ Implement a software infrastructure that facilitates event processing

▶ Integrate event processing into SOA initiatives

▶ Develop event models and manage events and event patterns

The remainder of this chapter explores these action items in more detail.

Acquire Event-Processing Skills

Business and system analysts, enterprise and application architects, project leaders, and anyone else involved in collecting application requirements, modeling business processes, and developing high-level system designs must understand when and how to use EDA and CEP.

Educate Your IT Staff

Simple, event-at-a-time EDA is underutilized in most companies because analysts and software engineers often fall back on more-familiar design patterns, particularly batch processing and request-driven design patterns. It's not that EDA is hard to understand—much of it is common sense. However, analysts and architects who haven't used MOM, document-driven systems, or similar techniques may be unfamiliar with some of the mechanical details of EDA. Chapters 3, 6, and 7 address these issues and clarify how to identify the parts of a business process that would benefit from EDA.

Application developers often build rudimentary forms of CEP into applications without realizing that they are doing CEP. Whenever you write application logic that combines two or more messages that contain data about business events, or use any other set of data that reports two or more events, you are doing CEP. When the logic is not complicated, there may be nothing to gain by calling it CEP or learning anything more. However, a formal understanding of CEP and the use of commercial CEP platforms are helpful if the volume of events is high, the latency of response must be low, and the rules for processing the event patterns will change fairly often. Chapters 3, 7, and 8 provide information on this subject.

CEP is taught in a few computer science programs, mostly at the graduate school level, sometimes under the label of "event stream processing" or "stream processing." The Event Processing Technical Society (see www.ep-ts.com) also has a workgroup that is developing a curriculum for event processing in collaboration with researchers and educators at a group of universities. Appendix A provides pointers to books and other resources that can help you if you want to learn more about this field.

Leverage Outside Expertise

Companies that want to accelerate the development or lower the risk of a project that involves event processing may hire architects, developers, or project managers from a system integrator or software vendor. Consultants at a system integrator with a background in EDA and CEP are typically associated with a BPM or SOA team.

Most CEP software vendors have consulting practices. These are usually good sources of product-specific advice and general help on CEP implementation. Virtually all vendors of MOM, enterprise service buses (ESBs), and other SOA infrastructure have consultants that understand simple EDA and its role in modern application development. Some software vendors and system integrators offer application templates or industry frameworks that include software products, data models, best practices, and sample application flows that incorporate event-processing features. Outside experts may help your staff learn more quickly, especially if your people actively work with them.

Incorporate Event Processing into IT Architecture

Some leading-edge corporate IT architecture programs are beginning to pay attention to event processing, although IT architecture historically did little or nothing to explicitly address EDA or CEP.

Companies that have formal enterprise architecture guidelines that prescribe design patterns should document their guidance on when to use event-, request-, and time-driven patterns (see Chapters 3 and 6 for a discussion of some of the basic principles). Some companies separate enterprise architecture from application architecture. Enterprise architecture is strategic and general in scope—it answers questions such as, "How should all of our systems work?" Application architecture (sometimes called solution architecture) is more tactical and specific—it answers questions such as "How should this system or set of systems work?" Both types of architecture should allow all three design patterns and provide advice on where to use each.

Companies that have a review process that verifies application system design as part of the development cycle should examine the conceptual design of every new system to confirm that EDA and CEP have been utilized where appropriate. The architecture review committee should expect almost every large application system to have some EDA components. Most large systems should also have some continuous-monitoring capabilities. These will leverage observational notifications and do some type of CEP, although commercial CEP platforms will appear in a minority of projects during the next several years.

Use Event-Enabled Packaged Applications

The presence of event-processing features should be a factor when selecting packaged applications, for the same reasons that it is a factor in the design of good custom applications.

Packaged applications were historically poor at emitting event notifications when a business event was detected or generated within the scope of their processing. They did a reasonably good job of accepting and responding to incoming events, but they didn't do as well for sending outgoing notifications to other applications. This has changed, however. Many packaged applications can now emit event notifications for many types of business events. This is usually a configuration option, so developers who are installing and tailoring the package must study the business requirements to iden- tify what type of notifications should be sent. Your other applications will have use for some, but not all, of the events that a packaged application could potentially send.

Some packaged applications are much better at event processing than others, so it's worth the effort to investigate how well it is implemented. EDA can be particularly important for application integration scenarios that require heterogeneous applica- tions of disparate origins to work together.

Many packaged applications have business dashboards or other continuous-mon- itoring and alerting features as part of the product. The vendor will rarely refer to these as "CEP" capabilities, although they technically would qualify as a limited type of CEP. Monitoring features are visible and generally desirable, so their presence will probably be pretty obvious if you get a demonstration of the software before you buy it. Most dashboard and monitoring features in packaged applications are fairly lim- ited in scope. They monitor activities and parts of business processes that are con- ducted within the package, but they are not designed to monitor events that occur in other applications or elsewhere in the company.

Implement an Event-Processing Software Infrastructure

Event processing is a design concept that doesn't necessarily require any particular type of middleware or development tool. However, many event-processing applica- tions would be impractical without the use of appropriate commercial middleware infrastructure or CEP tools.

Support for Event Communication

EDA and CEP systems need some messaging infrastructure to convey the notifications from event producers to event consumers. All large companies already use the Web, e-mail, and other basic message-capable communication protocols, and most already use MOM, ESBs, and SOAP in some locations. Therefore, more than half of all event-processing projects don't need any new messaging software, because they can use the infrastructure that is already in place. However, projects that are implementing demanding new applications that have high volume, low latency, high integrity, or other requirements may need to acquire commercial MOM, ESB, or other infrastructure products if they are not already present. From the network and middleware perspective, notifications are just messages. A company's event network is conceptual—it's physically just a part of the general network that carries voice, e-mail, web inquiries, remote procedure calls (RPCs), DBMS traffic, and other communication.

Guidance on selecting messaging technology should be part of your enterprise and application architecture programs, if you have such programs. Companies should also have a messaging technical support group equipped with configuration and monitoring tools for deploying the messaging infrastructure and managing it at run time.

CEP, Dashboard, and Other Monitoring Products

Before 2004, developers of applications that perform CEP usually wrote their own CEP logic, rather than buying a commercial CEP platform or other commercial product. Even today, some demanding CEP applications and most dashboards and other monitoring capabilities are built with standard application development tools or off-the-shelf utilities. For low volume or simple applications, this is usually still the best strategy. However, more-demanding CEP applications require sophisticated algorithms and purpose-built CEP architectures, so companies will sometimes be better served by commercial CEP technology.

Commercial CEP, dashboard, and monitoring technology can be acquired as part of a CEP-enabled application, such as a financial trading platform or supply chain management (SCM) product, or it can be bought as a dedicated CEP platform, business event processing (BEP) system, appliance, or other point product. Companies that acquire CEP, dashboard, or monitoring software generally make their decisions on a project-by-project basis. These products have disparate specializations, so they are chosen according to the unique requirements of each application.

Where practical, architects and project leaders should use the same CEP, dashboard, BEP, and monitoring products for multiple projects to minimize license fees and training and support costs. However, virtually all companies will acquire multiple, partially overlapping, event-processing-related products during the next five years. At some point in the future, some companies will designate a preferred CEP platform, dashboard-building tool, or monitoring product as part of their enterprise technology architecture for use in projects around the company. However, the nature of CEP projects varies so much that no one set of products will be right for all CEP applications in a large company.

Integrate Event Processing into SOA Initiatives

Many development projects that implement simple EDA, CEP, or both are promoted under the aegis of an SOA or BPM strategy. EDA, SOA, and BPM are compatible concepts that are often used together. An event-driven SOA application implements the principles of SOA and EDA simultaneously. Moreover, systems that leverage BPM generally use CEP in their monitoring capabilities (see Chapter 10 for more explanation of the links between BPM and event processing).

In view of these overlaps, companies should fold much of their EDA and CEP work into their SOA programs. Companies generally should not build a separate competency center (or "center of excellence") for EDA. The SOA competency center may have one or two architects or analysts who have more training or experience in EDA, MOM, or CEP than other members of the team, but they should all be part of one team.

Conversely, it is a mistake to implement an SOA program that can't support event-driven SOA and some type of continuous business monitoring from its inception. Some companies have shied away from event-driven SOA, consciously or not, to focus exclusively on traditional request-driven SOA. However, this results in overusing request-driven SOA and batch (time-driven) processing in new SOA systems. There is no benefit to deferring adoption of event-driven SOA—it's not a major burden to undertake and its advantages should be tapped even by the initial SOA applications.

Incorporating event-driven SOA and CEP-based monitoring into SOA and BPM initiatives involves more than just organizational and training issues. Many messages used in event-driven SOA should be implemented with the same management tools, industry standards, security mechanisms, and middleware infrastructure products that are used for request-driven SOA interfaces. For example, event-driven SOA is commonly implemented with XML messages, so the same metadata format (for example, XSD) can also be used for event notifications. An ESB- or MOM-based SOA infrastructure and protocols such as HTTP and SOAP can support both event- and request-driven communication. However, most commercial SOA registry and repository products are primarily designed to support request-driven SOA so developers may need to undertake custom extensions to fully support event processing.

Some CEP projects are too specialized to belong under an SOA or BPM program, for organizational and technical reasons. They may have specialized event sources (such as third-party event data feeds); their own ways to define event types; specialized communication protocols; non-XML (binary) data formats; and alternative monitoring tools and metadata management technology.

Develop Event Models and Manage Events

Event-processing functions coexist and are intertwined with transactional business functions, social application activities, office productivity applications, collaboration, and other kinds of application functions. With the exception of some pure-play monitoring systems (see Chapter 8), event processing is just a description of how part of an application system works.

The design of business events, notifications, and event patterns is partly a black art, like data modeling, form design, or designing SOA services. Analysts, architects, and software developers must determine all the following:

▶ Which business events are important and relevant

▶ What notifications should be generated to report those business events, and the topics (or "subjects") of the notifications

▶ What data items to include in the event types

▶ Which application components will produce each kind of notification

▶ What channels will transport the notifications

▶ What CEP algorithms to apply, and what event patterns to look for (this is pattern discovery; see Chapter 7)

▶ What the consumer components and people should do with the notifications and alerts once they get them

Events, notifications, and event patterns are designed at the same point in the development cycle that SOA services and databases are designed. This is typically after the business requirements and overall process model have been explored but fairly early in the development cycle. In modern iterative development approaches, this is a recurring activity. After some initial parts of a system are deployed, they are used, monitored, and periodically refined, and additional segments of the application are added.

An application system typically uses only a few kinds of event types—often under 10, and usually under 25. However, the business processes in a large department or business unit may collectively involve a dozen or more application systems with many dozens or even hundreds of events, channels, and event patterns. A large company will have hundreds of application systems and thousands of business processes, potentially requiring thousands of different event types, channels, and patterns.

A company's event traffic is an event "cloud," not an event stream, because it isn't organized in any systematic way. A company's event cloud is part of the larger event cloud of its virtual enterprise that encompasses some of its suppliers, customers, and other business partners. The virtual enterprise event cloud is, in turn, a subset of the global event cloud that includes all companies, consumers, governmental bodies, and other organizations that produce or consume events.

We are not aware of any company that has developed an enterprise-wide map or registry that documents all its events and event patterns. An enterprise event cloud is probably too complex to ever centrally manage at a detailed level. A company that formally documents and manages even some of its important events is ahead of the industry mainstream because many companies don't do any systematic event management. However, we are aware of some leading-edge companies who are beginning to manage their events in a federated fashion, similar to the way they manage their SOA services.

As indicated in the previous section, event management should usually be conducted by people within an SOA competency center rather than in a separate organization. Many large companies already have SOA competency centers in each division, subsidiary, functional area, or large department. These are typically federated and loosely overseen by a central, corporate-level SOA competency center. The central organization sets company-wide policies, provides architectural guidance, and coordinates the communication among the distributed competency centers. Managers try to balance the competing forces of central control and local autonomy.

A federated SOA competency center can be extended to cover event management. If a competency center faithfully collects and stores metadata for all notifications and event types in a registry or repository, project teams can use them in future application development wherever they are relevant to the new business requirements. Event streams used for one purpose will sometimes be relevant for new purposes. Systematic event management can reduce, although not entirely eliminate, redundant event data.

A significant amount of event sharing ("reuse") occurs after the fact with event logs. Numerous important applications are already in use that mine event logs from previous hours and days to provide insight into things that have happened. Customer buying preferences are detected, credit card fraud is discovered, and airline schedules are studied and improved by using event logs.

A person or group in a competency center should systematically collect and maintain metadata for all events types, notifications, and event patterns that are used in the applications and SOA services in the business unit. If an event is formatted in XML, its metadata can be managed in an XML Schema Description (XSD), Schematron, or similar mechanism, just as request-driven SOA documents are. However, the reports generated for developers and managers need a way to distinguish event notifications from other kinds of SOA documents. Moreover, events that use binary data will require different metadata mechanisms than those used for XML data.

Governance for events lags the governance of request-driven SOA services in its maturity. Leading-edge companies are beginning to systematically manage notification topics and event types, but we are not aware of any company that is managing event patterns, event-processing language (EPL), or event hierarchy metadata in a systematic way. Companies that use CEP may implement these things within individual CEP application projects, but don't document them elsewhere in an organized fashion. Neither are we aware of any features in commercial SOA-oriented registries and repositories for managing topic trees, event patterns, EPL, causality, or event hierarchies. Repositories are generally extensible, so it should be possible for an adroit event administrator to extend a repository to handle these things. It's also likely that repository vendors will add support for this in the future.

Companies should allow their portfolio of events and patterns to evolve organically, bottom up, as part of each application project's development process. We don't recommend developing a detailed company-wide "as is" inventory or "to be" architecture of event notifications and patterns. Similar activities for enterprise-wide SOA service models and enterprise data models were notoriously unsuccessful where they were attempted. Sweeping architecture projects require a large investment in staff time and have long-term payback, if they pay back at all. The resulting architecture documents don't age well—their value degrades rapidly because changes in the IT portfolio and the business make the information obsolete. Moreover, the documents are commonly underused or entirely ignored by the project teams building application systems. The value of enterprise-wide architecture is inherently limited because the needs of future projects cannot be accurately anticipated in advance. By the time developers begin work on a new project, events and patterns designed months or years earlier will usually need to be changed.

Summary

SOA and EDA are complementary—they can be used together as event-driven SOA. Event-driven SOA can coexist with request-driven SOA and time-driven designs in the same application. Event processing is a departure from traditional IT practices in certain ways, so it may require companies to acquire additional expertise and software infrastructure. Companies should modify their IT architecture and SOA governance practices to support event processing.

10

Positioning Event Processing in the IT World

In this chapter, we'll explain how event processing contributes to business process management (BPM) initiatives. We'll also look at the relationship between traditional business intelligence (BI) and business activity monitoring (BAM) systems. Finally, we'll compare and contrast complex event processing (CEP) technology with rule engines and business rule management systems (BRMSs).

Events in Business Process Management

BPM projects are more successful when they use event-driven architecture (EDA) and CEP appropriately. BPM encompasses two related concepts:

▶ In some contexts, it is a discipline for designing, simulating, monitoring, and optimizing systems in a deliberate and systematic way that is conscious of end-to-end business processes.

▶ Elsewhere, it refers to the use of BPM software, such as orchestration engines and workflow engines, at run time to direct the sequence of execution of software components and human activity steps in a process.

Both concepts of BPM always involve events, but they don't always involve event objects or the discipline of event processing. The next two sections explain the role of events in BPM initiatives.

The BPM Discipline

The BPM discipline is a collection of methods, policies, metrics, management practices, and tools used to design, run, and manage systems that support a company's business processes. Business managers, users, business analysts, and software engineers all have roles to play when using a BPM approach.

The life cycle of a business process begins with process discovery, analysis, and design. Process modelers develop an understanding of how the business should work, not just how it currently works. The goal is to avoid re-creating a suboptimal process in new technology ("paving the cow paths"). Business processes and data are modeled to develop a "to be" business architecture—a conceptual view of how things will be done in the future. A process modeler, usually a business analyst or system analyst, will take the lead in developing and documenting the logical rules for the sequence of activities and data flows. This is the basis for determining which aspects of the process should be automated in application software and which should be done manually or in a machine of some kind. This leads to subsequent steps in the development cycle, including detailed design, coding, testing, and deployment, and then maintaining application systems and databases.

Note: The maxims that system design should begin at a business level and that it should reflect a broad, end-to-end view of the process have been part of good IT practices for many decades.

The origin of systematic approaches to business process design can be traced to Frederick Winslow Taylor, the inventor of scientific management and the time-and-motion study, who did his major work between 1880 to 1915. Scientific management provided an early foundation to the much-later business process re-engineering (BPR) movement that was inspired by Hammer and Champy's seminal 1993 book *Reengineering the Corporation: A Manifesto for Business Revolution* (see Appendix A).

The underlying principles of modern BPM reflect the insights of scientific management and BPR. However, modern BPM puts more emphasis on continuous change and ad hoc variability. The process and the business environment in which the process lives are constantly monitored and measured. Business processes are adjusted frequently, and hence the terms "continuous process improvement" and "business process improvement" have become goals for many advanced development organizations. Processes are becoming better able to support instance agility because they allow certain flow decisions to be made by a person dynamically at run time. Activities may be skipped or executed out of order, or additional activities may be inserted into the process. This is especially important for semistructured business processes that cannot be fully planned in advance.

Software vendors offer a variety of sophisticated tools for business process analysis, modeling, and simulation. However, many BPM initiatives are still carried out with manual analysis and simple drawing tools.

BPM Software

BPM software manages the flow of business processes at run time. It keeps track of each instance of a business process, using rules to evaluate events as they occur and programmatically activating the next step for each instance at the appropriate time. Vendors offer several types of run-time BPM software products, including orchestration engines, workflow products, composite application tools, and other BPM tools. Orchestration tools primarily control activities that are executed by software agents. Workflow tools primarily control activities that are executed by people.

BPM software is sold as a separate product or bundled into a business process management suite (BPMS), enterprise service bus (ESB), packaged application suite, or other application infrastructure product. A BPMS is the most complete of the product types that offer run-time BPM software. It includes tools for all of the aspects of the BPM discipline, including process modeling, analysis, simulation, and run-time monitoring and reporting.

The sequence of execution and the rules for controlling the conditional flow of a process are mostly or entirely specified at development time by a software engineer or a business analyst. Most process development tools have a graphical interface, although sometimes a scripting language or traditional programming language can be used. Modern BPM also seeks to make it possible for power users and managers outside the IT department to directly modify a business process in certain, limited ways without the direct involvement of IT staff.

The BPM discipline doesn't require the use of BPM software at run time. A process can be designed with a formal BPM methodology and modeled and simulated with BPM design tools, but still be instantiated as an application system that doesn't use run-time BPM software. When run-time BPM software is not used, the process flow is controlled by scripts, application programs, or direct human control. Conversely, run-time BPM software can be used without a formal BPM design program. However, the trend in application development projects is toward using both.

BPM is naturally complementary to service-oriented architecture (SOA). SOA's modular nature and well-documented interfaces can reduce the effort required to modify or add activities in a business process. SOA applications are more likely to use BPM engines at run time than traditional (non-SOA) applications are.

....

Note: SOA can be successful without using either development-time BPM design tools or run-time BPM orchestration or workflow software. However, you should never develop an SOA application without considering the architecture of the business process and considering the end-to-end business process model prior to development.

BPM and EDA

Business processes always involve business events in a general sense. However, they aren't event-driven in every aspect, nor do they use EDA for every interaction. As you know, most processes are a mix of event-, request-, and time-driven interactions. We'll describe the relationship between BPM and EDA in this section. The next section describes the role of CEP in BPM.

The disciplines of event processing and BPM sometimes use different terms to describe the same phenomena. Consider an order-to-cash business process consisting of the five steps shown in the visible process at the bottom of Figure 10-1:

A. Capturing a customer's order

B. Performing a manual approval if the order has some unusual characteristics

C. Filling the order

D. Shipping the goods

E. Issuing a bill (concurrently with shipping)

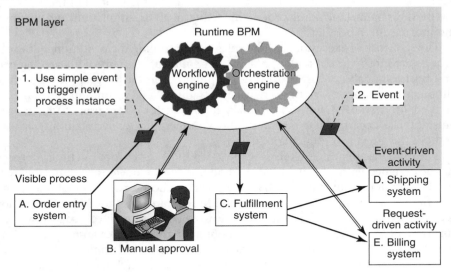

Figure 10-1: Using EDA with BPM.

In event-processing terminology, running through this whole process once to implement a specific action such as "Fred Smith buys a laptop" would be a coarse-grained business event. In BPM terminology, this would be a "process instance" or "business transaction."

In both BPM and event-processing terms, the process instance is initiated by a business event—capturing Fred's laptop order in the order entry system (A). The order-capture event is fine-grained. It is only one of many business events that take place within the larger "Fred Smith buys a laptop" event or process instance. In event-processing terms, manual approval (B), order fulfillment (C), shipping the goods (D), and issuing a bill (E) would also be business events. Within each, additional layers of more-detailed events might be identified, studied, and implemented. In BPM terms, each of these steps is an "activity." The event-processing perspective describes the change that occurs, whereas the BPM perspective describes the actions that carry out the change, but they're referring to the same part of the same process.

The relationships among agents that implement this business process can be structured in an event- or request-driven manner, or a combination of the two. Assume that BPM software is being used to orchestrate the flow of this process. The order-entry application (A) can inform the run-time BPM software that a new order has arrived by sending a notification containing an event object that says "Fred Smith just submitted an order for a laptop" (see "1. Use simple event to trigger new process instance" in Figure 10-1). Each event in an event stream from application A would trigger a new process instance (a separate order). Alternatively, application A could have triggered the start of a new process instance in a non-event-driven way by invoking a request/reply web service that instructed the BPM engine to "enter new laptop order for Fred Smith and send a reply back to acknowledge that the order had been received." Either way, the BPM software would create a new process instance and assume control of the process, triggering steps B, C, D, and E in succession until the process instance for Fred's purchase had completed.

The choice between an EDA or a request-driven style of interaction between application A and the run-time BPM engine has implications on the looseness of the coupling and the agility of the application. But either technique accomplishes the goal of signaling the occurrence of a business event that initiates a new business process instance. Similarly, the BPM software can trigger each subsequent activity step by issuing a request (steps B and E) or by sending event notifications (steps C and D). The notification that triggers step D is labeled "2. Event" in Figure 10-1. In some cases, an activity or the whole process can be time-driven rather than request- or event-driven (not shown in Figure 10-1).

The run-time BPM software (workflow engine or orchestration engine) must be aware of certain events to know when to start or stop activities. For example, it must learn that a previous step has concluded before it starts the next step. Again, an EDA-style notification can be used to convey this information within the run-time BPM software, or a request-driven mechanism may be used.

BPM and CEP

Conventional BPM engines control the process flow by applying rules that refer to things that have happened to the application software that is implementing the business process (in this case, it would be steps A through E). A recent advance in BPM technology involves the use of CEP software to augment the intelligence of run-time BPM software (see "1. CEP assists BPM engines" in Figure 10-2). The CEP engine gets information about events that occur outside this business process from sources such as sensors, the Web, or other application systems. It also gets information about events that are occurring within the business process from the BPM software. From these base events, it can synthesize complex events. These are forwarded to the BPM software to enable sophisticated, context-dependent, situation-aware flow decisions. Only a few BPM engines have this capability today, but we expect this to become more common in the future.

Most commercial run-time BPM software products have a BAM dashboard feature for process monitoring (this is sometimes called "process intelligence"). Run-time BPM software emits notifications to report events that occur in the life of each process instance. The monitoring software captures these events, tracks the history of each instance, calculates average process duration and other statistics, and reports on the health of the operation through the dashboard and other notification mechanisms. The monitor can give early warnings of anomalies for individual process instances and for aggregates (groups of instances, such as all orders for computers submitted in the past week). Process-monitoring dashboards generally enable the user to drill down into the detailed history of an individual process instance when necessary.

All process monitors implement a basic form of CEP in the sense that they apply rules and perform computations on multiple event objects to calculate what is hap-

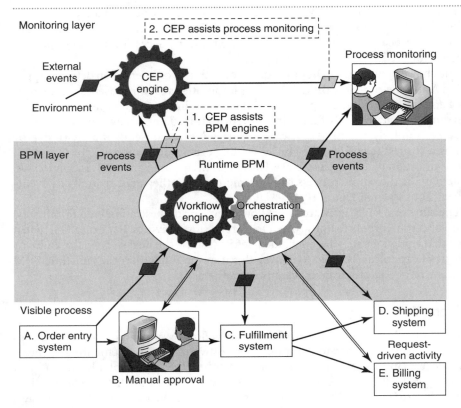

Figure 10-2: Using CEP with BPM.

pening in a business process. However, process monitors are not general-purpose CEP engines, and most process monitors don't listen to events from outside the managed business process (that is, all of their input is derived from internal process events happening within applications A through E). However, a few leading-edge projects have linked CEP engines with process-monitoring tools (see "2. CEP assists process monitoring" in Figure 10-2) to provide a broad, robust, situation-awareness capability that encompasses both internal process events and external business events. We expect that this will become more common in the future.

Process monitoring can also be implemented in scenarios where there is no runtime BPM software (not shown in Figure 10-2). Business processes that are not controlled by run-time BPM software are more common than those that are. Businesspeople still want visibility into what is happening in those processes so that they may deploy a process monitor and BAM dashboard. Supply chain management is a type of process monitoring that usually is implemented without run-time BPM software, or with only small parts of the supply chain under the control of run-time BPM software.

Summary of Event Processing in BPM

The BPM and event-processing disciplines evolved independently, but they are beginning to influence each other more heavily as CEP moves beyond technical domains to support business applications, and as BPM becomes more sophisticated and dynamic. The relevant technologies are a good fit with each other, and the resulting synergy produces better process management and business decisions (see Figure 10-3). A combined discipline is forming under the label "Event-Driven Business Process Management" (EDBPM) encompassing a body of work on technology and best practices.

Relevance of EDA to BPM	Relevance of CEP to BPM
Single event can trigger new process instance	Business process monitor can use complex events to track and report the health of a process and its individual instances
Single event can trigger new activity step within a process	Run-time orchestration or workflow engine can make decisions on process flow based on complex events
Activity can emit a new event notification to trigger another process or activity	CEP software can identify a threat or opportunity situation that triggers a new business process instance

Figure 10-3: Summary of event processing in BPM.

Event Processing in Business Intelligence

Enterprises use business intelligence (BI) systems to make better decisions. BI applications can be categorized as analyst-driven, process-driven, or strategy-driven. Analyst-driven systems, the most common type of BI applications, rarely use event-driven CEP. Some process-driven BI systems deal with near-real-time information—these are known as business activity monitoring (BAM) systems. BAM systems leverage event-driven CEP extensively. Strategy-driven BI systems, including performance management systems, occasionally use event-driven CEP. This section explains these three kinds of BI in more detail and then describes the relationship between BI and event processing.

Analyst-Driven BI

Analyst-driven BI applications primarily serve analysts and knowledge workers. They provide in-depth, domain-specific analysis and information delivery using ad hoc queries, periodic reports, data mining, and statistical techniques. This style of BI answers questions such as:

▶ Do we have enough account executives on the street to meet our sales quota?

▶ Which customer segments are buying the most?

▶ Should we retire a product line because it is underperforming?

BAM

BAM provides situation awareness and access to current business performance indicators to improve the speed and effectiveness of operations. It's a type of continuous intelligence application and it uses CEP in most usage scenarios.

BAM differs from analyst-driven BI in fundamental ways:

▶ BAM systems are typically used by line managers or other businesspeople charged with making immediate operational decisions. In contrast, analyst-driven BI systems are used mostly by staff people preparing recommendations for strategic or tactical decisions.

▶ Much of the input for BAM is event data that has arrived within the past few seconds or minutes. Historical data is used to put the new data in context and to enrich the information before it is distributed. The event data is often in a fairly raw form—it's observational notifications, sometimes with missing, out-of-order, or unverified messages. BAM data is often held in memory for immediate processing, and in some cases, it isn't saved on disk. However, some BAM applications need access to vast amounts of historical data. They may use in-memory databases with specialized data models such as vector database management systems (DBMSs) or real-time, in-memory variants of online analytical processing (OLAP) technology. In contrast, analyst-driven BI relies mostly on historical data from previous days, weeks, months, or years. Analyst-driven BI data is a mix of event, state, and reference data. Most data used in analyst-driven BI has been validated, reformatted into a database schema that is optimized for queries (such as conventional OLAP), and stored in a data warehouse or data mart on disk.

▶ Most BAM systems run continuously, listening to incoming events and communicating with businesspeople through dashboards, e-mail, or other channels. BAM systems typically use a mix of event-driven (push) and request-driven (pull) communication to interact with users. The event-driven communication alerts people when something significant happens. Users then make requests to drill down into root causes or look up information needed to formulate a response. In contrast, most analyst-driven BI is request-driven, where the end user submits ad hoc queries or asks "what if" questions through a spreadsheet that sits in front of a database. Alternatively, analyst-oriented BI is sometimes time-driven, using periodic batch reports.

▶ Some BAM systems execute a response through a computer system, actuator, or other fully automated mechanism. In contrast, analyst-driven BI always involves a human decision maker.

Strategy-Driven BI

Strategy-driven BI, the third category of BI, is used to measure and manage overall business performance against strategic and tactical plans and objectives. These applications typically serve corporate performance management (CPM) and other performance management purposes. They provides visibility into such issues as

▶ Are we on track to meet our monthly sales targets?

▶ Will any of our operating divisions overspend their capital budgets this quarter?

Formal performance management applications are less common than analyst-driven BI or BAM systems. Most managers still use less-systematic approaches to performance management, such as spreadsheets or manual analysis of traditional reports. However, performance management systems for sales, marketing, supply chain, HR, and others areas are becoming more common for the same reason that operational decision-making BAM is becoming more common—the growing amount of data available in electronic form.

Performance management systems differ from BAM systems in several ways:

▶ Performance management system users are typically at a higher level in the organization than BAM system users. Executives, senior managers, and department heads use performance management systems, whereas lower-level line managers or functional decision makers are more likely to use BAM systems.

▶ Performance management dashboards differ drastically from BAM dashboards, although most of the input data for both kinds of dashboards are event data. Performance management dashboards generally show summary-level data from one or more business units collected over many days or weeks. Totals and averages are compared against targets, often using scorecard-style displays. In contrast, most data used in BAM systems is a only few seconds or minutes old and the data is summarized at a lower level.

▶ Decisions made on the basis of performance management systems typically have a medium-term time horizon. If nothing is done for a few hours or days, it often doesn't matter. In contrast, BAM systems are generally targeted at more-urgent, although often narrower and less consequential, decisions. Decisions made on the basis of BAM may only affect a small part of the company's work, such as one or two customers or one day's results.

▶ Performance management systems are used by people. The issues tend to be complex and require human judgment. In contrast, some BAM decisions are simple enough to fully automate. The majority of BAM systems still involve human users too, but automated decisions and responses are becoming more common over time.

Positioning BI and Event Processing

In the language of event processing, all three kinds of BI systems perform CEP because they compute complex business events from simpler base events. However, BI users and developers rarely think of events or CEP in a formal or explicit manner. They are aware that they are dealing with things that happen, such as business transactions, but they don't think of them as "event notifications," "business events," or "complex events."

Note: Typical Interaction Patterns Used in Business Intelligence Systems

▶ *Analyst-driven BI is usually request-driven, but occasionally time-driven.*

▶ *BAM, the near-real-time aspect of process-driven BI, relies heavily on event-driven CEP for data collection and the initial notification, and then supports request-driven inquiries for subsequent drilldown.*

▶ *Performance management and other strategy-driven BI uses time-driven, periodic reports as its primary mode of interaction.*

BAM is the only type of BI that makes heavy use of message oriented middleware (MOM), low-latency event-stream processing (ESP) engines, real-time, in-memory DBMSs, and other trappings of event-driven CEP. Other kinds of BI are more likely to leverage traditional BI analytical tools and DBMS technology that can support very large databases and OLAP data models. Those technologies provide rich analytical capabilities for ad hoc inquiries into historical event data and other data.

Companies that invest in formal, systematic BI programs generally try to standardize BI data models, metrics, and tools across a broad swath of their business units and management levels. However, BAM initiatives are generally outside the scope of such programs. Most BAM implementations are "stovepiped"—they are associated with a single functional area, process, or application system. The most common way of acquiring BAM capabilities is to buy a packaged application that includes a dashboard as an accessory. The second most common way of acquiring BAM is to implement a dashboard or other monitoring capability as part of a custom application development project.

Piecemeal, stovepiped BAM can be quite valuable because it provides timely visibility into the key metrics that matter to a particular task. However, it falls short of providing the comprehensive situation awareness that is helpful for certain decisions. Even today, some businesspeople use two or three different BAM systems as part of their job. As the number of stovepiped BAM systems grows within a company, the company naturally acquires MOM, CEP suites, visualization tools, analytical tools, and, most importantly, experience in implementing BAM. This provides the foundation for more-improved, holistic BAM systems. Over time, we expect that BAM stovepipes will become somewhat more integrated. It will be more common to see a single BAM dashboard (or "cockpit") provide monitoring that spans multiple application systems and business units.

This doesn't mean that one dashboard will satisfy the needs of everyone in a company. BAM dashboards must implement very different views of the situation for each business role. The view of a supply chain will look different on a BAM dashboard on the loading dock than it does on the sales manager's BAM dashboard or the fleet manager's BAM dashboard. And the performance management dashboards for mid- and upper-level managers will inherently differ from the BAM dashboards used by lower-level managers and individual contributors.

BI professionals and BAM developers will need to collaborate more often in the future. Businesspeople are pressing BI teams to provide more-current data, and they're also pressing BAM developers to use more historical data to put real-time event data into context. Most of the underlying business-event objects and other data are the same for conventional BI and BAM systems. Both kinds of systems ultimately draw from the notifications that are generated in transactional applications. Architects and data administrators will be able to improve both types of applications by developing their understanding of the flow of transactional and observational notification data between applications. Conventional BI and BAM won't merge, because the kinds of decisions and the end-user interaction patterns are inherently different. However, they will need to exchange data more often and cooperate more closely on defining data semantics.

Rule Engines and Event Processing

In Chapter 1 we observed that CEP software is a type of rule engine. In this section, we'll clarify the similarities and differences between CEP software and other kinds of rule engines used in business applications.

Business Rule Engines

A business rule engine (BRE) is a software component that executes business rules that have been segregated from the rest of the application software. Most rules are expressed declaratively rather than procedurally, which implies that the developer has provided a description of what is supposed to be done rather than providing a step-by-step sequential algorithm for how to perform the computation. The BRE maps the declarative rules into the computer instructions that will implement the logic. A BRE can be physically bound into the application program or it can run independently and communicate with the application by exchanging messages at run time (regardless of whether it runs on the same computer or elsewhere in the network). BREs evolved from expert systems that originally appeared in the 1980s.

Business Rule Management Systems

BREs are often packaged into larger, more-comprehensive BRMS products that incorporate a variety of complementary features. A BRMS is more than a rule execution engine and development environment. It facilitates the creation, registration, classification, verification, and deployment of rules. It incorporates support for:

▶ A BRE execution engine

▶ A rule repository

▶ An integrated development environment (IDE)

▶ Rule-model simulation

▶ Monitoring and analysis

▶ Management and administration, and

▶ Rule templates

A BRMS contains development tools to help power users, business analysts, and software engineers specify and classify the business rules. It stores rules and checks them for logical consistency. For example, a rule that says "if the credit verification system is down, no purchase over $100 can be approved" would conflict with another rule that says "if the customer is rated as platinum level, they can buy up to $500 of merchandise without credit verification." In practice, most company's business rules, whether on paper, in computer systems, or just in people's heads, are rife with logical inconsistencies of this type. One of the major benefits of a BRMS is that it can identify the relationships among rules, expose many of the inconsistencies, and make it easier for users to resolve them.

A BRMS is based on the premise that business rules usually change more often than the rest of the application, so the application will be easier to modify if the rules are managed and stored separately from the other logic. When business conditions change, the rule can be modified on-the-fly without recompiling the rest of the application system. Moreover, the rules are shareable among multiple applications so that when the rules change, all applications that use the same rules automatically begin using the new version of the rules.

BRMS and CEP Engine Similarities

CEP software has many characteristics in common with BRMS BREs. Both are rule engines that externalize business rules and both are commonly packaged as discrete software components. Much of the data that is processed by a BRE or CEP engine is event data. Businesspeople must be involved in preparing the rules for both types of engines, although BRMS products have a longer track record for providing development tools that are used directly by power users. Both types of engines can be used to support human decision making or to compute fully automated decisions. Both have database adaptors that allow them to look up historical or reference data as part of their processing logic. BREs are sometimes used to complement the operation of run-time BPM engines in a manner that is similar to the way CEP engines complement them (see Figure 10-4). However, because BREs and CEP engines serve different purposes, they use different algorithms and are constructed differently.

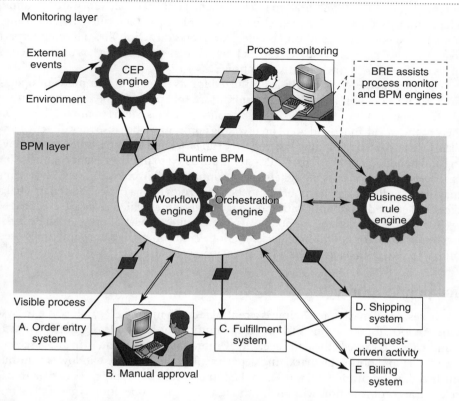

Figure 10-4: Using a BRE and CEP engine with run-time BPM.

Request-Driven vs. Event-Driven

BREs are typically request-driven. An application program working on a business transaction needs to make a decision on how to proceed. Instead of having the business rules embedded in its application code, the application invokes the BRE to derive a conclusion from a set of premises. The BRE, called a production system or inference engine, then swings into action to perform the computation and return the result to the application. The general model for a BRE rule is "If <some condition> then <do action X> or else <do action Y>." In many applications, multiple if-then-else rules must be resolved to make one decision—in some cases, hundreds of such rules.

By contrast, CEP engines are event-driven. They run continuously, processing notification messages as soon as they arrive, in accordance with the principles of EDA. Recent events are stored in the CEP engine, and additional input event data may arrive every second or minute. The notion of automatic, implicit inference does not exist in most CEP engines. However, a CEP engine can compute a complex event that is then fed into another CEP computation to implement a type of explicit forward chaining. The counterpart to a BRE if-then-else rule is a CEP when-then rule: "When <something happens or some condition is detected> then <do action X>." The counterpart to a BRE "else" clause is a CEP clause that says "When <something has not happened in a specified time frame> then <do action Y>."

The internal design of a BRE is optimized for its request-driven mode of operation. A BRE functions as a service to applications that perform the input and output (I/O) to messaging systems or people. By contrast, CEP systems maintain their own view of the world, independent of an invoking application. Because they directly handle I/O to and from messaging systems, they run faster and are more efficient at receiving and handling notifications. CEP systems can listen to multiple event channels (for example, multiple messaging systems) to get input from diverse sources. CEP systems may also handle a larger number of independent rules than a typical rule engine handles. The event data in notification messages determines which rules are executed.

BREs and CEP engines are not always used online as part of an immediate business transaction or operational decision. Both kinds of engines are sometimes used offline to process data at rest in a file or database.

Temporal Support

As we described in Chapter 7, time is a central focus in many CEP systems. A CEP system can look for situations such as "If the number of hits on this web page in a 5-minute period exceeds the daily average by more than 50 percent, bring up a second web server and notify the marketing department." The 5-minute window is continuously sliding or jumping forward into the future. BREs can apply rules to data that is selected according to time windows, although this type of operation is generally cumbersome to specify at development time in a BRE. Moreover, BREs typically have more overhead (and thus higher latency) for handling incoming messages. This makes them less applicable for demanding ESP applications that must carry out computations on large sets of event messages in a few milliseconds. Some BREs demonstrate high throughput (they can scale up to many hundreds of rule requests per second and tens of millions of requests per day), but their latency is not as low as in purpose-built CEP engines for this type of application.

Individual vs. Set-Based Processing

BREs are designed to operate on a working set of data. The input data is passed in as part of a transaction, or is retrieved from a database (it is not stored in the BRE between requests). BREs are commonly used to apply known insights and data to transactional business processes with a modest amount of data that applies to each rule.

For example, about 90 percent of all credit card transactions in the United States are checked for fraud as they take place. A BRE validates the card number and amount against a database of account numbers to determine if the card is good or bad. The databases are typically updated nightly. BREs are also used in online, event-based "precision marketing" strategies where cross-selling and upselling opportunities are identified as the customer interaction is taking place. BREs are sometimes used immediately after a transaction has executed to check for regulatory compliance. Any of these applications may involve hundreds or even thousands of individual transactions per second, and the logic must execute within a second or two. However, each transaction is logically independent, so the work can be spread across dozens of copies of the BRE application on dozens of systems.

CEP engines are appropriate when large amounts of potentially related data must be quickly manipulated as a set. For example, CEP engines are used in context brokers for location-aware applications that monitor the movement of thousands or tens of thousands of people. The CEP system can track where each person is by tapping into the cell phone network. It ingests thousands of messages per second and correlates the event data so that it can notify a person if any member of his or her personal network is within one-quarter mile of his or her current location. This involves immediate pattern detection across a huge set of data—it cannot be accomplished by viewing data items individually.

The distinction between individual and set-based processing extends to offline applications as well. BREs are used in nightly batch systems that check each transaction from the previous day for regulatory compliance, fraud, opportunities for personalized, follow-up marketing activities, or other transaction analytics. CEP systems may also be used offline, but they still deal with large data sets simultaneously rather than individually. Offline CEP applications may replay the event log from a previous day to detect correlations and patterns that were overlooked earlier by the online CEP application. In this scenario, the CEP engine is still seemingly event-driven by the notifications as they arrive, although the event data may represent things that happened at a much earlier time.

Overlap

The technology that is used in typical BRMSs is inherently different from that used in most CEP engines, although they are both rule engines. Nothing prevents a vendor from creating a single BRE/CEP product that is good at both kinds of rule processing. However, it needs to implement both sets of algorithms and technical architectures.

A few anti-money-laundering, fraud-detection, pretrade-checking, network-monitoring, and other applications can be implemented with either kind of rule engine, so there is a minor overlap in their usage scenarios. In general, BRMSs and CEP systems are complementary notions. Together, they are the core technology needed to implement intelligent decision management (IDM) programs (sometimes calls enterprise decision management [EDM] programs). IDM programs are, as their name implies, systematic ways to provide computer support for making better business decisions. The terms IDM and EDM originated in the rule engine market, but they can encompass BI (including BAM and CEP) because they all are ways to use computers in decision making.

Summary

The discipline of event processing is related to several other major IT-based initiatives found in many companies. Business events are inherent in BPM, although event objects and notifications are not always used when BPM tools deal with business events. CEP technology is used for process monitoring and for some sophisticated, new types of run-time BPM flow management. CEP has introduced a new decision management technology that complements other types of BI tools and rule engines.

11

Best Practices

"It's the economy, stupid!" was a phrase that drove design choices in President Clinton's 1992 campaign. "It's about the business!" is the phrase that determines design choices for event-processing applications. Most of the benefits in implementing event-processing applications come from transforming, or significantly improving, the business.

In this chapter we apply the concepts and ideas of the previous chapters to propose a collection of best practices in event processing. We also draw upon our experiences working with different companies in different domains. The chapter is organized in the following main parts:

▶ **Starting out**—Starting out with developing an event-processing application for the business: points to keep in mind.

▶ **Pilot project**—How to select a pilot project for an event-processing application.

▶ **Best practices**—Best practices to set up in your business for designing and implementing event-processing applications.

Starting Out

The following points are self-evident but should be kept in mind when building applications for an enterprise that has not, as yet, acquired software tools that are explicitly labeled "event processing," "EDA," or "CEP":

▶ The enterprise is already event-driven—it has event-driven business processes even if IT applications explicitly called "event processing" don't exist in the enterprise. The organization may not, however, have systematically evaluated the types of valuable event-driven business processes that it can implement today or that it will be able to implement in the near future.

▶ Most IT applications in the enterprise are, and will remain, hybrid systems with time-, request-, and event-driven components. Event-processing applications are built using mature IT technologies that already exist in the enterprise and (possibly) new components. Event processing adds value to earlier investments in IT technologies.

181

▶ Some enterprises have developed event-processing components, including CEP components, for their businesses. For example, defense departments and space organizations have immense expertise in event processing in their domains. Existing components and expertise within the enterprise should be used in developing new applications.

▶ The benefits and costs of event-processing technologies are directly related to the business. Justifications of conventional IT projects don't emphasize benefits such as situation awareness, event detection, and accurate response, which are central to event processing (see Chapter 4).

Next, we discuss the following steps in developing event-processing applications:

1. Identify applications suitable for event processing.

2. Identify user communities.

3. Identify scenarios and responses.

4. Identify data sources.

5. Identify events and data transformations.

6. Estimate costs and benefits and plan for the future.

Identify Applications Suitable for Event Processing

Two early steps that help introduce applications that are explicitly labeled CEP, EDA, or event processing are to identify the applications in your enterprise that are most likely to benefit from the addition of event-driven components, and identify the different communities of users in your enterprise who will benefit from the addition of event-driven functionality.

A first step is to determine whether a new business application or functionality can benefit from event-processing technologies (see Chapter 5). Here we summarize the main points. As you saw in Chapter 1, the system drivers for event-processing applications are timeliness, agility, and information availability. The technology-push and consumer-pull drivers for event-driven interactions are summarized in Chapter 2 by the PC-cubed (price, pervasiveness, performance, connectedness, celerity, and complexity) trends; these trends influence the role that EDA will play in the future. The informal expectations that people have about event-driven interactions are different from those for time- and request-driven interactions. The expectations that businesspeople have about components of a proposed application indicate whether time-, request-, or event-driven processing is appropriate for those components. The presence of several A-E-I-O-U features, described in Chapter 5, in a business domain indicate that EDA is suitable for that domain. Chapter 5 also shows how the framework is applied to evaluate the suitability of EDA for a variety of business domains. The effort that goes into this initial screening of a business problem will yield returns in later steps.

Identify User Communities

The value proposition of EDA is a business value proposition. EDA applications have a visible impact on people in lines of business. Even applications in which the entire process, from data acquisition to response, is automatic have a tangible impact on the business. A place to start identifying business domains that benefit from event processing is with the businesspeople who will be most affected.

Multiple Roles Impacted by Event-Driven Functionality

People in different roles are affected by the addition of event-driven functionality. Some roles benefit in the short term and others over the longer term. Consider, for example, the installation of smart electric meters as the electric grid is upgraded to the smart grid. Smart meters provide an immediate, visible benefit to the metering and billing part of the business because smart meters communicate to computers in the utility, obviating the need for meter-readers to travel to customer sites. Smart meters also enable new applications that provide greater benefits over the longer term. Two-way communication between meters and the utility enables the utility to control appliances in the home, and this allows customers and the utility to jointly reduce demand when the system is about to get overloaded. Responsive demand allows the utility to build fewer power-generation plants and transmission lines and reduces carbon emissions. These savings are much higher than the savings from fewer meter-readers; however, these savings accrue over the longer term. The grid is getting "smarter" in stages, with different groups of people benefiting at different points in its evolution. Similarly, EDA functionality installed at trading desks provides immediate benefits to traders, whereas functionality added later also benefits other groups of users such as corporate risk managers.

....

Note: Multiple groups of people will be affected by the addition of event-driven functionality. Some groups benefit in the short term while others benefit over the longer term.

EDA applications can be transformational and provide significant benefits to many different constituencies in the enterprise. When a business unit identifies the benefits of event processing, the benefits become apparent to related business units. For example, farmers put National Animal Identification System (NAIS) RFID tags on their livestock to help officials track infected animals; but farmers use the same tags to improve management of their animals. An application that uses accelerometers in buildings to identify areas damaged by earthquakes can also be used to study building dynamics and weaknesses in welds. Components such as sensors used in an application for one business unit can be used for a different kind of application for a different unit. Managing staged rollout of integrated enterprise-wide EDA applications that deliver tangible benefits to different groups at each stage is a business, technical, and project-management challenge.

Users Outside the Virtual Enterprise

Many event-driven business processes interact with people outside the business. (The "O" in the A-E-I-O-U list of features stands for "outside.") The smart grid has different types of user groups, including rate payers, the metering and billing organization in the utility, the transmission and distribution organization, power-generation companies, and the Independent Systems Operator (ISO) that coordinates operations on the grid. Some user groups, such as the metering and transmission organizations, are within the utility, and other user groups, such as rate payers, the ISO, and power-generation organizations, are outside the utility. Early steps in developing an event-driven application are to identify the user communities within and outside the enterprise and then estimate the different measures of business benefits that each of these groups derives from the application.

The complexity and the uncertainty of design parameters and cost/benefit measures depend, in part, on the type of application. Likewise, the business case for an event-processing application depends on its characteristics. Next, let's look at two characteristics of the applications and their impact on the business cases for the applications and cost/benefit measures:

▶ Is the application a new ("greenfield") application or an improvement to an existing application?

▶ Does the application respond continuously to events or does it respond only to rare, but critical, events?

Is the Application New or an Improvement to an Existing One?

The strategy for developing event-processing functionality depends on whether it improves existing processes or enables entirely new processes. Technologies such as RFID (radio frequency identity) can transform business processes but can be understood, nevertheless, within the framework of more familiar devices such as barcode readers. The benefits and costs of applications that improve existing business processes are clearer than for applications that enable totally new processes. For example, the return on investment (ROI) from using RFID bands on patients in hospitals can be estimated with greater certainty than the ROI from EDA technologies to manage wind energy.

Many business applications, such as the smart grid, have both types of features: they improve existing processes and enable new solutions. The smart grid improves existing metering and billing processes by automatically transmitting meter readings to the utility. Some features of the smart grid are totally new because technologies—such as distributed energy resources from wind—are being deployed on scales never seen before or because new technologies, such as phasor measurement instruments, are becoming available as commercial off-the-shelf (COTS) devices.

The grid that has operated with truly remarkable success for a century has to become "smarter" and more event-driven to deal with the issues of large amounts of transient "green" power, reduced standby capacity from fossil fuel generators, and increasing peak demand. As reported by Reuters (see Appendix A), system operators curtailed power to interruptible customers by over 1,000 megawatts within 10 minutes when wind dropped dramatically in Texas in February 2008; the operators sensed a change—reduction in wind power—and responded in an appropriate, timely fashion.

The ROI of smart meters, purely from a billing perspective, can be estimated from records of costs before and after traditional meters are replaced by smart meters in target areas. Predicting ROI from making the grid smarter to deal with distributed resources such as wind and solar energy is more difficult; however, these resources cannot be exploited without adding "smartness" and more event-processing capability to the grid.

An advantage of using event processing to improve existing functionality, as opposed to developing totally new business processes, is that changes in business processes engendered by incremental additions of functionality are less radical than those engendered by completely new functionality. This allows application developers to expend more effort on technology and less on the difficult problem of managing change to the business. On the other hand, an advantage of using event processing to create totally new business applications is that doing so demonstrates the transformative power of event processing, and the benefits are huge. A good practice is to demonstrate ROI from event-processing technologies by first taking less-risky, more-technology-oriented steps to improve existing functionality, and then taking more-difficult, business-oriented steps to develop new transformative processes.

....

Note: You can demonstrate ROI from event-processing technologies in stages by first taking technology-focused steps to improve existing functionality and then developing transformative event-driven business processes.

Does the Application Respond to Events Continuously or Rarely?

RFID applications—whether for tracking patients in hospitals, palettes in warehouses, packages in transshipment points, or other objects in different tracking applications—respond to events continuously. By contrast, applications that warn about shaking during earthquakes respond rarely. Some applications combine routine responses to frequent, customary events with critically important responses to rare, unusual situations. For instance, smart electric grids upload energy consumption recorded in smart meters on a routine basis and also help manage rare brownout situations.

Applications that provide the greatest benefit by responding to critical rare events can be designed to also provide value by detecting, recording, and exploiting information in frequent, routine events. Routine events are used to develop models of the enterprise and its environment. All of us observe and record (subconsciously) events in dealing with our families and colleagues, and we use the recorded events to build informal models of them; then we use these models to predict (informally) how they will behave in different situations. Enterprises use business intelligence to build models from logs of recorded events. Scientific instruments that provide immense value when they detect critical rare events also provide value from continuous measurement. The Large Hadron Collider in Switzerland will provide colossal value when (and if) it is used to detect the Higgs boson particle; however, the instrument also provides great value from its continuous ongoing measurements. Seismological networks provide the most value in identifying regions of the greatest shaking after rare, severe earthquakes; however, commonplace events, continuously recorded by the networks, are the raw materials from which seismological models are built. Airplane cockpits display continuous measurements and also issue alarms. Business activity monitoring (BAM) dashboards provide value when they display key performance indicators (PKIs) that indicate situations that require response; however, dashboards also deliver benefits on a continuing basis because they provide evidence that nothing that requires immediate action has occurred.

Applications that are required to respond to routine events can be extended, often with little additional cost, to also respond to rare but important events. The initial specification of the application may have restricted attention to routine operations; however, a little creative analysis may show how the same application can be used to respond to exceptional threats and opportunities. A baggage-handling application that responds to the routine events of baggage movement can be extended to intercept packages containing contraband or dangerous material in seconds. Advanced metering infrastructures for electricity and water that routinely detect and record the resources consumed can be used to detect unusual situations. Demonstrating ROI for an application that responds both to routine and rare events is easier than demonstrating ROI for an application that responds only to rare events; likewise, the ROI for an application that responds to routine events can be increased by extending it to deal with massive, but rare, threats and opportunities.

Tip: Extend applications required to respond to rare, critical events to also respond to frequent, routine events. Likewise, extend applications required to respond to routine events to detect and respond to rare events that may occur.

Identify Scenarios and Responses

After identifying the application domain, continue the emphasis on users by identifying the scenarios and responses that are most valuable to them. The practice of identifying use cases and scenarios is especially important when developing event-processing applications because many scenarios are driven by natural agents or adversaries over which the enterprise has no control. Scenarios for intrusion detection describe different types of intruders and their strategies; scenarios for smart homes describe the many situations in which older people may need help; and scenarios for the smart grid specify a variety of natural and manmade conditions. The scenarios describe what nature may do (windstorms, earthquakes), what hostile people may do (attempt to manipulate your customers' bank accounts and appliances), and what systems may do inadvertently.

In some cases clients are unwilling to describe scenarios in any detail. Traders in energy, stock, or foreign exchange may refuse to describe the scenarios they care about, the responses they wish to take, the events they want to identify, and even the data sources they want to monitor. In these cases, designers work with generic or "sanitized" scenarios, and this is often difficult especially when debugging applications that cannot be revealed entirely.

Scenarios Include Responses to Events

Responses are also events, and responses are intertwined with other steps in event-processing applications. A system that secures an area from intruders must initiate a response when a possible intruder is detected; however, the application's function doesn't end with the initiation of the response—the application continues to respond to events such as movements of the intruder, movements of security personnel, and alarms being turned on. Applications that alert traders about opportunities also respond to actions that the trader takes in response to the alert. Since the event-processing applications are so tightly interwoven with business problems (detecting intruders and exploiting trading opportunities), businesspeople have to put in a lot of effort to identify and describe scenarios.

....

Note: The effort that goes into specifying scenarios is primarily for describing the business aspects of the scenarios and only secondarily for describing the IT aspects.

Scenarios Dealing with Alerts to People

A common response of EDA applications is to inform people about events by updating BAM dashboards; sending alerts by e-mail, instant messaging, phone calls, or audible alarms; and providing tools, such as maps, for dealing with the event. For example, an accounting application responds to deviations of actual and planned expenditures by sending alert messages that contain locations in data cubes that help resolve the problems. When radioactive material is moved from a safe to an unsafe location in a hospital, an application responds by generating audible alarms and sending alert messages containing information about the situation. Spend time to identify the scenarios that describe how people want to be alerted, the devices that they want used, the situations under which they want to be alerted, and the times at which they want to be interrupted.

Scenarios about Social Networks

Many people use event-driven processing to monitor their social networks. Twitter is an example of a "social activity monitoring" application that displays information about people that a user is interested in (or to use the vernacular, the people that the user is "following"). The number of participants in social networks has increased dramatically in the last 5 years, and the number of social activity monitoring dashboards now exceeds the number of BAM dashboards. A generation has grown up with interactive games that process thousands of events per second. People use event processing routinely in nonwork settings such as news alerts. When you identify scenarios and responses, you should also look at the ways in which customers of your proposed application use event processing in social settings.

Scenarios for Automatic Sense and Respond

Some EDA applications respond without human intervention. Cross-trading applications, described in Chapter 2, match buy and sell orders in milliseconds without human interaction. Search engines automatically select advertisements to be displayed on the web pages in a second. Some software enterprise applications have interfaces that automatically trigger workflows when specified events occur, and responses for most applications include automatic updates to information repositories. Even for applications that respond entirely automatically, the scenarios must identify the business benefits of proposed applications, such as the expected revenue from a different advertisement-selection algorithm.

Scenarios for Interacting with the World Outside the Virtual Enterprise

Best practices in developing event-processing applications are the same as those for any other application except that event-processing applications emphasize different benefits and costs than those emphasized in conventional IT applications. Responses in event-processing applications usually result in action—not merely in the transfer of information—and this action often involves interactions with the world outside the enterprise. Thus, an event-processing application may change the ways in which the enterprise interacts with the outside world. A goal of this step is to understand how the dynamics of interactions between the enterprise and its environment will change as a consequence of the event-processing application.

Identify Data Sources

The first three steps in developing event-processing applications, covered in the previous sections, identify what the needs are: the business applications for which event-processing components are appropriate, the different user communities, and the responses the users need. The next steps identify how those needs can be met. Of course, application development doesn't (and shouldn't) progress in a strict waterfall from one stage to the next.

Variety of Sources of Data

The variety, number, and cost-effectiveness of data sources are increasing by the day. Sensors are becoming more sensitive and accurate even though they consume less power and have smaller form factors than ever before. The costs of sensors such as temperature, pressure, and strain gauges and accelerometers have dropped substantially compared to the costs of other goods and services. Increasing numbers of products have event emitters built in at the factory—building event emitters into a product, as it is being manufactured, is cheaper than inserting emitters into finished products. Vendors are implementing more software products, such as business processes and databases, with event emitters. Some enterprise software applications have publish-and-subscribe interfaces that allow other components to subscribe for events generated by the applications.

Data Sources on the Web

Many organizations offer web services or other application programming interfaces (APIs) for accessing valuable information, including news, blogs, business data, prices, trends, weather forecasts, journal papers, abstracts, and patents. Websites can be "screen scraped" even if they do not provide APIs for acquiring information. (Screen-scraping is best avoided, because it is unreliable; if screen-scraping is necessary, the results should be checked frequently in case the schemas at the website change.) Enterprises have access to a great deal of valuable information on the Internet, and the quantity continues to grow dramatically. Event-processing applications that could not have been built just a few years ago because data sources didn't exist have become viable today. The PC-cubed trends tell us that event-processing applications will become even more cost-effective in the future.

Crowd Sourcing Event-Processing Components

Some applications delegate the acquisition of information to the public; this delegation is sometimes called "crowd-sourcing." The idea is similar to the "wisdom of crowds"—use the collective intelligence of a lot of individuals. The idea in crowd-sourcing information acquisition is to use the "senses of crowds." The U.S. Geological Survey's website includes a "Did You Feel It?" page (http://earthquake.usgs.gov/eqcenter/dyfi) that gets data from thousands of people to estimate where shaking occurred after an earthquake. Some applications detect traffic congestion by fusing data from hundreds of drivers. Crowd-sourcing is invaluable in many applications.

The application must have enough data sources to ensure high accuracy and completeness. The application can improve accuracy by verifying information from one data source with information from another. "Sanity checks" of data acquired from external sources also help weed out errors. The application must also have enough data to detect significant events. It is helpful to list the possible sources that an enterprise could use for a given application and then cull the list later.

Though the numbers and varieties of data sources continue to grow at explosive rates, an enterprise may not have creatively and systematically attempted to identify the data sources that can help it. There are beneficial data sources within and outside the enterprise, in hardware and in software, with and without APIs, generated by devices and generated by people.

Tip: Identify invaluable, unexploited data sources that are available today and that will become available in the near future by encouraging business and IT people to brainstorm together.

Identify Events and Data Transformations

Now that we have identified the input (data sources) and output (desired responses), we next design the steps that process the input to produce the output. Initially, we merely sketch the steps in the computation to determine whether the desired output can be computed from the given input in the specified time, or whether we need more or different data sources, or whether we need to modify responses.

Many of the steps that transform input to output may be implementable using components already in your enterprise's software stack. An inventory of the enterprise's IT components—such as BAM portals, business intelligence (BI) tools, rule engines, databases, and enterprise service buses (see Chapters 9 and 10)—helps in determining the additional components, if any, that are required. Your enterprise may have high-performance versions of these components (such as real-time BI, low-latency rule engines, and in-memory databases) and may have in-house expertise in these technologies. Moreover, your enterprise may have developed highly tuned event-processing applications in its core competence. A component that builds shake maps (that identify the degree of shaking at different points due to earthquakes) is highly specialized; it is unlikely that there is any benefit in reimplementing the component by tailoring other COTS components. You can leverage specialized components by implementing the application using architectures that allow you to snap in the different types of components required by your application (see Chapter 8).

A preliminary mapping of computational steps to resources in the enterprise, and components that the enterprise can acquire, helps in estimating the feasibility and cost of the proposed application.

....

Tip: Make an inventory of the enterprise's existing event-processing applications, the IT technologies (including high-performance versions) that it already has, and its expertise in technologies related to event processing.

Many commercial and open source components for event processing have been developed recently. For example, alert engines are components that gather news (including events about crises such as hurricanes), organize and display information on mobile phones or desktops, and send alerts to devices based on the user's preferences (such as, mobile phone during the day, e-mail messages at night). Communication-enabled business process (CEBP) systems identify the best group of people to deal with an event based on which people are available at the current time, their locations, and their skill sets. CEBP also sets up collaboration tools such as teleconferences, calendars, e-mail, and wikis for the taskforce created to deal with an event. You can acquire software tools or use publicly available services for a wide variety of technologies, including natural-language processing, image and video analysis, geospatial analysis and display, time-series analysis, and signal processing. The variety and power of specialized components for event processing continues to increase, driven partially by growth in consumer applications. The design challenge is to select a proprietary or open source service or component from a vendor for each component in the design and then to integrate these new components with components in the enterprise's portfolio.

The events generated by an application may be valuable to other applications, possibly in other divisions of the enterprise. The event objects that describe these events may prove to be invaluable in the future; applications that are not even on the drawing board could find these event objects to be useful. Furthermore, event objects stored in repositories could be used later by BI, statistics, and model-building tools. You saw in the example of the smart grid that enterprise-wide event-processing applications can be developed in stages over decades, and certain types of events generated by an application for smart metering today may be used by very different applications in 5 or 10 years.

Tip: Assess the value of monitoring events in a business application so that the information can be used by applications in other divisions in the enterprise, by BI, and by future business functions.

Estimate Costs and Benefits and Plan for the Future

The benefits of EDA applications—such as event detection, faster response, accurate responses, and situation awareness—are not emphasized in project justifications for conventional IT applications. The business case for an event-processing project is similar to that for other IT projects but the relative emphases on different benefits are important.

The PC-cubed trends—technology push for lower price, greater performance, and increasing pervasiveness of EDA technologies coupled with consumer pull for technologies that deal with greater complexity, connectedness, and celerity—tell us to expect substantial changes during the lifetime of an EDA application. The lifetime of a smart electric meter is at least a decade; in that time, home energy-management systems, electrical appliances, and communication technologies connecting homes to utilities will change. Utilities cannot postpone installing smart meters. Overdesigning today's meter to deal with possible new requirements in the next decade is expensive. On the other hand, replacing millions of meters in a utility's service area, when the meters no longer meet requirements, is expensive, too.

Estimating the benefits and costs of any IT system over its lifetime is a challenge. This estimation is, however, particularly difficult for event-processing applications because IT components are often intertwined with long-lasting infrastructures and business processes. Bridges last for centuries, and smart bridges, by virtue of their smartness, will last even longer. Computers, however, become obsolete within 5 years.

A design question that impacts the long-term benefits of an event-processing application is: How general-purpose should the application be? A house remains much the same over the decades of its life, but a smart house is a programmable house: it can be changed by reprogramming, possibly by a programmer at the opposite side of the globe. A door is a door, but a "smart" door is configurable and reconfigurable. Should you design a smart door for today's requirements, or should it have general-purpose sense-and-response capability to satisfy requirements over the door's lifetime, or should it be a plug-and-play door so that sensors, responders, and processing units can be plugged in and popped out of the door? How much work will a home-owner or "smart" handyman or handywoman have to do to reprogram a smart door? The different measures of benefits and costs, described in Chapter 4, can be estimated only approximately over the long lifetimes of these systems; nevertheless, the estimates help in scoping out the proposed application.

Note: Estimating the benefits and costs of event-processing applications over their lifetimes is difficult because the applications are often tightly intertwined with long-lasting infrastructures and business processes.

An event-processing project in one division of an enterprise serves as a catalyst for other divisions to rethink the structures of their business processes. Making business event objects in one division visible to other divisions leads to integration of event-driven business processes across multiple divisions; this, in turn, makes the entire enterprise more responsive and agile. The potentially transformative power of event processing can result in viral dissemination of the technology. The potential benefit of event objects generated in one business unit for units across the enterprise makes design and estimation of benefits difficult. It also makes managing mission-creep important since multiple business units may want to add functionality to initial designs. Issues about uncertain requirements during the lifetime of the application (think smart grid) are bound to be raised. So, complete the implementation of event-processing applications in stages, and demonstrate the tangible business benefits of each stage before going on to the next.

Pilot Projects

An incremental, layered approach to implementing event-processing functionality reduces risk. A pilot project or proof of concept (PoC) at each stage helps to demonstrate that the functionality for that stage can be implemented and integrated into the business. Evaluations of costs and benefits after a pilot project is completed help determine whether initial cost/benefit estimates were reasonable.

Pilot Projects for Well-Defined Applications

Less time is required for a pilot project for a well-defined, "shrink-wrapped," mature application in a vertical business domain than for a new application implemented by integrating application-independent components. For example, today electric utilities put a great deal of thought and effort into designing test systems for evaluating advanced metering infrastructures (AMIs) that collect and analyze data from smart electric meters. That's because the utilities are integrating components such as smart meters, communications networks, and billing systems to form advanced-metering applications. They are pioneers. In a decade, professional services companies, products companies, and electric utilities will have developed expertise in implementing AMI systems. At that point, smart metering will have become a well-defined business application with generally accepted design principles and standards; so, much less effort will be required to implement proofs of concept. Many utilities, however, do not have the luxury of waiting for a decade.

Effort Required from Business Users for a Successful Pilot Project

A pilot project must be a sufficiently complete representation of the actual task so that extrapolations from the pilot project to the actual task are credible. On the other hand, the pilot project should be small enough that it can be finished quickly. This tension is common to all system development; however, there are some issues that are accentuated when developing event-processing applications. One of these issues is the effort required from the businesspeople in specifying and evaluating the pilot project. Since the benefits of EDA applications are directly visible to people in lines of business, the evaluation of a pilot project must be carried out with the aid of businesspeople; however, they often have more-pressing responsibilities.

The authors have participated in, or observed, designs of pilot projects in many business domains, including electricity power trading and commodity trading. In some cases, the decision to evaluate event-processing software for trading was taken by management—not by the traders themselves; however, the value of the application is that it helps traders. An event-processing vendor insisted on commitments of time from a few representative traders to help design and evaluate the PoC. They provided critical feedback about what they did and did not want in the application. The commitment from the traders proved absolutely necessary for a useful PoC.

Getting commitment from management for evaluating a trading PoC is sometimes easier than getting the same commitment from the traders themselves. There are many reasons for this, including the manner in which managers and traders are compensated for their work. Traders are under pressure to go back to their trading and get immediate results rather than spend time on a PoC for an application which may provide value months later. A best practice is to get commitments of time from end users as well as management to specify and evaluate pilot projects.

....

Note: Getting commitment from management for time from end-users to specify and evaluate a pilot project is sometimes easier than getting the same commitment from end-users themselves; a best practice is to get commitments from both users and management.

Estimating Return on Investment from Pilot Projects

Another characteristic of a proof of concept for an event-processing application is that benefits and costs of the PoC must be evaluated along multiple dimensions such as better situation awareness and more rapid, accurate responses. Evaluating each of the REACTS (relevance, effort, accuracy, completeness, timeliness, and security) benefits provided by a PoC helps in estimating the ROI of the final application. For example, a PoC evaluation for a trading application should measure, or estimate, parameters such as: How much time does a trader need to tailor the application to satisfy that trader's specific needs? What is the change in risk exposure due to traders using the application? What are the security weaknesses of the application exposed by the PoC? There will be cases where the PoC delivers inaccurate data, doesn't detect events, and reacts late—the value of a PoC is in measuring how much better the proposed system is than current business practice. The REACTS metrics aren't usually emphasized in justifications for conventional IT projects.

Size of a Pilot Project in Event Processing

The size and duration of a pilot project for any application should be determined carefully; this is especially true for an event-processing application because it interacts with the environment outside the enterprise. A pilot project for an AMI for electricity must evaluate the ability of the system to get measurements from meters to the utility in a timely fashion under different environmental conditions such as thunderstorms and windstorms. These pilot projects span thousands of homes over many months to ensure that likely natural and manmade situations are experienced. Designs and redesigns of some applications never stop. For example, applications to detect movement of hazardous radiation material are improved continuously to deal with new types of threat scenarios.

Best Practices

This section looks at how material presented from previous chapters is used to design event-processing applications systematically. Best practices are derived from the apparently trite, but useful, dictum: "It's all about the business!" There are many best practices in designing event-processing applications; we focus attention on the following:

▶ **Stepwise development of event-processing functionality**—The activities of validating assumptions, testing implementations, and measuring benefits and costs are particularly important for event-processing applications because they are so intertwined with business activity. The assumptions that must be tested are not merely about the software but, more importantly, also about the business. Stepwise development validates assumptions about the business, tests implementations of changed business processes as well as software, and measures or estimates business benefits at each step.

▶ **Using models of the business and its environment**—Models play a central role in event-processing applications. An application that triggers business processes to check on events that appear to signal fraud uses a model of what is, and is not, fraudulent. Alerts to traders about opportunities are based on models of the market. The development and use of models are critical parts of designing event-processing applications.

▶ **Designing for long-term business benefits**—Business event processes are useful to the business for the long term. Event-processing applications in healthcare, pharmaceuticals, smart bridges, smart grids, trading, and national security will remain critical for decades; however, the requirements for these applications will change with changing business conditions. A good practice is to design event-processing applications for the long term. Business event processes must be designed so that they can be monitored, administered, configured, and reconfigured over a long term.

Stepwise Development of Event-Processing Functionality

Stepwise development adds functionality incrementally and validates or modifies assumptions at each step before going on to the next. There are some situations for which stepwise development is inappropriate, and we discuss those situations later in this section. Where possible, a good practice is to follow the sequence of steps outlined next.

Business application monitoring (BAM) applications are good candidates for adding event-processing functionality in steps because they can be overlaid on top of existing applications. A BAM application acquires and processes raw events and displays KPIs. It provides visibility into a business process without controlling it. The response of the IT part of a BAM application is to display information—the response does not trigger workflow, invoke web services, or take other active steps. The active response of a BAM application, however, consists of the actions executed by the person who sees the KPI display.

The advantages of stepwise development of BAM applications are that each step has bounded scope; each step delivers tangible business value; and each step focuses on different concerns. We recommend that each step focus on the following concerns:

1. **Data sources and display**—The initial BAM application focuses on acquiring and displaying data. At this step developers identify data sources, build connectors to the data sources, and organize and display the data. Performance indicators at this step are simple aggregates of the acquired data. The value proposition of this initial application is better situation awareness and consequently more accurate, timely responses to situations that may arise. At this step, the person with the display acts not only as the component that detects events from patterns of data but also as the component that responds to the detected events.

2. **BAM networks**—The next steps deal with integrating multiple applications into BAM networks that mirror the organization of the enterprise. System-wide situation awareness requires events from multiple applications to be fused together to provide a holistic picture. Information local to a specific business unit is shown on displays for people in that unit, whereas displays for executives who manage multiple units show aggregate information across all the units that they manage. The value proposition for this step of application development is that the organization, as a whole, has better situation awareness of itself and its environment.

3. **Detecting events**—In the first step ("Data sources and display") and the second step ("BAM networks") people are responsible for detecting patterns in the data that indicate significant events, and they are responsible for initiating responses to these events. The technology in the first two steps merely aggregates and displays data—it doesn't detect patterns. In the next step, the application uses algorithms for detecting patterns in the data to identify significant events and then sends alerts about events to different people and different devices depending on the time of day, business roles of people, their skill sets, and the type of the alert. In this step, the application also proactively determines and displays the tools and data that a user will need to respond to an event. For example, an application may point to locations in repositories, such as data cubes, containing information helpful in responding to the event. At this step, responses to alerts are still carried out by people though detection of events is done with the aid of software.

4. **Automatic responses**—The final steps focus on triggering automatic responses to detected events. In this step, the application automatically invokes business processes, triggers workflows, and initiates other activities automatically, in addition to displaying data and sending alerts.

The approach given here is cautious and incremental: crawl before walking, walk before running, and evaluate return on investment at every step. There are, however, many problems for which the business case for a complete event-processing solution is so compelling, that directly implementing step 4—a full event-processing solution with automatic support for sensing, analyzing, and responding—is the right thing to do. Further, some applications cannot be implemented in a sequence of incremental steps. For example, a first incremental step of developing a BAM application is not helpful for businesses, such as algorithmic trading, that require responses in less than a second.

Using Models of the Business and Its Environment

Event-processing applications rely on formal or informal models of the business and its environment. In Chapter 2 we discussed a model that a mother on a trip has about her family. The model allows her to conclude that no emergencies have happened at home if she hasn't heard from her family. Your colleagues, friends, and doctors have informal models of you, and these models play key roles in their interactions with you. Routine medical checkups provide data that doctors use to build baseline models of your health. Your doctor's actions are based on this model: for example, your doctor may recommend, based on the model, that you do not run a marathon.

Event-Processing Applications Are Based on Models

An event-processing application that supports trading is based on a model of markets and trading. When a trader specifies that a certain pattern of stock prices signals a buy opportunity, the trader is using a model to predict the probable direction of stock prices. Applications that warn about impending hurricanes are based on weather models. When the Food and Drug Administration decides that spinach from certain regions of the country needs to be destroyed because of salmonella, it makes the decision based on a model of food distribution and disease.

You have expectations of an airline's behavior when you register for alerts at the airline's website—for example, you expect to be alerted within minutes if your flight is canceled. You estimate the current state of your flight and take actions based on your expectations. In the absence of an alert, you drive to the airport, expecting that the flight is operational. If you find when you get there that your flight had been canceled several hours ago, you conclude that your model of the airline is inaccurate, and you update it.

Identify the Implicit or Explicit Models that Users Employ

A key aspect of designing an event-processing application is identifying the implicit or explicit models that users of the application employ. The application uses the models to estimate the current situation and predict the future. The model, as a central construct, helps guide systematic design even when users don't couch their requirements in terms of models. The construct helps designers determine whether data sources are adequate and whether expectations of system, environment and user behavior are accurate enough to execute responses effectively.

Models of hurricanes, earthquakes, electricity distribution, air traffic, and many other systems are complex. An event-processing application may require powerful computers to execute models and compare what-if scenarios so that the system can respond to events with celerity.

....

Note: The model, as a central construct, helps guide systematic design even when users don't couch their requirements in terms of models.

Designing for Long-Term Business Benefits

Event-processing applications are used for many years. They are built so that they can be administered and reconfigured while they are in operation. You should keep the different business benefit measures in mind when you design a system. We now focus attention on a few issues that we haven't covered in detail: designing for performance, tailoring the application to suit the user, systems administration including security issues, and build versus buy tradeoffs.

Designing for Performance

Most event-processing applications can be executed on parallel computers. An event-processing network (EPN) can be mapped naturally onto a network of computers, with each node of the computer network being responsible for executing a phase of the EPN. Event objects are processed in a series of steps, and while one step of an event object is being executed, another step of a different event object can be executed concurrently in a different computational thread or process. Clusters of computers and multiprocessors are becoming commonplace, powerful, and inexpensive, and they are suitable platforms for event processing.

Many EDA applications are distributed systems, because sensors are located where data is generated and responders are located where responses are executed. An important aspect of design is defining the distributed structure—determining what information should be sent where, and what computations should be done at each location. There is a conceptual simplicity to designs in which all components, apart from sensors and responders, are located at a single site.

Storing all data at a central site simplifies replay, because computations can be replayed by data from central event logs. Central events logs also simplify debugging, forensics, and what-if analyses. On the other hand, sending all data to a central site may require excessive communication bandwidth and consequent expense. In many applications, satisfactory accuracy is obtained by sending summary data from the periphery of the network to internal nodes. For example, seismological applications can have thousands of sensors deployed over a wide region, with each sensor being capable of sending measurements several times per second. The system can function effectively with each sensor sending infrequent short messages containing summary data except when a sensor detects an unusual pattern. Since unusual patterns are infrequent, the system needs low average bandwidth. Similarly, there are applications in telecommunications, homeland security, and defense that function effectively with only fractions of sensor data sent to processing nodes.

One approach for dealing with the tradeoff between easy replay and forensics on the one hand and costs of communication on the other is as follows. Each site sends only summary information to central sites but stores information about all events that occurred at that site during a time window. The sites ship data logs to central sites when bandwidth is available. Simulations, what-if analyses, and forensics studies are executed using data stored at central sites except in those relatively rare cases where that data is insufficient.

Business costs and benefits are also used to determine what information to save and what to discard. Cameras connected to traffic signals, at airports, at border crossings, and aboard unmanned aerial vehicles record information at enormous data rates, millisecond by millisecond, and year by year. Science experiments, such as the Large Hadron Collider and telescope networks, also capture information at high bit rates for years and decades. Even though costs of storage continue to decrease, storing all information in perpetuity is not always cost-effective. Here, too, a best practice is to estimate the probable business benefits from alternatives such as storing all the raw information, storing only summary information, or storing detailed recent information and coarse-grained summaries of old information.

The performance of event-driven systems benefits from technologies such as in-memory databases and streaming databases. In-memory databases can operate an order of magnitude faster than conventional databases, and streaming databases offer high-performance operations on streams of events. The design decision of whether or not to use these technologies depends on the business benefits of timeliness (see, for example, the value-time functions in Figure 4-2). For some applications, the rate-determining component may inherently require seconds to complete; so, reducing the time for a database operation from a second to a millisecond may only reduce the overall response time by a tiny fraction.

Note: A best practice is to sketch all the steps in an event-processing flow; estimate— however approximately—the times required for each step; estimate the value-time function that determines the value of a response as a function of the time to respond; determine the performance requirement for each step; and only then select the technologies appropriate for each step.

Tailoring the Application to Suit the User

An important aspect of design is determining how to help end users tailor an application to meet their own individual needs. As we discussed in earlier chapters, if end users cannot tune applications to satisfy their changing requirements, then the applications may provide irrelevant, inaccurate data. A best practice is to work with business users to understand their willingness to configure and reconfigure an application. What are the user interfaces and programming notations with which different groups of end users are familiar? Are they power users of spreadsheets? Do they prefer SQL? Or do they not have the time or inclination to configure the application? Do users want to turn data sources on and off based on their levels of trust? Can IT staff or professional services develop business templates that users can fill in, or do users need more flexibility? These questions are important in designing any system, but they are particularly important in event-processing systems.

Note: A best practice is to design configurability into every component and to think, at every stage of design, about how business users will tailor the system to meet their needs.

Systems Administration

Features for administering and managing an event-processing application are similar to those for any continuously running application. Long-running applications should have plug-and-play capability that allows components such as sensors to register with the application and then interact with it. For example, a seismic application that allows any accelerometer to send signals to the application must have mechanisms for registering new sensors, where registration steps include giving each distinct sensor a unique ID and recording sensor parameters such as the type of sensor, the owner, and location.

A key aspect of plug-and-play is security; for example, an application must identify and discard information from clearly faulty sensors, and it must ensure that a single device cannot act as though it is thousands of different devices. Many event-processing applications are mission critical. The consequences of successful attacks by hackers or inadvertent failures are enormous in defense, national intelligence, financial trading, and smart systems such as smart grids, smart homes, and smart roads. Fraudulent activities that manipulate event-processing systems have been carried out by insiders familiar with system operation.

Note: You have to pay attention to security at every step of the design.

Buy-Versus-Build Tradeoffs

"It's about the business!" is the phrase that determines design choices, including the build-versus-buy choice, for event-processing applications. The effort, time, and costs of understanding and transforming the business far exceed the costs of buying or building software components.

Much of the effort in implementing event-processing functionality is expended in integration—integrating new event-processing components with other components in your enterprise's software portfolio, and integrating new event-processing functionality with the rest of the business. The buy-versus-build decision depends in part on the ease with which the components you buy or build can be integrated with the enterprise's existing IT infrastructure. (Of course, the buy-versus-build tradeoff for a shrink-wrapped application that contains event-processing components is the same as for any other shrink-wrapped application.)

There are several reasons to buy event-processing software and hardware components, including the following:

▶ A vendor may have specialized expertise in a business domain, such as financial trading, and demonstrated understanding of the many important business issues in event-processing applications in that domain.

▶ The application may require very rapid response times and the ability to serve high data rates. Some vendors have software tools that have been honed, over years of experience, to deliver extremely high performance. Developing equivalent tools in-house will take time.

▶ An event-processing component may be used by many different types of users who need to tailor the component for their specific roles. Developing flexible interfaces for business users to configure components takes time. Buying a component with a very flexible configuration mechanism is likely to save money in the long run.

Summary

The central point of this chapter is to focus on benefits and costs to the business at every stage of implementing an event-processing application. There are many different axes along which costs and benefits of EDA applications are measured, and you should consider all of these axes.

The success of an event-driven application depends on how well the application is integrated with the business. Effective application integration into the business takes time and effort from different groups of people, including IT staff and people in lines of business. Event-driven applications transform business processes—they don't merely improve current practices. As a consequence, the development of event-driven applications must be careful and systematic.

The chapter suggested a sequence of steps to take in implementing an event-driven application. Developing applications in a sequence of steps reduces risk and helps ensure that the final applications are efficient. There are several reasons for considering acquisition of specialized event-driven software components, and some of the key reasons were highlighted.

12

The Future of Event Processing

Where is event processing going? What new technologies will drive event processing forward? What consumer and industry demands will lead to more event-processing products and businesses? What are the barriers to adoption of the technology? What are the dangers of event-processing technologies? Let's answer these questions based on the material in the previous chapters.

All animal species—from bacteria to humans—are event-driven. They sense and respond to threats and opportunities as well as routine events such as heartbeats. Storks that do not detect frogs in the reeds die of starvation. Frogs who are forever jumping away from imagined storks die of exhaustion. Let's learn from nature.

Packs of animals—herds of zebras, prides of lions, schools of fish, and tribes of humans—detect events collectively. To use the vernacular, they "crowd-source" events. When a white-tailed deer runs from danger, its white tail signals others in the herd about danger in the vicinity. The presence of buzzards in the sky informs others about food in the area. The "wisdom of crowds" starts with the "sensing of crowds" and leads to collective responses of crowds.

Information technologies help societies advance by amplifying their collective intelligence and by facilitating time-, request-, and event-driven interactions among their members. Let's look at how we can help solve (some of) the world's problems using event processing in conjunction with other information processing technologies. Nature suggests how we should use event-processing technologies: we should amplify our collective ability to sense, analyze, and respond to situations appropriately. The key word is "appropriately." There is no point in responding faster than is appropriate, in using more energy than is appropriate, or in responding to situations that need no response. Peace of mind and a balanced view are no less important than speed and responsiveness.

Ancient man, hunting on the savannah, obtained situation awareness by using his sight, hearing, and smell and signals from members in his hunting party. In the next decades, we will achieve global situation awareness by using event-processing technologies and our collective ability to sense, analyze, and respond. Buildings will respond in seconds to slippage along earthquake faults; electric grids will respond to shifts in wind and clouds; governments will respond to *E. coli* contamination in food supplied from anywhere on the globe; telescope systems will respond to events in the far reaches of the universe; and parents on trips will remain aware of the situation at home.

Solving the World's Problems One Application at a Time

What are the scarcest resources on the planet and how can event processing help husband them?

Surely, one of the most precious resources is your time: time in which you can think, do activities, relax, and enjoy things *without interruption*. We let ourselves be driven by events that should be handled later or ignored altogether. Devices spawned by information technology are driving us to distraction. A frog that continually jumps away from imagined threats, or jumps toward imagined opportunities, suffers from exhaustion; so do we. The most significant scarce resources of the 21st century are your time and attention. We are beginning to realize that we are frittering away this precious nonrenewable resource. Event-processing technologies will save the day: they can help give you undistracted time during which you can pay attention to things that matter.

Your Attention

An attention amplifier that helps you pay attention to what matters to you now must know what *does* matter to you now: the application must know your current context. Do you want to pay attention now to your sales forecast, to your presentation on enterprise software, to reading a book, or to finding a proximate restaurant? Applications will estimate your current context by analyzing your history—the items you've searched for in web searches, the books you've read, the movies you've downloaded, your pattern of movements—and by monitoring your current activity—what you are doing now, what documents you are working on now, what web searches you are conducting now, where you are now and where you came from. Applications will proactively acquire information and tools you need, and either push them to you or have them ready the instant you ask for them.

Personal information managers will become attention amplifiers. They will distinguish events that you care about from those that you don't care about; they will determine whether you should be interrupted immediately or not; and they will organize information about events that don't merit your immediate attention into documents for your later perusal. Our sensory capacity will be magnified manyfold by thousands of sources of information across the globe, and attention-amplifier applications will help us process the information without suffering from sensory overload.

Expert Attention

Attention from experts is a scarce resource. Event-processing applications will deliver expert attention to where it is most needed.

The old and infirm need attention, but costs of caring for the aged threaten treasuries of many nations. Getting expert medical attention to the aged immediately when they need it—such as after a fall—is difficult. The costs of home-healthcare nurses have been increasing exponentially while the costs of event-processing devices have been dropping exponentially. Supporting experts (social workers, nurses, and doctors) with event-processing technologies will improve quality while reducing costs. Sensors in smart wheelchairs and smart houses will help direct expert attention to where it is needed urgently. Blood sugar levels of diabetics in Washington D.C. will be monitored by health centers in Maryland or even in the Philippines. Long-term-care insurance will promote use of smart walking sticks, smart pill dispensers, and other sensor-rich devices.

Commercial off-the-shelf (COTS) devices and applications will monitor internal events; provide plug-and-play interfaces that enable other applications to listen to events; and have dashboards that display key performance indicators (KPIs). Air conditioners, refrigerators, washers, dryers, cooking ranges, and cars will monitor and report internal events. Appliances are getting more complex, and most people don't want to analyze data generated by hundreds of sensors monitoring the internal workings of their appliances; however, maintenance experts can exploit such detailed information. The costs of experts to maintain increasingly complex appliances are increasing too. So, appliances and cars in expensive areas such as Manhattan will be monitored from less expensive locales such as Detroit, Biloxi, and Sarajevo.

You will gain situation awareness about your entire home and family by means of applications that integrate and display information about events from multiple appliances, people, and pets. This integrated display will help you manage power, gas, and water consumption and keep track of children, dogs, and things that are important to you. (A downside, however, is that the technology will enable couch potatoes to remain on their couches even longer! Imagine having a remote control that not only allows you to surf hundreds of TV channels and thousands of YouTube videos but also allows you to check on your children, pets, and spouse and whether the washer has finished its load.)

Nonrenewable Resources

Some resources cannot be renewed. World reserves of petroleum, particularly light sweet crude, are shrinking. Several hundred animal species and plant species are endangered. Recovering carbon dioxide from the atmosphere is expensive, and so the atmosphere cannot be renewed and returned to its state of 100 years ago. Event processing will help humanity manage its precious nonrenewable resources.

Sensors in critical habitats of endangered species will detect poachers and other threats. EDA applications will detect schools of fish in rivers and respond by turning off water intakes of factories to ensure that fish are not sucked in. Sensors and satellite tags on animals will enable scientists to see and hear what sharks, turtles, and other animals see and hear. Data gathered about animals over their lifetimes coupled with CEP will help scientists manage recovery of threatened species. Event-processing applications will help reduce consumption of fossil fuels by enabling effective use of renewable—but occasionally erratic—energy resources, such as wind and solar power. Humankind's increasing awareness of the fragility of planet earth will drive use of event-processing technologies.

Renewable Resources: Food, Water, and Energy

The essentials of life include clean water, food, energy, health, shelter, security, and peace of mind. In the next decades event-processing technologies will help conserve and replenish these essentials.

Departments of agriculture will rely on event-processing technologies—sensors, simulation models, pattern detection, and machine intelligence—to ensure the quality of food delivered to tables in London from farms in Chile, Australia, and Israel. Event-processing applications that detect and analyze events over the lifetimes of farm animals in herds in different states and countries will help prevent substandard meat from reaching supermarkets.

Clean water is essential for life but is in short supply in many parts of the world. Regions of the world suffer from drought. Irrigation is being threatened by demands from rapidly-growing cities. In the next decades you will see massive efforts to improve water supplies and to help humanity consume water more wisely—and event-processing technologies will play a major role in those efforts. Uniform irrigation over large regions will be replaced by location-specific irrigation tailored to the needs of small areas. Data from sensors that measure soil conditions, flow rates in rivers, snow packs in mountains, and weather forecasts will be fed to computational models to determine the ideal amounts of water to use and the ideal times to irrigate.

Event-processing technologies enable the use of renewable, intermittent, energy sources by detecting and responding to changes in demand and supply. The smart grid cannot function without these applications. The next quarter century will see massive use of event-processing applications for managing power generation, power markets, power transmission and distribution, across the world.

EDA applications will reduce energy consumption in homes and offices by monitoring activity and turning appliances on and off appropriately. These applications will detect from GPS readings when you are on your way home and turn on heaters, air conditioners, computers, and other appliances. Humankind has been profligate in its use of energy—from cutting down trees for firewood to burning coal in power plants—and event-driven systems can help humanity consume this resource wisely.

Healthcare

Countries around the globe will make hard choices about healthcare in the next quarter century. Healthcare costs have been rising faster than the rate of inflation for decades while the costs of sensors, responders, and computers have been dropping. U.S. healthcare costs are expected to grow to 20 percent of gross domestic product (GDP) in a decade. Companies are going bankrupt because they can no longer afford the costs of providing healthcare to their employees.

Governments and companies want individuals to take more responsibility for their own health. Better healthcare begins with self-awareness—knowing what you eat, how much you exercise, and what your blood pressure, pulse rate, and blood sugar levels are. Your self-awareness will be raised by using applications that detect, record, and analyze the events you generate. Devices ranging from software that logs the foods you consume to exercise calorie counters are mechanisms for monitoring and recording events. Noninvasive, or minimally invasive, sensor devices will become available in the next decades that monitor a variety of physiological vital signs. The costs of these devices will keep decreasing and their power will keep increasing, enabling employers to reduce the healthcare dollars spent on employees.

Feedback control theory tells us that the way to improve the quality of actions is to measure KPIs and then make corrections to actions based on the deviations of measured values from ideal values determined by a model. Future healthcare applications will embody control-theoretic principles. Sensors will measure your physiological vital signs and send data to computational engines that analyze deviations of measurements from desired values; based on this analysis, the computational engines will send recommendations to you and, when appropriate, send information to your doctors. Unfortunately, event-processing applications are limited: they do not solve the overwhelming problem of making us follow recommendations!

In the next 20 years, you will benefit from plug-and-play connectivity standards for medical devices. Event objects generated by different medical devices will be encoded using standard data structures. This will help provide holistic situation awareness of a patient by fusing data from all the devices monitoring the patient. In the next decade, hospitals will deploy complete, shrink-wrapped applications for monitoring and managing patients, hospital resources, and medication. These applications will use RFID tags and will have event-, time-, and request-driven components.

Jet travel has increased concern that healthcare systems have insufficient time to respond effectively to new contagious diseases. Swine flu in Mexico or avian flu in Southeast Asia can spread to Europe in weeks. Event-processing systems will be used (sometimes inappropriately) to reduce spread of contagious diseases. Airports will have sensors that screen arriving passengers for above-normal temperatures, and passengers with symptoms detected will be required to undergo further tests on the spot. Concerns about pandemics as well as bioterrorism will result in the development of sensors that can make measurements some distance away from the subject so that people can be analyzed as they walk through doors. Healthcare will be a fruitful area for event-processing technologies in the next two decades.

Security

Unfortunately, antisocial elements use technology, too. Without a doubt, antisocial elements will exploit event-processing technologies just as they exploit the Internet and mobile phones. Progress promotes a technological arms race between those who would protect society and those who would destroy it—and this is no less true of progress in event processing.

Event processing will be widely used in the next decades to protect countries against adversaries with dangerous technologies. EDA applications will be used by customs and immigration agencies to combat terrorists with access to nuclear material, drug lords with "narco-subs" (crude submarines built surreptitiously) and planes, and people smugglers.

The defense industry and the military have been pioneers in event-driven systems and will continue to lead in the future. Departments of defense have been drivers for global situation awareness and for integrating event-driven applications across multiple services and "stovepipe" applications within services. Companies, nongovernmental organizations, and other agencies of government, such as Homeland Security, will adopt technologies and procedures pioneered by the Department of Defense. Little further needs to be said about the future of EDA and CEP applications in the Defense industry; however, a point worth mentioning briefly is the use of EDA and CEP in robotic systems and in the exploitation of space.

Several books have been written recently on robots in warfare. The books predict that the number and variety of robots used in defense will increase in the coming years. Robots extend military sense and response capabilities: robots detect and defuse remote improvised explosive devices (IEDs), and unmanned aerial vehicles (UAVs) provide reconnaissance from battlefields across the world. Networks of military reconnaissance satellites are sophisticated remote-sensing devices that provide detailed images of the earth using different types of imaging sensors. UAV and satellite reconnaissance applications are prototypical examples of streaming intelligence—they derive intelligence continuously from data streams generated by video cameras and other sensors. Increased resolution of ground images from cameras in satellites and UAVs provides invaluable information, but the total volume of data generated is overwhelming without efficient CEP analysis.

The Workforce and Science in the 21st Century

The workforce of this century will have to deal with developing and maintaining increasingly complex products, from credit default swaps to pluggable hybrid electric vehicles. New employees will have to be trained quickly; lifetimes of service in steel mills, coal plants, and automobile factories are giving way to mastering complex new situations rapidly. Just-in-time information will enable the workforce to manage complex systems. Some just-in-time learning will be request-driven and some will be event-driven. When an electric utility worker inspects a transformer, all the information about that transformer will be pushed to the worker; the system will detect where the utility crew is and what components are being inspected and respond by pushing information to help the crew solve the particular problem that they are facing at that point.

Science progresses, in part, by observing and then understanding the unexpected. Telescopes will become even more event-driven as they are retargeted to follow unexpected transient phenomena. Biological instruments will become event-driven as biologists focus their measurements on interesting but infrequent intervals of activity interspersed among long periods of less interest. Instrumentation in high-energy physics will also have more embedded event-driven capability that detects significant events and retargets instruments to track significant events when they do occur.

Infrastructure

Road travel is fast and pleasurable when roads aren't congested, but can be a prolonged nightmare otherwise. The transition from acceptable to excruciatingly slow occurs as traffic increases by the small amount that takes the system from uncongested to congested states. The same situation holds in the electricity grid: the system works perfectly when demand is less than capacity, but a small surge in demand or a small cut in supply can push it over the edge.

Infrastructure is expensive. Moreover, construction of infrastructure such as prisons, freeways, and transmission lines in many regions is limited by the not-in-my-backyard (NIMBY) syndrome. Infrastructure usage is getting perilously close to its limits in many areas, and this will increase demand for dealing creatively with the tensions between "nimbyism" on the one hand and poor service on the other. Event-processing applications will help deal with this tension.

Users of certain types of infrastructure, such as roads, have an incentive to use the infrastructure when it is not congested. In other cases, users are given incentives—for example, you can get paid for allowing the electric utility to turn off your air conditioner during peak loads. Event-processing applications will detect and respond to congestion. A response might be to raise rates for using the infrastructure; inform potential users of the congestion so that they can delay their use of the infrastructure or choose alternates; or manage demand by disallowing customers from using the infrastructure for short periods.

A resource that is increasingly congested is the sky. There were about 13 million commercial flights in the United States in 2005 and about 9 million in 1985. The demand for more flights is likely to increase. The next generation of air traffic control system, called Next Generation Air Transportation System (NextGen), uses satellite navigation systems to keep pilots in planes in touch with each other and with ground controllers. Distributed event processing is an important component of NextGen. You will see increasing use of event-processing technologies as NextGen is deployed over the next quarter century.

An example of the NIMBY syndrome is the aversion that communities have to prisons and convicted sex offenders in their neighborhoods. For example, sex offenders in Dade County, Florida, are reported by National Public Radio and the *Miami Herald* as living in tent cities under a causeway because living anywhere else is difficult given county ordinances (see Appendix A for references). Electronic monitoring of people on probation can help ensure that they don't enter designated areas such as schools while giving the probationers more flexibility. Given growing costs of managing prisons and people on probation, governments will use sense-and-respond applications to help deal with the problem.

Businesses

Online retailers already use event processing extensively and will increase use of the technology in the future. Retailers monitor customer behavior at their websites and make recommendations that help steer customers to valuable interactions. EDA, CEP, and real-time response will become absolutely critical for successful retailing.

Web portal and search companies attempt to deliver advertisements that are meaningful to you, and what is meaningful to you depends on your context. Web portal companies will use increasingly sophisticated, near-real-time CEP to estimate your long-term interests and your current context and determine the advertisements that are most likely to result in sales.

The more a business knows about you, the better it can estimate your context and your needs. So, businesses have an incentive to provide you with services such as e-calendars, e-mail, and document storage that enable them to learn more about you. These services are useful to the business to the extent that they can use business intelligence (BI) to offer you the services and products you want just when you want them. Web-based companies will use BI to build models of your long-term behavior and use CEP to estimate your current context; knowing your long-term range of interests and your current focus will enable them to give you information that both interests you and is relevant to your immediate needs.

Finance and logistics applications will increasingly use event-driven components. Mutual fund companies, banks, package-shipping companies, and airlines will allow you to specify events that interest you and the actions to be taken in response to those events. Today, responses to events are mostly notifications by e-mail or text messaging. In the future, companies will offer responses that are more varied, such as triggering adjustments to your investment portfolio when specified events occur or changing your flight schedule when a plane is late.

Impact on Society

People have always depended on others—the hunting party, tribe, or town—to look out for dangers and alert the community. In the future we will depend on social networks to inform us about threats and opportunities. An alert may be as commonplace as being told that an author will autograph books at the local bookstore or as important as being warned about an armed deranged person on the loose. Indeed, people will join social networks partly because they can collectively sense and respond to situations better than they can individually.

EDA applications will promote even more globalization. Events in one part of the world will create responses in another part. A patient in San Francisco may depend on doctors in the vicinity and also on a team of nurses in the Philippines dedicated to monitoring that patient for 24 hours each day. Round-the-clock care in San Francisco is expensive, and getting work visas to enter the United States is hard; so, EDA applications will be used to help deal with the problem. Likewise, IT systems in Frankfurt will be managed by engineers in Bangalore.

A great deal has been written about the digital divide: the poor have less access to information technology; as a consequence, they don't acquire adequate IT skills and thus can't compete as well at school and work. The "event divide" will become an aspect of the digital divide. Those who master event-driven technology will be able to better focus their attention on the things that matter to them, sense situations that are important to them, and respond more effectively.

Barriers and Dangers

Concerns about security and privacy are major barriers to the adoption of event-processing technology. Security is a concern because successful attacks on systems such as air traffic control, medical devices, finance, and the electric grid will be devastating for society. A related concern is that insiders, or others who learn how the systems work, will exploit their knowledge to misuse the system for their own ends. Organizations will postpone implementations of event-processing applications until they are sure that the threat to security can be reduced to manageable levels, and they will exercise constant vigilance after the application is deployed.

Event-processing applications push relevant information to you by knowing what information is relevant to you. The more that the application knows about you the better it will serve you. Many people are willing to cede private information to an organization if the organization promises not to release the information to anybody else or misuse the information; however, once private information becomes public it may remain nonprivate forever. Somebody who obtains a copy of your private information may hold on to it despite copyright rules and privacy laws. You have to trust the organization as an entity, the individual people in the organization who have access to your information, and governments who can demand that information.

Most people in well-governed countries trust that companies will obey laws and keep private information private. This trust is essential for growth of event-processing web applications.

A danger of widespread use of event processing is system fragility. Water, food, health, security, energy, shelter, and finance may be controlled by software applications that have components in common. Systems that appear to be independent will, in reality, be dependent on common substrates. A failure of—or a successful attack on—some components may affect all the applications that use those components. These applications may include those on which life depends. Therefore, government agencies for verifying and testing critical components will enforce regulations that are shared by many applications.

Drivers for Adoption

The adoption of event-processing technologies is driven by several forces, including the PC-cubed (price, performance, pervasiveness, celerity, complexity, and connectedness) trends discussed in Chapter 2. The prices of sensors, responders, communication bandwidth, and computing devices in event-processing systems will continue to drop for several reasons. Consumer applications, such as computer games and mobile phones, increase demand for sensors, responders, computers, and displays. The use of accelerometers in phones and car airbag systems has increased demand and reduced price for them. GPS devices are now commodity items. Instant messaging systems are almost universally available. Consumer electronics and consumer Internet applications will keep driving down the costs of components used in event-processing systems.

The integrated circuit industry may be reaching the limits of Moore's Law—the number of transistors on an integrated circuit may not double every two of years—but that limit will not hinder the growth of event-processing applications. Unlike many applications that are inherently sequential, event-processing applications can exploit increasing numbers of processors by executing different steps concurrently on different processors. Even if single processors do not double in speed every two years, the cost of processors will drop, and thus hardware platforms for event-processing applications will continue to get more powerful and less expensive.

Models play central roles in event-processing applications. Solutions for problems in business, social, or natural systems are based on models of these systems. Some models are complex and require a great deal of computing power. For instance, models of stock markets, roads, water systems, hurricanes, food transportation, and the spread of disease require high-performance computing. Great strides in computer modeling and simulation over the past 25 years will pay off for event-processing applications.

Massive efforts have been made in neural networks, machine learning, BI, statistics, natural-language processing, and rule engines. Powerful tools have been encapsulated as services, and some of these services can be used free of charge. The availability of tools (especially open source) and services is increasing interest in these areas. The technology-push trends for event processing have been growing stronger.

The PC-cubed trends of celerity, connectedness, and complexity show no signs of abating. The celerity trend is not that systems and people will respond faster year after year, reducing responses from seconds to milliseconds to microseconds; rather, the celerity trend is that increasing numbers of systems will respond in a timely fashion whether timeliness requirements are in microseconds or hours.

The interconnectedness of people and systems across the globe drives demand for event-processing applications that enable systems in one part of the world to respond to events in another part. Event-processing technologies, in turn, create more interconnectedness. Event-processing technologies will also drive demand for a different form of interconnectedness: location-based, opportunistic connections. When two mobile phones are near each other, one of them can be used to relay messages to the other. Networks of mobile phones will be used as publish-and-subscribe systems. Cars on a road will communicate information to each other about accidents and congestion.

Event processing will be used to monitor and respond to complex systems. Detecting fraud and noncompliance will get more complex as rules get more intricate and rule evaders exploit technologies more skillfully. Smart buildings, smart electricity grids, and smart management of water resources are complex, event-driven systems.

Consumer applications are driving development and innovation in many components of event-processing applications. Features of instant messaging systems are used in alert engines. Applications such as Twitter that support social networks can be thought of as social activity monitors analogous to business activity monitors. Massive multiplayer online games process high volumes of events each second. Many consumers use event-processing technologies such as instant messaging routinely. Technology support for event-driven processing was rare 50 years ago; today, the young in many countries cannot function without it.

Most people have heard the adjective "smart" applied to nouns such as the electric grid, building, city, phone, and healthcare. A characteristic of smartness is the ability to sense and respond to events. Event-processing businesses—customers, vendors, and products—will gradually become more mature in the next decade. One indication of market maturity is widespread acceptance of standards, nomenclature, and reference architectures. The U.S. National Institute of Standards and Technology (NIST) is developing standards for the smart grid, and organizations such as the World Wide Web Consortium (W3C) are developing standards for events (see Chapter 9).

Technology push, enterprise pull, widespread consumer demand for event-processing features such as agility and celerity, and a generation growing up with event-processing consumer applications all suggest that the use of event-processing technologies will continue to grow rapidly.

Summary

Event-processing technologies will play critical roles in managing the essential stuff of life—water, food, health, security, energy, and shelter—as well as activities that are not necessary for basic survival but are extremely important such as finance, logistics, sales, and marketing. Growth will be driven by advances in technology, reductions in price, demand from enterprises, and increasing familiarity with event-processing applications.

The introduction of powerful technologies can have dangerous side effects. The dangers of event processing include possible loss of security and privacy, and a possible increase in fragility of the systems that serve society. Moreover, antisocial elements will acquire this powerful, but low-cost, technology. Deployment of event-processing applications must be done carefully, with particular attention paid to security, privacy, and reliability.

People who master event-processing technologies will have an advantage over those who don't. Just as mastery of request-driven applications such as search engines, online encyclopedias, and online forums provides an advantage to people today, facility with using event-processing services will provide an added advantage in the future.

Event processing will have a marked impact on society over the next quarter century. Companies in IT as well as in other businesses will incorporate event-processing technologies into their services and products. All government agencies and many nongovernmental organizations will provide essential services by using event-driven components. The IT industry and educators have the opportunity and the responsibility to ensure that this powerful technology helps deal with society's most pressing problems.

A

Books and Other Resources

Books

Ash, David J., and Vlad G. Dabija. *Planning for Real Time Event Response Management.* Upper Saddle River, NJ: Prentice-Hall, 2000.

Biske, Todd. *SOA Governance: The Key to Successful SOA Adoption in Your Organization.* Birmingham, PA: Packt Publishing, 2008.

Chakravarthy, Sharma, and Qingchun Jiang. *Stream Data Processing: A Quality of Service Perspective.* New York: Springer, 2009.

Covey, Stephen R. *The 7 Habits of Highly Effective People.* New York: Simon and Schuster, 1989.

D'Amario, Alfred J. *Hangar Flying.* Bloomington, IN: AuthorHouse, 2008.

Eckerson, Wayne W. *Performance Dashboards: Measuring Monitoring, and Managing Your Business.* Hoboken, NJ: John Wiley, 2006.

Faison, Ted. *Event-Based Programming: Taking Events to the Limit.* New York: Springer-Verlag, 2006.

Fingar, Peter, and Joseph Bellini. *The Real-Time Enterprise.* Tampa, FL: Meghan-Kiffer Press, 2004.

Fowler, Martin. *Patterns of Enterprise Application Architecture.* Reading: MA: Addison-Wesley Professional, 2003.

Haeckel, Stephan. *The Adaptive Enterprise: Creating and Leading Sense-and-Respond Organizations.* Boston: Harvard Business School Press, 1999.

Hammer, Michael, and James Champy. *Reengineering the Corporation: A Manifesto for Business Revolution.* New York: HarperCollins Publishers, 1993.

Hohpe, Gregor, and Bobby Woolf. *Enterprise Integration Patterns: Designing, Building and Deploying Messaging Solutions.* Reading, MA: Addison-Wesley Professional, 2003.

Jackson, Maggie. *Distraction: The Erosion of Attention and the Coming Dark Age.* Amherst, NY: Prometheus Books, 2008.

Luckham, David. *The Power of Events: An Introduction to Complex Event Processing in Distributed Enterprise Systems.* Reading, MA: Addison-Wesley Professional, 2002.

McGee, Kenneth G. *Heads Up: How to Anticipate Business Surprises and Seize Opportunities First.* Boston: Harvard Business School Press, 2004.

Muhl, Gero, Ludger Fiege, and Peter Pietzuch. *Distributed Event-Based Systems.* Berlin: Springer-Verlag, 2006.

Ranadive, Vivek. *The Power to Predict: How Real-Time Businesses Anticipate Customer Needs, Create Opportunities and Beat the Competition.* New York: McGraw-Hill, 2006.

Stojanovic, Zoran. *A Method for Component-Based and Service-Oriented Software Systems Engineering.* Delft, The Netherlands: Delft University of Technology, 2005.

Szyperski, Clemens. *Component Software: Beyond Object-Oriented Programming,* 2nd ed. Reading, MA: Addison-Wesley Professional, 2002.

Taylor, Hugh, Angela Yochem, Les Phillips, and Frank Martinez. *Event-Driven Architecture: How SOA Enables the Real-Time Enterprise.* Reading, MA: Addison-Wesley Professional, 2009.

Tufte, Edward R. *Envisioning Information.* Cheshire, CT: Graphics Press, 1990.

Westerman, George, and Richard Hunter. *IT Risk: Turning Business Threats into Competitive Advantage.* Boston: Harvard Business School Press, 2007.

Widom, Jennifer, and Stefano Ceri. *Active Database Systems: Triggers and Rules for Advanced Database Processing.* San Francisco: Morgan Kaufman, 1996.

Articles and Other Works Referenced in the Text

Allen, Greg. "Sex Offenders Forced to Live Under Miami Bridge." *National Public Radio,* May 20, 2009. https://www.npr.org/templates/story/story.php?storyId=104150499.

Baran, Daya. "False Google Story Triggers Massive Stock Sell Off." *Searchonomics,* September 9, 2008. https://www.webguild.org/2008/09/false-google-story-triggers-massive-ual-stock-sell-off.php.

Chatterjee, Bikash. "Security and RFID's Place in the Pharmaceutical Supply Chain." *Pharmaceutical Processing,* May 11, 2009. https://www.pharmpro.com/ShowPR~PUBCODE~021~ACCT~0000100~ISSUE~0905~RELTYPE~ATO~PRODCODE~0000~PRODLETT~BO.html.

Johnson, Carolyn. "Medical Devices Lag in iPod Age." *Boston.com,* December 29, 2008.

https://www.boston.com/news/health/articles/2008/12/29/medical_devices_lag _in_ipod_age.

National Science Foundation, Division of Astronomical Sciences, Senior Review Committee, "From the Ground Up: Balancing the NSF Astronomy Program." Report of October 22, 2006. https://www.nsf.gov/mps/ast/seniorreview/ sr-report.pdf.

O'Grady, Eileen. "Loss of Wind Causes Texas Power Grid Emergency." *Reuters,* February 27, 2008. https://www.reuters.com/article/domesticNews/ idUSN2749 522920080228.

Samuels, Robert. "A Life of Tension, Fear for Sexual Predators Living Under Miami Bridge." *Miami Herald,* May 2, 2009. http://www.miamiherald.com/460/story/ 1029919.html.

Stevenson, Richard W. "Fraud Inquiry on Barings in Britain." *New York Times,* March 4, 1995. http://query.nytimes.com/gst/fullpage.html?res= 990CEFD91F3 8F937A35750C0A963958260.

U.S. Department of Agriculture. "USDA Implements Key Strategy from National Animal Identification System Business Plan." News Release, April 15, 2008. https://www.usda.gov/wps/portal/!ut/p/_s.7_0_A/7_0_1OB?contentidonly= true&contentid=2008/04/0102.xml.

U.S. Food and Drug Administration. "Prescription Drug Marketing Act—Pedigree Requirements under 21 CFR Part 203." CPG Sec. 160.900. https:// www.fda.gov/ICECI/ComplianceManuals/CompliancePolicyGuidanceManual/ ucm073857.htm.

http://www.iht.com/articles/ap/2008/01/25/business/EU-FIN-France-Societe-Generale-Fraud.php—International Herald Tribune, January 25, 2008.

Web Resources

Amazon Elastic Compute Cloud (Amazon EC2; http://aws.amazon.com/ec2) This is one of the Amazon Web Services infrastructure services.

Complex Event Processing (www.complexevents.com)   This is the most extensive website dedicated exclusively to CEP. Moderated by Dr. David Luckham, Professor Emeritus of Stamford University, it includes information about event processing technology, best practices, case studies, and commercial products.

ebizQ (www.ebizq.net)   This website covers a very broad range of architecture and middleware issues, including SOA, BPM, messaging, EDA, and an increasing amount of CEP coverage.

Elemental Links, Inc. (www.elementallinks.net)   This website, moderated by Brenda M. Michelson, addresses a range of architecture and middleware issues, including EDA and CEP, from a practical, implementation-oriented point of view.

Event Processing Technical Society (www.ep-ts.com) This is the official website for the EPTS, a technical society founded to facilitate the successful use of EDA and CEP. Society members include users, academics, vendors, and industry analysts. The EPTS provides information about event-processing use cases, reference architectures, languages, and terminology.

Gartner, Inc. (www.gartner.com) Gartner is the world's leading information technology research and advisory company. It offers technology-related insights on virtually every facet of IT and has been very active in event-processing research. It covers strategic and tactical management concerns, technology trends, best practices, and vendor and product selection issues.

Mobile Health (mHealth) Alliance (www.unfoundation.org/global-issues/ technology/mhealth-alliance.html) The webpage says "At the GSM World Mobile Conference in February 2009, the Rockefeller Foundation, United Nations Foundation and Vodafone Foundation announced an agreement to form the mHealth Alliance to facilitate global innovation and ensure maximum impact in the field of mobile health (mHealth)."

Washington State University, CASAS Smart Home Project (http://ailab .wsu.edu/casas)

B

Glossary

The following is a summary-level explanation for some of the key terms and concepts used in this book. Their meaning in the context of event processing differs from their meaning in other realms in some respects.

A-E-I-O-U features: Five kinds of business requirements that indicate the need to use event-processing techniques: adaptability with respect to change, management by exception, instrumentation of a system to measure and record events, responding to situations from outside the virtual enterprise, and responding to unanticipated situations.

agent: An entity, such as a person or software component, that is capable of action.

alarm fatigue (also called alert fatigue): The condition of a person who has received too many false alerts. This is a common issue in event-processing system design and operation because people tend to turn off systems that cause this problem. *See also* false positive.

alert: An event notification intended to cause a response.

business activity monitoring (BAM): A kind of business intelligence that provides access to current business performance indicators to improve the speed and effectiveness of operations. It is sometimes called operational intelligence or near-real-time, process-driven business intelligence. BAM uses CEP in most applications.

business event: Anything that happens that is significant to a company, governmental agency, or another organization in the course of its business. Examples of business events include placing a customer order, delivering a shipment, changing an address, executing a bank transaction, experiencing a power outage, and hiring an employee.

business event processing (BEP): 1. Any computing that deals with business events. 2. Event-driven CEP in which some of the application development is performed by people who do not work for the IT department (for example, businesspeople specify some event-processing rules or patterns).

causal: Necessary to have occurred first. Causality is an important kind of relationship that can be present between events. Event A is causal to event B if A had to happen before B could happen. Causality is necessary but it may not be sufficient. If A and C are causal to B, then B will not occur if A occurs but C does not.

CEP platform (also called CEP suite, event-stream processor): A software subsystem that includes CEP software and is designed to support event-driven CEP applications.

CEP software: Any computer program that can generate, read, discard, or perform calculations on complex-event objects.

communication-enabled business process (CEBP): A business process that leverages telephony or telephony-related technology. CEBP applications typically use a mix of web, Short Message Service (SMS), or other integrated computer and telephony technology to notify people or arrange joint conference calls to respond to a situation. CEBP is often used with directory services such as LDAP (Lightweight Directory Access Protocol).

complex event: An event that is an abstraction of one or more other events. It represents the collective significance of those events. Complex events represent summary-level insights that are more meaningful and helpful for making decisions than are the simpler events that contribute to it. "Complex event" can refer to an event happening or to a complex-event object. *See also* simple event.

complex-event object (also called complex event): An event object that is an abstraction of other events or event objects. Most complex-event objects are synthesized by performing CEP computations on base (input) event objects. *See also* composite event.

composite event: A kind of complex-event object that is synthesized by combining member events using a specific type of computation. Member events are any base events used in creating a composite event. A composite event includes its member event objects, whereas most complex-event objects include only a unique identifier for their base events or don't contain generic information about their base events at all.

continuous intelligence system: An event-driven system that supports automated or partially automated decision making and runs in an uninterrupted manner. It is a complement to periodic intelligence systems that are request-driven or time-driven. Situation awareness relies on continuous intelligence systems.

contract: A statement by the developer of a component about what the component does; users of the component rely on this statement to design systems using the component.

crowd-sourcing (also called sensing of crowds): Obtaining information by tapping the collective knowledge of many people.

cyber-physical systems: Systems that conjoin information systems with physical systems, typically by leveraging event processing.

derived event: *See* synthesized event.

dissemination network: A set of channels and event-routing intermediaries that moves events among event producers, consumers, and event-generating EPAs. A dissemination network can filter events and route them intelligently but does not alter them.

event: 1. Anything that happens. 2. A state change. 3. A detectable condition that can trigger a notification. *See also* event object.

event channel: Any means of conveying event notifications from producers to consumers. A channel can carry events of multiple types. Events transported by a single channel may be consumed by multiple event consumers (the channel is said to fan out). Events transported by one channel may originate in multiple producers and be delivered to one consumer (the channel is said to fan in).

event cloud: A set of event objects that is not completely organized in any systematic way. It typically encompasses multiple event streams and channels.

event consumer (also called event sink, event handler, event listener): An event-processing agent that receives event objects.

event-driven: A characteristic of a person, software module, or other entity that acts when it detects an event. A person is event-driven when he or she reacts immediately upon finding out that something has happened, perhaps by seeing it or hearing about it. When software is event-driven, however, it is event-object driven—it has received news about an event in a notification.

event-driven architecture (EDA): An architectural style in which one or more components in a software system are event-driven and minimally coupled. "Minimally coupled" means that the only relationship between the event producer and the event consumer is a one-way, "fire and forget" notification. The producer does not get a response associated with the notification back from the consumer, and a notification does not prescribe the action the consumer will perform. Something is event-driven without being EDA if it is not minimally coupled.

event-driven SOA: An architectural style in which the principles of EDA and SOA are implemented together.

event object (also called event, event entity): A record of an event. Intent is essential to the definition of event object—it is intended to convey information, not just store information.

event pattern detection: Searching a set of events (an event "space") to find matches to a pattern.

event pattern discovery: A process of finding new event patterns. This is generally accomplished by people with the assistance of software. In machine learning, software can discover a pattern based on positive and negative examples and feedback such as thumbs-up and thumbs-down responses to categorizations made by the software.

event processing: 1. Any computation that involves event objects. 2. The design discipline of event processing, encompassing the principles, reference architectures, design patterns, and best practices related to computing with event objects.

event-processing agent (EPA): An agent that creates, discards, or performs calculations on event objects. A physical EPA is a software component. A conceptual EPA is an abstraction that performs logical functions. An EPA can be an event producer, consumer, or both. An EPA can be a consumer relative to one event and a producer relative to another event.

event-processing language (EPL): A high-level computer language for defining the behavior of event-processing agents.

event-processing network (EPN): A set of EPAs and channels connecting them. An EPN has at least one event producer, one consumer, and the dissemination network between them.

event producer (also called event source, publisher): An agent (EPA) that emits event objects. Producers include devices in the physical world, transactional applications, and continuous intelligence applications.

event provenance (of an event object): 1. A description of the sequence of steps by which an event object is generated. 2. Data items used to record the steps in the process by which an event object is generated.

event stream: A sequence of event objects arranged in some order, usually the order of arrival at a consumer. Event streams are usually in motion—for example, arriving in notification messages. However, an event stream can be at rest in a file or database.

event-stream processor (ESP): 1. CEP platform. 2. A CEP platform that is optimized for handling one or a few event streams, each of which has a high volume of events (thousands or hundreds of thousands of notifications per second) that must be processed very quickly (for example, in a few milliseconds each).

event type (also called event class, event schema): A description of the data items held in a particular kind of event, including their structure, the manner in which the data is encoded, and the operations that can be performed on them. All event objects are instances of an event type.

false negative: Failing to report an event that should have been reported.

false positive: Incorrect reporting of an event that does not occur.

fat-finger trade (in trading operations): An erroneous trade in which the amount or price is different from what the trader intended. For example, a fat-finger error may result in a trade of a million shares of a stock when the desired trade was only a thousand shares. The name "fat finger" derives from possible errors caused by a person with a fat finger who accidentally types extra zeros in the amount to be traded or leaves his finger on a key for too long.

instance agility: The ability to handle each instance (iteration) of a business process in a unique manner.

instantaneous event: An event whose beginning time is the same as its end time. It is the opposite of an interval event. In some approaches to event processing, all events are instantaneous (each happens at a point in time).

interval event: An event whose beginning time is different than its end time. It is the complement of an instantaneous event.

intermediary (in an event-processing network): A software agent that is interposed between two or more EPAs. Channel intermediaries provide message-handling services but don't perform any computation on event objects within notifications. An EPA intermediary is an event consumer and event producer that performs computation on event objects.

latency: The time it takes for a system to respond to an input.

notification: 1. An event object packaged in a form that can be conveyed from an event producer to an event consumer. 2. An event-triggered signal sent to a runtime-defined recipient. *See also* transactional notification and observational notification.

observational notification: A notification that reports an event but doesn't directly change anything in a transactional application or in the physical world.

PC-cubed: Six factors that are increasing the prevalence of event processing. Suppliers are offering products with improved price, pervasiveness, and performance. This results in technology push. Consumers are seeing a growing amount of celerity, connectedness, and complexity in their business activities. This results in demand pull.

process agility: The ability to change a whole process to support new kinds of products or services.

publish-and-subscribe: A pattern for decoupled communication in which the identities of the consumers are defined in independent entities, subscriptions, rather than being built into the publisher or the channel. Publish-and-subscribe systems consist of publishers, subscribers, consumers, event-generating EPAs, and dissemination networks. Publishers generate data, such as event notifications. Consumers receive data. Dissemination networks include channels, subscriptions, and subscription managers. Subscribers send subscriptions to the subscription manager at run time or startup time. Subscription managers ensure that published information that matches each subscription is delivered to the corresponding consumers. A subscription manager is usually an event-routing intermediary agent, but a publisher sometimes acts as the subscription manager. *See also* subscription and subscriber.

REACTS: Six sets of metrics relevant to cost/benefit analysis of business problems that may be suitable candidates for event-processing approaches. REACTS encompasses the relevance of information, effort in tailoring a user's interest profile, accuracy of detected events, completeness of detected events, timeliness of responses, and safety, security, privacy, and provenance of information, and system reliability.

request-driven: A characteristic of a person, software module, or other entity that acts when it receives a request from a client or consumer agent.

service-oriented architecture (SOA): An architectural style in which software systems are modular and some components (service providers) are distributable, discoverable, substitutable, and shareable.

simple event: An event that is not a composition of other events and is not synthesized or otherwise abstracted from other events (the complement of a complex event).

situation: A combination of circumstances that is meaningful to an observer. In the discipline of event processing, a system is said to detect a situation when it finds a simple or complex event that a user of the system deems to be meaningful for any reason. A situation reflects the fact that some event data item, combination of data items, or pattern match instance has met some criterion that indicates a threat or an opportunity. A situation may be inferred from the occurrence of an instance of an event pattern. A situation typically leads to a response.

situation awareness (also called situational awareness): Knowing what is going on so that you can decide what to do.

smart infrastructure: Infrastructure augmented by information technology, typically including EDA and CEP.

spam: Information received by an agent that is unsolicited and irrelevant to the agent.

subscription (in publish-and-subscribe communication): A specification that defines which messages should flow to which consumers. It contains instructions to be used by the dissemination network that delivers the messages. A subscription is a discrete entity, separable from the publisher and consumer components. In some publish-and-subscribe systems, subscriptions make it possible to add, drop, or change publishers and consumers dynamically at run time. In others, subscriptions are determined at startup time.

subscriber (in publish-and-subscribe communication): An agent that generates a subscription. In many systems, the consumer is also the subscriber. However, in other systems, the subscriber is the event publisher or a third party.

synthesized event (also called derived event): A complex-event object that is generated as a result of applying a method or process to one or more base event objects.

time-driven: A characteristic of a person, software module, or other entity that acts at a specified time. A clock notifies the entity when to commence action.

time stamp: A data item in an event object that records the reading of a clock. Time stamps typically refer to when the event occurred, when the event object was created, or when it arrived at a consumer.

transactional notification: A notification that reports an event and directly causes something else to happen in a transactional (operational) application.

window: A bounded segment of an event stream. For example, the events in the last ten minutes are a moving window.

Index

References to figures are in italics.